May the Best Man Win

May the Best Man Win
Sport, Masculinity, and Nationalism in Great Britain and the Empire, 1880–1935

Patrick F. McDevitt

MAY THE BEST MAN WIN
© Patrick F. McDevitt, 2004

First published 2004 by
PALGRAVE MACMILLAN™
175 Fifth Avenue, New York, N.Y. 10010 and
Houndmills, Basingstoke, Hampshire, England RG21 6XS
Companies and representatives throughout the world

PALGRAVE MACMILLAN is the global academic imprint of the Palgrave Macmillan division of St. Martin's Press, LLC and of Palgrave Macmillan Ltd. Macmillan® is a registered trademark in the United States, United Kingdom and other countries. Palgrave is a registered trademark in the European Union and other countries.

ISBN 1–4039–6552–8 hardback

Library of Congress Cataloging-in-Publication Data
McDevitt, Patrick F.
    May the best man win : sport, masculinity, and nationalism in
Great Britain and the Empire, 1880–1935 / by Patrick F. McDevitt.
        p. cm.
    Includes bibliographical references and index.
    ISBN 1–4039–6552–8
      1. Sports and state—Great Britain. 2. Nationalism and sports—Great Britain.
    3. Great Britain—Colonies—Race relations. 4. Masculinity. I. Title.

GV706.35.M38 2003
796'.0941'09041—dc22   2003065635

A catalogue record for this book is available from the British Library.

Design by Newgen Imaging Systems (P) Ltd., Chennai, India.

First edition: April 2004
10 9 8 7 6 5 4 3 2 1

Printed in the United States of America.

For Sheila, Sinéad Ophelia, and Seamus Toussaint

The 1898 All-Ireland Hurling Championship Team from Tubberadora, Co. Tipperary.

CONTENTS

ACKNOWLEDGMENTS

The seeds of this book were planted while I was at the University of Canterbury in Christchurch, New Zealand where I first met historians who viewed the study of sport as a serious field of historical inquiry. From that early starting point to this completed book, I have amassed more personal and professional debts than I could ever hope to begin to repay. While inadequate, I hope that these acknowledgments will go some way toward expressing my immense gratitude.

My deepest debt is to John Gillis who has been an advisor, mentor, and friend since I arrived at Rutgers University in spring of 1994. This work would never have come into being without his unceasing support, intellectual stimulation, wisdom, and enthusiasm. Second, I would like to thank Bonnie G. Smith for her continually astute commentary, her unending patience, and her faith in me. Likewise, I would like to especially thank Michael Adas, Antoinette Burton, and Susan Kingsley Kent. Their careful and constructive criticism was indispensable to this project and the time that their repeated readings of numerous drafts took away from their own scholarship is enormously appreciated.

Furthermore, I would like to thank all my colleagues in the Center for Historical Analysis and the history department community at Rutgers University. Particular thanks to Richard I. Jobs, Kimberly Brodkin, Roxanne Panchasi, Matthew Guterl, Carol Helstosky, Omer Bartov, Mia Bay, Herman Bennett, Rebecca Boone, Rene Burmeister, Christie Cox, Allen Howard, Matthew Matsuda, Tammy Proctor, Martin Summers, and Deborah Gray White.

Likewise, I am substantially indebted to the following people who have been generous with their time and criticism throughout the years: Martin Berger, Joanna Bourke, Susan Cahn, Bill Carrigan, Ian Catanach, Margaret Cordi, Alastair Davidson, Paul Deslandes, Jonathan Dewald, John Dugan, Edward Farrell, Heidi Gengenbach, Elizabeth Gilbert, Natasha Glaisyer, Stephen Heathorn, Rebecca Krawiec, Jonathan Lindroos, J.A. Mangan, Grey Osterud, Eleanor Parry, Tammy Proctor, Sandra Quick, Elihu Rose, Jay Rosen, Weiland Ross, Tony Rotundo, Claire Schen, Kelly Smith, Patience Smith, Tamara Thornton, Luke Trainor, and Liana Vardi.

It is traditional for authors to claim sole responsibility for all the faults that remain in a text despite innumerable readings by others; I wish to forgo that tradition and state my belief that whatever the book's failings, they should be shared by everyone listed herein. That's why I asked for their help in the first place.

Versions of chapters two and three first appeared in *Gender and History* and the *International Journal for the History of Sport*, respectively. Various incarnations of parts of this book were presented at numerous forums, including the Institute for Historical Research, the Sir Robert Menzies Centre for Australian Studies, the Southern Ontario Modern British History Seminar at McMaster University, the International Security Studies Conference at Yale University, Centre d'Etudes Afro-Americaines at Université Paris 7—Denis Diderot, the American Conference for Irish Studies, the North American Conference on British Studies, New York State Association of European Historians Conference, and the Association of Caribbean Historians Conference. Thanks are due to the numerous valuable comments and questions that substantially improved this book over the years.

My numerous trips to Ireland and England would have been not only less fruitful but significantly less enjoyable without my family and friends there; thanks to all the Farrells, especially Michael, Jean, Sinéad, Niamh, Eddie, Irena and Kasia, and Janet and Diarmuid Heafey. In a similar vein, I would like to acknowledge the debt both personal and intellectual to the members of the University of Canterbury C rugby team who first introduced me to the universe of imperial sport and its attendant world of ritual male behavior and bonding. Particularly, I would like to acknowledge those stalwart C-Men who transferred with me to the London French R.F.C. in the fall of 1996; namely, Mark Leary, Michael McDermott, and Brendan Ryan. Lisa Jordan, Stephen Dickson, and Robin McCone also helped make London feel more like home, even though Steve and Rob were too old and slow to join us on the pitch any longer.

In conclusion, I would like to thank my family for their unflagging belief in my abilities. For their love and support, I thank my parents John and Joyce McDevitt, my siblings and siblings-in-law, Michael and Janet McDevitt, Beth and Sean Depew, and Joelle Lemmons. Finally, my love, devotion, and admiration for my wife, Sheila Zamor McDevitt, are unending and total. This work, which would never have been finished without her support—in both the metaphysical and material senses—is dedicated to her and our children Sinéad and Seamus.

P.F.M.
Buffalo, NY

CHAPTER ONE

Gender and Imperial Sport

In the winter of 1906, the national rugby team of South Africa, the Springboks, traveled to Britain for a series of matches. Twenty-five games later, they had lost just two and drew one, all the while outscoring their opponents 553 to 79. The trouncing, though decisive and embarrassing, may not have been as newsworthy as it proved to be had the same thing not happened the year before, when the New Zealand All Blacks took 31 of their 32 matches in the British Isles by an aggregate score of 830 to 39. Within a year, then, two teams from the Empire came to Britain, the home of organized sport and the birthplace of athleticism, and earned victories that resonated not just with fans of rugby but also with the culture at large. In contrast to earlier colonial victories, most notably the Australian success at cricket against England, had been explained away by stressing the "Englishness" of the Australians, the rugby defeats struck a warning chime among English commentators and were seen to be a portent of doom for the future of the British Empire, especially in the wake of the perceived poor showing of the British army in the recently concluded Anglo-Boer War.[1] Organized games and the doctrines of Muscular Christianity, which held that athletics in general and team games in particular were uniquely able to foster the manliness which an Empire needed in order to prosper, had been exported over the second half of the nineteenth century.[2] These rugby tours and the British and colonial responses to them were emblematic of a larger process of interaction between metropolitan Britain and the colonies that continually redefined what those games, and indeed manliness itself, meant.

At stake for the British was much more than simply a loss of face over the results of some rugby matches. Rather, the overwhelming success of colonial teams was taken to be a sign of British physical and moral degeneration in a time when Social Darwinism clearly foretold the fate of those who were not the "fittest." The All Blacks and Springboks did not just overpower and outlast their opponents, they also employed innovative playing styles and tactics, which left the insular world of British rugby badly shaken and competitively deficient. Unlike the elite, public school, Old Boy constituency of English and Scottish rugby, the South Africans and New Zealanders were more egalitarian in their athletic pastimes and rugby was enjoyed by a wide swath of the New Zealand population and of the white South African population. Furthermore, the All Blacks included both Maori and Pakeha (i.e., white New Zealanders) and the Springboks comprised both Afrikaner and British South Africans. After these resounding defeats, the British media began to question whether elite British men had degenerated, and if so, what that degeneration would mean for the future of the Empire.

The tours highlighted the manner in which organized sport, which was widely perceived as the great bond of Empire, was also at times a weakening agent of that Empire. As the twentieth century progressed, open physical competition between the men of different nations, like much shared imperial culture, undermined the status quo of gender, race, class, and metropole/colony relations as frequently as it reinforced it.[3] "May the best man win" was a common sentiment in imperial Britain and the Empire, but this was not simply a paean to fair play and clean sport. It was also an expression of a worldview which held that participation in and success at athletic endeavors were primary measures of the worth of a man *as a man*. Games playing as defined by English rules and standards set the British and their subjects apart from effeminate continental Europeans, subjugated Africans, and effete Asians, and provided a forum for intra-imperial communication between the metropolitan center in England and the colonial periphery, as well as between peripheral nations themselves.

Various communities of men in the British Empire used sport to construct, propagate, and maintain national conceptions of manhood. To many observers, it seems commonsensical that issues surrounding manhood would permeate the world of sport and that success at games would relate to perceptions of manliness and virility. However, sport and masculinity are not necessarily inherently connected and the meanings attached to constructions of athletic masculinity are not self-evident. In the seventeenth and eighteenth centuries, nonelite women at times participated in the free-for-alls that comprised various popular, traditional games of football played throughout Europe. Likewise, women also participated in bat-and-ball games like cricket, rounders, and stool ball, and ran competitive races. Working-class women challenged and fought other women to settle disputes or points of honor, and aristocratic women often engaged in archery practice.[4] It was only over the course of the nineteenth century that, consistent with the general domestication of women and the gradual removal of women from the public sphere, women were pushed out of the world of recreational physical activity.

During the later nineteenth century, the pastimes of throwing, kicking, and hitting balls around a clearly defined playing field under specific and standardized rules were deemed a male preserve. More importantly, the British and their colonial subjects increasingly viewed these games as transformative endeavors that actively created men out of boys. Upper- and middle-class women who sought access to physical culture ultimately found themselves embroiled in what has been called a system of athletic apartheid. This athletic world consisted of allegedly "safe" athletic activities, such as golf or tennis, which would not threaten women's reproductive capabilities. Women who transcended these limitations were customarily suspected of being "mannish," thus casting into doubt either their desirability to men or their desire for men.[5] For example, one observer in 1905 argued, "It is one of the first duties of woman to look nice, it is but an extension of that duty for her never to do anything unnecessary which will prevent her looking nice."[6] Team games were one of the main activities, in that author's opinion, that prevented women from "looking nice." However, while it often seems axiomatic that sport and manhood are inherently connected, this is not a universal truth but rather is the product of a specific historical moment in the development of Western society. Yet, the fact that the assumption of intrinsic association is so often made, nevertheless illustrates the tremendous success of the games revolution, which produced sport in its modern form and provided a new institutional framework for the dissemination of normative manhood ideals.

Sport has been more than just a mirror to society; it has also been an active engine in the creation and preservation of power relationships. If, a sporting event is a tale that people tell about themselves, then the stories that the British were telling did not always mesh with the stories British colonial subjects were telling.[7] For the British administrators of the Empire who did so much to bring their games to the world, the value of the games was to be found in the moral lessons they taught. By spreading these games, they held that they were spreading civilization.[8] However, as any teacher can attest, the lessons one teach are not always the same as the lessons students learn. The spread of organized games did manage to create a wide knowledge of the ideals of British sport and by extension of British manhood. However, just as frequently, the colonial pupils took these basic lessons, read them through the prism their own experience and developed a culture and athletic masculinities which were something new, a mixture of British and colonial. Just as different British men played and promoted games for varied personal reasons, colonial subjects also brought their own agendas and meanings to the playing fields of the Empire.[9]

This was the case whether one looks at the creation of completely new games, such as the Irish did with Gaelic games and the Australians did with Australian Rules football, or if one examines the modification of long-standing athletic practices such as was seen around the Empire with the adoption (and adaptation) of cricket by local communities. Repeatedly, one sees how varied groups of men around the Empire inscribed common practices with unique significance. To be sure, British army officers and Indian princes played polo with and against one another on the same grounds, but the symbolic meanings they attached to this shared activity varied as widely as their respective cultures did. The core of this study will analyze the processes through which the British propagated and colonial subjects shared and contested imperial sporting values and the varied nature of imperial masculinities thus produced.

Sport as a Cultural Phenomenon

Historians of popular culture in general, and sport in particular, face numerous challenges when trying to understand the creation of something as nebulous and variable as gender roles, national ideals, or popular consensus. An investigator working from a Marxist perspective might see sport largely as a form of false consciousness by which the working classes were distracted in a bread and circuses manner. Marxist accounts of sport can see athletic activity as wholly alienating and simply a reproduction of the relationship of the dominant and working classes. In this view, sport is simply another form of labor.[10] In contrast, a postmodern, particularly a Foucauldian, point of view might focus on the ways in which power has been exercised by institutional and societal norms; sporting culture could thus be viewed primarily as a site of surveillance and discipline. From this perspective, the broad category "sport" acts to organize various institutions (such as the media, governing bodies, science, technology, and medicine) into a more or less coherent whole, which, in turn, produces a diverse assortment of bodies (variously raced, gendered, classed, sexualized, aged) that can be classified and placed in a hierarchy.[11] Both these approaches run the risk of falling into the trap of ahistoricity by failing to account for change over time and location. Likewise, by viewing all sport as a static form of elite social control, the actions and reactions of subalterns (i.e., nonelites) are rendered invisible beyond either accepting or resisting elite values.[12]

Sport was not a matter of mere imperial domination or indigenous subversion; participation in sport was not simply an acceptance of the colonial or class order. Influences moved both from the top-down and from the bottom up. Sport also came to be supported by colonial subjects for reasons that were indigenous and which neither supported nor challenged the British. How sport acted as a tool of legitimation of elite domination, the role of accommodation and half-conscious complicity by all classes and races of the indigenous populations, as well as the unintended consequences of actions, must also be considered. Organized games functioned crucially within imperial contexts as a means for disseminating British ideals of masculinity as well as constructing alternate and contrasting masculinities around which colonial subjects could mobilize.

By and large, false consciousness and social control are inherently specious explanations for popular enthusiasms and actions. Working-class and colonial spectators were not duped into caring about sports as a way to distract them from revolutionary activity; rather, it is clear that a passion for sports was genuine and deeply held across the Empire and the class spectrum. Even so, although elites might have promoted the game for one set of reasons and the subordinate parts of society might have embraced them for another, there was a certain amount of common ground, which is evident in newspaper accounts, letters to the editor, sporting memoirs, and the like. Therefore, while many aspects of the middle-class athletic philosophy came to be considered universally "true," most notably that athletic competition was beneficial to the community as a whole and was instrumental in the creation of true manhood, many of the details of the ethos and the manner in which it was lived on a daily basis were tempered by working-class and colonial contributions, ideals, values, and practices. What was produced was thus not an instrument of social control per se, but a product of consensus and continually shifting, dialectical transformation of sport from an elite to a mass pastime.

Generally speaking, as sport evolved in the nineteenth century, it helped maintain the status quo of late industrial capitalism and imperialism and largely benefited the elites of that system. Despite the fact that working class and colonial subjects at home and in the Empire largely accepted this sporting philosophy, there was still resistance to some aspects of the ethos. Agreement on fundamental values and conceptions of sport overshadowed class, race, and ethnic divisions along with the exclusion of women from the games that men played and the manner in which they played them. Even nationalists in Ireland, who steadfastly rejected British sports and viewed them as an Anglo-Saxon plot to strip Ireland of its Irishness, still viewed sport as being intimately tied to masculinity and agreed that to be a free nation, a country needed athletic men.

To date, histories of imperial sport have at times employed diffusionist models in which class, race, or empire elites, created and disseminated games. Eventually, those lower on the social and economic scale learn the sport and become competitively dominant. This pattern can be seen in cricket and Association Football (i.e., soccer) spreading to the English working class, and cricket and rugby spreading to Australasia and South Africa. Elite male responses to the adoption of their games by social inferiors have been varied. For example, men from the upper classes of England and Scotland abandoned soccer in favor of rugby union once those elites could no longer easily defeat their social underlings on the playing fields. In cricket, at first the social etiquette and class divisions embodied in the Gentleman/Player divide allowed English elite men to maintain their supremacy. When this ceased to be sufficient, they sought other means to reassert English dominance, namely the tactics that resulted in the Bodyline Affair, during which the English resorted to the less than sporting tactic of bowling at the unprotected heads of Australian batsmen in an effort to intimidate them into defeat.

In the process of diffusion of middle- and upper-class games to the men of the working class, it was generally assumed that at the same time that the games were adopted, the associated middle-class values of honesty, playing the game, and respecting hierarchy would be passed on to the lower classes as well. While some characteristically bourgeois attitudes did come eventually to pervade all sports as they spread to men of other classes and peoples, the games themselves took root much more solidly than the ethos of sportsmanship did. Sportsmanship is a code of conduct that must be taught and constantly reinforced. It does not flow naturally from the games themselves.

Indeed, for most in the working classes, it was not a matter of how one played the game, but rather whether one won or lost. Jim Bullock, in writing of the sporting life in the Yorkshire mining village in which he was raised, drew a stark contrast between middle-class sport and what he knew growing up. First, there were material differences; for example, only the village's representative cricket team had grass while everyone else played on barren earth. Moreover, village contests rarely witnessed an overabundance of "sporting" practices. Batsmen given out would routinely argue, glare, and threaten the umpires. Threats to the other team and accusations of bribery were common. Rather than suffer questionable calls in stoic silence as would be expected in middle-class cricket, village matches would regularly end in fisticuffs on the field, in the dressing rooms, or in the pub. "Many times the visiting teams had to make a dash from the vicinity, pursued by a hostile crowd," recalled Bullock. Likewise, the middle-class practice of not taking advantage of an adversary's weakness would have been completely alien in mining village matches where "no quarter was asked for, expected or given. It was a fight from start to finish. The crowd of spectators would yell their encouragement for their own team, greet the visitors with howls of derision, and every time a ball hit a visiting batsman on any part of his body there would be a great yell from the crowd."[13]

While mainstream, or rather middle class, sporting relations rarely deteriorated to that level, increasingly, middle-class men's behavior departed from strict nineteenth-century codes of sportsmanship. Therefore, it is necessary to explore the manner in which working-class men responded to middle-class ideology and in turn influenced middle-class sport. Over the course of the twentieth century, middle-class male athletes have increasingly abandoned the attitudes toward professionalism and fair play, which had been at the heart of the games revolution and adopted instead a more traditionally proletarian attitude toward games. Money began to figure more prominently and winning became the primary goal in elite as well as popular sport.[14] In cricket, this drive for victory at all costs came to a climax in the Bodyline Affair in 1933. This study seeks to rework the traditional top-down bias and address the manner in which the Empire and the working classes talked back, or often simply ignored, the metropolitan elite.

Athletic Masculinities

Although much recent literature on imperialism in general convincingly illustrates the profoundly gendered nature of imperialism; in the historiography of imperial sport, the role of gender (and especially masculinity) is noticeably underrepresented.[15] While it has been argued that the effeminization of colonial men was a key factor in rationalizing imperialism, the issues of how colonial men constructed their own masculinity as well as their perceptions of British masculinity still beg attention.[16] Sport functioned in a pivotal manner within imperial contexts as a means for constructing alternate athletic masculinities to counteract British ideology. Sport came to act as a sort of cultural cement holding together the imperial edifice, which had been cobbled together, often violently, out of multiform societies, each with a distinct relationship to the metropolis. However, sport also proved to be a source of substantial tension by providing a site where the foundational ideologies of British imperialism, such as race, nationalism, and manhood, were contested and challenged. Attitudes and impressions formed on the playing fields and in the boxing ring affected economic, political, and social relations by changing the way one group of people perceived other groups.

Until historians recognize the centrality of gender relations to wider society, their understanding of the processes of imperialism and nationalism will be fundamentally incomplete.[17] In his discussion of Welsh rugby before World War I, David Andrews contended that gender and national identity are implicitly related because "this association is habitually characterized by male identification with and access to, and female estrangement and exclusion from, the culture of the national community."[18] This pattern was repeated throughout the British Empire and is most fully illustrated in sport and war heroes. The All Blacks came to act as personifications of New Zealand, equaled only by the soldiers of the Australia New Zealand Army Corps (ANZACs) who fought and died in the Great War. Since the All Blacks and the ANZACs were all-male institutions, both of these embodiments of New Zealand, excluded women from active participation.[19]

Similarly, games legitimated and sustained a status quo, which deemed men and women to be different and unequal. This can hardly be seen as accidental in an era in which women were denied the franchise and economic equality. At the same time and in the same classes that produced organized games, the women's movement for suffrage was also born. If organized games came to be considered masculine or manly, then they were by nineteenth century a definition antithetical to womanliness and femininity, which were held to be the negation of masculinity. Mary Poovey has argued that the separate spheres of ideology, which came to characterize Victorian society, was central to the growth of commercial capitalism and bourgeois power because it permitted families to retain moral authority, which was safeguarded by women, while not inhibiting competition, productivity, and profit, which were deemed to be the preserve of men.[20] Throughout the world of imperial sport, men were praised and feted for behavior which would cause women to be ostracized or ridiculed, most importantly violent athletic competition.

If something is unmanly or feminine it is because there is a system that defines and classifies things into masculine and feminine or manly and unmanly.[21] While such a "system" of classification existed in imperial Britain and drew heavily on the symbols and ethos of sport, the "system" was also variable and under constant revision. That is, appropriate behavior in one time or social setting might be inappropriate in another. For example, if the ability to drink alcohol to excess without losing consciousness was an ideal trait for a coal miner, it was not necessarily one for a London clerk. Likewise, the sporting dictum that everyone deserved an equal opportunity to compete and prove themselves was widely accepted enough in the 1880s to allow black West Indian-born Australian fighter Peter Jackson to fight freely in London, although he never got a title shot. However, by the time that the African American heavyweight champion Jack Johnson sought the right to fight white Englishman "Bombardier" Billy Wells in 1911, the perceived necessity to defend white manhood against possible public failures to a representative of black manhood outweighed the English sporting instinct and British officials banned the fight.

It was never exactly obvious what it meant to be a man or manly or masculine. Nonetheless, varied communities continually enlisted sport to demonstrate and display the "appropriate" characteristics of a man at any given time. While in the nineteenth century, the term "manliness" was often used to describe characteristics of the ideal of a moral and civilized man, increasingly in the twentieth century there was a noticeable shift from a dominant discourse of "upright manliness," to one of "virile masculinity." Masculinity can be seen as the more expansive term of the two since it generally speaking takes into account the traits, good and bad, which are to be seen in real men.[22] Nonetheless, masculinity still implied a privileging of some forms of male behavior over others; it still posited a hierarchy of values and behaviors attached to biological maleness. Consequently, it is possible that some men might not be masculine; they might not have the traits that all men should have according to whichever individual or group is judging.

In writing his book *Manhood in the Making*, David Gilmore hoped to find universally held ideals of manhood. He concluded, however, that there was a ubiquity rather than a universality in the "concepts, symbolization, and exhortations of masculinity." That is, according to Gilmore, in numerous societies, whether they be warrior or pacifist, European, African, Asian or North American, pastoralist, hunter-gatherer or postindustrial, manhood ideals were deemed important for the continuity of social systems and the psychological integration of males into their communities. However, rather than a consistent set of traits that were prized, Gilmore argued that there was a recurring belief "that real manhood is different from simple anatomical maleness, that it is not a natural condition that comes about spontaneously through biological maturation, but rather is a precarious or artificial state that boys must win against powerful odds."[23]

Therefore, despite similarities across time and cultures, there is no universal ideal of masculinity. The late nineteenth and early twentieth centuries however were not a time of cultural relativism. Promoters of an imperial gender ideal encouraged the belief that the values of that system were "natural" and by extension universal, at least as a model. When men from another culture or class did not live up to normative British perceptions of gender, it was determined not that they had different gender assumptions, but that they were in fact not real men. Sport in the British Empire helped to define that normative idea. Nonetheless, the creation of a consensus of "what it means to be a man" was a process of competition and perpetual reinforcement and revision.[24] Contradictions constantly arose. For example, if both winning and playing fairly were held to be admirable traits of a man and one was faced with the necessity of choosing one over the other, the choice that was made and how that choice was received in wider society tell us a great deal about the collective attitudes toward manliness. As this study will argue, when faced with that dilemma, the choice of various groups of British men changed over time, as did the reaction of the public.

Gender played a central role in the cultural skirmishes through which various ideologies of race, morality, and civilization were challenged, interwoven, and negotiated. In the Empire, certain cultural practices, sexual mores, and gender constructions helped colonizers distinguish themselves from the colonized and allowed colonial elites separate themselves from those beneath them in the imperial power structure.[25] The constantly shifting nature of sporting relations and practices in the British Empire and emerging commonwealth provides concrete examples of the process by which the British imbued cultural practices with biological meaning. These practices in turn defined and supported the related racial and gender hierarchies at the root of British political and social authority. As colonial elites initially, and later the masses of imperial subjects, adopted the games and some of the associated cultural practices, the effect was not a lessening of hierarchy and difference between colonizer and colonized, but a state of ambivalence and a continual need to reformulate what indeed was truly "civilized."[26]

Frequently, mutating definitions of masculinity were at the heart of these discussions concerning which values deserved to be privileged. It might be helpful to envision gender in terms similar to those used by E.P. Thompson to describe class. In other words, gender norms arise when a group of persons as a result of shared experiences articulate and feel a common identity as different from and often opposed to those of another group.[27] By the late Victorian and Edwardian age, a dominant vision of athletic masculinity in the British Empire was characterized by the ideals of sportsmanship, strength, and endurance. However, within that general conception of masculinities were many different shades and manifestations of alternate masculinity. For example, in the West Indies in the 1930s, one could envision an individual identifying with (and rebelling against) depending on the situation, certain attributes of imperial British masculinity, white West Indian elite masculinity, and black

West Indian popular masculinity more or less simultaneously. In his autobiography, *Beyond a Boundary*, C.L.R. James relates how he struggled with the question of identity when choosing which cricket club he should join after leaving school.[28] Although James portrayed the agonizing decision as one concerned with color and class, not gender, the gendered implications of the choice are obvious. When James asked himself with which group he most closely identified, he was clearly making a statement of the type of man he perceived himself to be. Scholars speak of a "double consciousness" as a way to describe multiple points of identification commonly experienced by black people in the modern world. Similarly, it is appropriate to see a similar process at work with relation to gender and masculinity.[29]

This study explores several different counter-hegemonic conceptions of masculinity, which, while working within a general framework of British masculinity, rejected large and important parts of that ethos. A significant part of this process is the manner in which various groups attempted to uphold what they perceived to be the status quo in gender relations. Sport therefore was (and is) not related to masculinity, but rather to masculinities; different games produced different masculinities. Likewise, the same sport in different locations produced distinct masculinities. The various masculinities produced by sport in the British Empire were dependent on political power, age, race, class, which are all intersected by gender.

The Games Revolution

Before there can be a reaction, there must be a widely recognized dominant idea in place. The hegemonic masculinity that colonials alternately resisted and accommodated was produced by the games revolution of the mid-nineteenth century in England. The founder of the reform movement, which swept the public schools in the mid-nineteenth century, was Hely Hutchinson Almond, headmaster of the Loretto School in the 1860s, who took an unknown Edinburgh school and made it famous by basing his curriculum on physical education. In his seminal work on the games revolution, J.A. Mangan wrote, "From health came courage, temperance and *esprit de corps*—a trinity of moral virtues which comprised his Sparto-Christian ideal."[30]

Tom Hughes, in his widely read novel, *Tom Brown's School Days*, published in 1857, promoted the educational vogue of the day in his fictionalized account of a "reformed" school. The book depicts a schoolboy's vision of his days at the Rugby School under the guiding hand of Thomas Arnold, the headmaster there from 1827 to 1841. Education, according to Arnold, should endeavor to create "Christian gentlemen," a task that transcended the purely academic task of learning. For Arnold success in academic pursuit was of less importance than the creation of morally upstanding young men. Hughes, in the novel, portrays organized team games as an integral instrument in the instillation of the desired gentlemanly traits. Although it was largely responsible for the popularization of Arnold and his school, *Tom Brown's School Days* was a complete misrepresentation of the man's life and work. Hughes was not the only proponent of the games revolution to consistently use Arnold's name and reputation to promote a movement that Arnold did not create and would have opposed had he not died in 1842. Despite being widely credited with creating the athletically centered public school, Arnold was at best ambivalent about games, and most likely largely hostile to them. In Arnold's conception of a Christian gentleman, physical exercise was to be enjoyed as a tonic for good health, but not as an avenue to enlightenment or spirituality. For his part, Arnold much preferred brisk walks with a companion with whom he could engage in intellectual conversation. Nevertheless, his stewardship of the Rugby School did provide a major impetus for the growth in the popularity of the public schools amongst middle-class parents and this swelling of attendance led directly to the institutionalization of organized games as formal components to public school curricula.[31]

This educational credo was neither a fad nor a passing fashion. Cyril Norwood, headmaster of Harrow 1926–34, firmly believed that the Empire was the product of the English public schools and that education should be centered around games. There was an instant connection between the playing field and the battlefield, although this was a more popular and common connection before World War I than after. Sir Henry Newbolt's famous poem, "Vitai Lampada" which alternated verses about the cricket pitch and a desert battlefield, was emblematic of this correlation. Each verse ends with the same exhortation from the captain/officer: "Play up! play up! and play the game!" and thus clearly couples the lessons of the sports fields with the success of the British army on the battlefields.[32] The belief that skills were transferable from the playing field to the Empire was virtually unquestioned before 1916. Lord Baden-Powell, in a letter to the pupils of his old school, reminded them of their duty to the Empire. He concluded, "And in thus doing your duty whether it be to the Captain of your team, to your masters, or to your Queen—remember that at the same time you are carrying out a higher work because you are doing your duty to God."[33] This unique educational ideal was promulgated throughout the British Empire; the belief that games created the hardy, quick-thinking men who would run the Empire, dominated elite education throughout the realm in the second half of the nineteenth century through World War II.[34]

The Australians, who viewed themselves as the main inheritors of British civilization in the Empire, particularly trumpeted the connection between the games field and the battlefield. One Victorian newspaper, while defending Australian Rules football, stated that "it is the very element of danger in our own out-of-doors sports that calls into action that noble British pluck which led to victory at Agincourt, stormed

Quebec, and blotted out the first Napoleon at Waterloo."[35] In 1908, Sir Alfred Deakin stated his belief that "a nation's very safety—its name and its existence staked, as it must be staked, upon its young men—and when the tocsin sounds the call to arms, not the last, but the first to acknowledge it will be those who have played, and played well, the Australasian game of football before they played the Australasian game of nation-making and nation-preserving- to stand by the old land."[36] By the turn of the twentieth century, some classes of British society believed that British sporting philosophy was the backbone of the Empire and by extension, the British way of life. The elites of British society held games to be "as important as institution in the British system as trial by jury or *habeus corpus* because it taught teamwork and the subservience of the individual to the team."[37] Similarly, Mangan wrote, "Imperialism, Education and Games were an Imperial Trinity, as sacred to the upper-class Victorian educator as Liberty, Equality and Fraternity were to the Revolutionary Jacobin."[38] Belief in the Empire and the British race's fate to hold dominion over lesser peoples was in the fashion of the day in the schools and out. In this they echoed the intellectuals and statesmen of the day, notably Sir John Robert Seeley, Charles Wentworth Dilke, and Sir Halford MacKinder.[39]

White Australia welcomed this imperial creed; there, the ideology of imperialism, racism, and Muscular Christianity reminded them that through British culture they could recreate Britain in the South Pacific. Success at vigorous games was taken as a sign of community moral health and placated concerns that questionable immigrant (and worse, convict) stock might have produced an inferior race that was then further weakened by the enervating climate of Australia.[40] Even Australians of Irish descent, many of whom retained the anti-English sentiments of their forefathers, seemed to embrace British games with an enthusiasm equal to their English-descended countrymen. Australians apparently took great pleasure in beating the English at their own games. In contrast, for the Irish in Ireland, the automatic connection between English games and unwanted imperialism made the British games distasteful for many nationalists. The relationship with England and English games was also ambiguous for Indians and West Indians who, depending on class and color, had greatly differing places in the hierarchy presumed by the games ethos. Finally, while the working class in England adopted many of the games of the elites, there was less acceptance of the attendant values associated with the games.

Conclusion

The main theme of this book is one of dialectical communication not only between the metropolitan center and the imperial periphery, but also between various locations in the periphery. While British elites certainly sought to use sport and the attendant conceptions of masculinity to help them maintain a dominant position in imperial relations, they also provided colonial peoples with an opportunity for self-expression and resistance to British control and influence. There has been significant debate about the meaning of the term "cultural imperialism," yet Martin Barker's definition provides a good starting point. Following Barker, this study of cultural imperialism will proceed from the assumption that "the process of imperialist control is aided and abetted by importing supportive forms of culture."[41] The main danger that exists when employing a concept of cultural imperialism is that one is apt to elide from a narrative of metropolitan influence to one of metropolitan domination. Frequently, in the historiography of cultural imperialism, domination remains at the center of the imperial relationship.[42] This is problematic because it limits the possibility that the recipients of this cultural propaganda could fruitfully resist and/or reciprocally influence the metropolitan center. As will be illustrated throughout this study, the imperial periphery did resist totalizing British ideologies and did "talk back" to England. Cultural imperialism, even successful cultural imperialism such as the exportation of English games philosophy, should not be conflated with social control.

Organized sport and the ideology of Muscular Christianity were initially the product of the elite public schools, and the games, which resulted from these trends, came to be associated with male virility. Elite British society identified manliness with upper-class men who generally enjoyed more leisure time to devote to training and were consequently the most successful group in early organized sport. In a society such as industrial Great Britain, which placed a premium on the status of men, the popularization of a national recreation, which bolstered the perceived manliness of the males of the ruling class, could only be viewed as a benefit to that elite. As organized games spread from the confines of the recently reformed ancient public schools to wider society, it was almost inevitable that groups other than the English elites, whether they be colonial subjects or the British working-class, would begin to excel at games and challenge the notion that elite men were the best men. What was not challenged however was the belief that sport was a measure of a man's valor, capabilities, and virility.

Hegemony rather than social control characterized the relationship between British games philosophy and the athletic world of the British Empire.[43] At the root of this hegemonic resistance were competing senses of what was meant by the cultural construction of manhood prevalent in distinct groups within the Empire; these groups were differentiated by nationality, age, race, gender, and class. The various sporting practices which came to occupy an important place in the cultural life the Britain and her Empire in the late nineteenth and twentieth centuries, occupied more attention than simple pastimes would have, had they not been intimately related to much larger issues. Sport allowed cultural differences to be displayed and nurtured through the propagation of variegated discourses of masculinity and the relationship of those masculinities to wider issues of class, race, nationality, and age.

CHAPTER TWO

Strong Men, Free Men: Gaelic Team Sports and Irish Masculinity

Looking back from the 1930s, P.J. Devlin, a prominent Irish sportswriter wrote, "It was from the countryside that had become as graveyards, from this atmosphere, pestilential and maddening, that the soul of our race arose with revivified body and answered the call of the Gaelic Athletic Association."[1] The creation of the Gaelic Athletic Association (GAA) in 1884 and the subsequent standardization of hurling and Gaelic football marked nothing less than a nationwide campaign to resurrect the physical stature of the manhood of Ireland, which was deemed debilitated due to the combined effects of British rule and the Great Famine. The choice of hurling and Gaelic football by GAA founder Michael Cusack and the game's subsequent immense popularity offer valuable insight into Irish-Catholic conceptions of gender, nationalism, and embodiment in turn of the century Ireland. The games assisted in the formation of an Irish conception of a nationalist masculinity during the period from 1884 to 1916 by providing a public forum where conflicting symbols associated with manhood and Irishness could be produced, contested, and synthesized.[2] This unique "Gaelic" manhood was then utilized to reject the English belief that Irish men were inferior.

Hurling has always been a dangerous game.[3] Contemporary commentators remarked on the fact that hurling matches before the founding of the GAA in 1884 resembled nothing more than a faction fight, with large, uneven groups of men hacking and wrestling as often as they followed the ball. Referees had no whistles and often "controlled" the game by riding the sideline on horseback and interfering like riot policemen only under the most extreme circumstances.[4] Likewise, the ancient law of Ireland specifically enumerated compensation for death caused in hurling matches, thus illustrating the game's long pedigree as well as its extreme potential for violence. Football in Ireland only dates to, at the earliest, the seventeenth century, whereas hurling has a millennia-long tradition. Later, opposition to games by clergy and magistrates coupled with the

Famine led to dwindling participation. By the 1860s, English games became well established in towns, albeit with mainly loyalist participation.[5] However, a leading nationalist newspaper in Ireland reported that memories of this unpleasant past of wildly violent and uncontrollable Irish men were "completely obliterated" only three years after the founding of the GAA. Described as being of "national importance," the 1887 Gaelic football championship game provided such an excellent exhibition of "skill, science, speed and stamina that it was a model in every respect."[6]

Gaelic football and hurling in their modern forms are similar in pace, tactics, and objectives; widely dispersed players use open-field running and passing to move the ball toward the opposing team's goal. Hurling can best be described for non-initiates as a combination of lacrosse and field hockey in which a hard, leather ball (called a "sliotar") is struck with a wooden, ax-like club (called a "caman") toward an "H"-shaped goal. When not passing the ball to teammates, who can catch the ball with bare hands, hurlers run with the sliotar balanced on the end of their caman. The game is characterized by long hits, massed jumps, and scrambles along the ground for loose balls. Gaelic football is similar in structure, but lacks camans and uses a large, inflated ball the size of a child's soccer ball. Running in Gaelic football is limited by the requirement that players alternately kick the ball back to themselves and bounce the ball on the ground every few steps, a feat which demands coordination, dexterity, and a tremendous amount of practice. In both games, a "goal" (worth 3 points) is scored by propelling the ball via the feet (or caman) beneath the crossbar (as in soccer), and a "point" (1 point) is scored by propelling the ball over the crossbar and between the uprights. Neither hurling nor Gaelic football allow tackling in either the rugby or soccer sense however both incorporate a large amount of physical contact and hurling allows for vast "incidental" contact between one player's caman and another's body.

Spanning four decades from the 1880s through the 1910s, a diverse movement that came to be called the Gaelic Renaissance sought to create an Irish nation by emphasizing a living Irish language, a national theater, and "native" Irish culture. This movement gained particular prominence in the 25 years between the death of Home Rule leader Charles Stewart Parnell in 1891 and the Easter Rebellion of 1916. English politicians on both sides of the political fence saw Home Rule as a threat to the Empire as a whole. This Victorian "domino theory," which was championed most vigorously by Lord Salisbury, and the problems posed by the Protestant majority in Ulster, combined to repeatedly defeat the movement for Home Rule.[7] During the period after 1891, there seemed to be a retreat from explicitly political agitation in Ireland in favor of the ideological work of building a nation from the bottom up. These years were characterized by a "shift of interest from Westminster to Ireland, from the source of constitutional reform to the breeding-ground of rebellion."[8] In the face of failed political efforts to achieve independent nationhood, nationalists sought to demonstrate that even in the absence of a unified polity, a unified and unique culture marked Ireland as a true nation and not simply a region of the United Kingdom.[9] The revival of the Gaelic games was a hallmark of the Gaelic Renaissance and a strong pronouncement of Irish nationalism, but the highly gendered nature of this experience has been largely ignored by scholars.

Setting Irish Men Apart

Updated and revised, hurling and Gaelic football produced an image of Irish masculinity of which the nationalist community could be proud. The random violence of the earlier games, which had led English ruralist Arthur Young to describe hurling in 1780 as the "cricket of savages," was nominally replaced with order and virtuous manliness.[10] To a greater degree than many other games, the everyday coverage of Gaelic sports was couched in gendered language and the issues surrounding Irish "manhood" implicitly and explicitly dominated the commentary. Whereas the highly specialized language of cricket, for example, allowed matches to be described in primarily technical terms, the newly codified Gaelic sports lacked an established vocabulary and thus were largely discussed in relation to moral, social, and gender systems. Through this gendered language, the games acted as crystallizations of Irish views of themselves and of the British.

Richard Holt, while noting the importance of the GAA as a unique example of resistance to English hegemony, concluded that "the study of sport and imperialism leads naturally to nationalism."[11] The most detailed work on Gaelic games, by W.F. Mandle, is primarily an institutional history of the GAA, in which "nationalism" provides the primary explanation for why these sport were so symbolically powerful in Irish society at this time.[12] However, this is inadequate. Mandle and Holt accept "nationalism," "politics," "Irishness," and "manliness" as uncontested and self-evident entities. The case of hurling and Gaelic football provides an excellent opportunity to reconfigure this constellation of issues, as well as illustrate and advance the hypotheses advanced by Eric Hobsbawm in his oft-cited and influential introduction to *The Invention of Tradition*.[13] Gaelic games, which were clearly "invented," referred to earlier practices as a means of establishing themselves as authentically Irish and were openly crafted to inculcate specific values and political goals, specifically to forge an Irish nation by creating a new Irish man. Furthermore, since lack of initiative and originality were key characteristics ascribed to colonized peoples by imperial powers, the act of invention itself is important because it countered English stereotypes of the Irish.

Mandle argued strongly that "much of what the G.A.A. regarded as distinctive about the meaning and development of its games, and of their morality was, to only slightly overstate the case, merely substituting the word Ireland for the word England."[14] In fact, although the reorganization of Gaelic games was based on an English model and the two countries' sporting lives were similar in broadly defined self-image, the fact that the

Irish saw themselves as unique and actively opposed to the British is significant. The potent mix of masculine sport and national identity was seen in a variety of forms throughout the Empire, although most nations hoped to claim a place of honor within the British Empire. The Irish, on the other hand, sought to remove themselves from it completely. Rather than adopting the English sport of cricket, rugby, and soccer like the Welsh, Scots, Australians, Indians, South Africans, and New Zealanders did, the Irish created their own games to symbolically refute British influence.[15] At the end of the nineteenth century, an era marked by the heretofore greatest homogenization and internationalization of popular culture that the world had ever seen, the Irish self-consciously opposed this trend and promoted their "native games" and the image of an Irish manhood which would stand apart from British or imperial manhood.

Gaelic games, while culturally importing much of their foundation from the British, provided the Irish with a novel form of self-expression through which they foregrounded the differences between themselves and the British and shaped a masculine identity which they viewed as uniquely "Irish."[16] The supporters of the GAA could be said to have fashioned a philosophy of "Muscular Catholicism" to counter the "Muscular Christianity" doctrine which was the driving motivation behind the development of modern sport in England.

Irish men sought to distinguish themselves from the British through anti-imperialism, Catholicism, Irish culture, egalitarianism, and fraternal solidarity; these marks of distinction coexisted with an emphasis on morality, codification, and competition that was shared with the British. Distinct images of manhood were created; a British one based on Protestant elitism and class, while the Irish version was dominated by Catholic communalism. Although Roman Catholicism and the GAA were intimately tied, the association's relationship with the clergy was often stormy in its first decade, due to clerical opposition to the Irish Republican Brotherhood.[17] For lay Irish men, one of the most readily accessible manners of defying the British and celebrating one's "Irishness" was participation in Gaelic games. Sport can be viewed as a medium for self-expression in many ways; impressions of the self and the other are linked inextricably in the evolution of sport within a given locality and society.[18] This can be seen quite dramatically in Ulster where Catholic boys played Gaelic games and Protestant boys played English football. Many Ulster communities maintained the practice of surrounding their games with full-scale Gaelic festivals much longer than they did in the three southern provinces.[19] For the men of the nationalist community, the concepts of manhood, patriotism, and resistance were so interconnected as to be almost conflated, and these three ideals of nationalist philosophy are drawn together most dramatically by the national pastimes.

The games provided Irish nationalists with a symbolically defiant act broad enough to encompass aspects of ritual, nostalgia for a legendary Irish past of united independence, physicality (with its attendant discipline and ordered violence), and strict differentiation of gender roles. The athlete's beautiful, healthy, and vigorous Irish male body counteracted the Victorian English characterizations of the Irish as either simian, drunken ruffians, or effeminate and feckless, childlike inferiors in need of Anglo-Saxon domination. The charge of infantalization was an important component in defending the imperial mission.[20] The fully formed, athletic bodies produced and displayed in hurling and Gaelic football provided muscular counterimages to the memories of weakened and emaciated Famine victims. This was a profound moment of self-definition: first and foremost, the English and Anglo-Irish were excluded and thereby deemed "un-Irish"; second, Irish men were distinguished from Irish boys; finally, Irish women were excluded from the centers of action and power. If communities, whether a nation or a fraternity of sportsmen, are symbolic constructs created via cultural imaginings, then the example of hurling and Gaelic football allows us to see this cultural imagining in its making and in its most naked and powerful form.[21]

As in other parts of the modern sporting world, the Irish emphasis on the paramountcy of manhood vis-à-vis womanhood was not without costs. The cost of constructing a powerful masculinity was largely borne by women. Post-Famine Irish society was characterized not only by the radical separation of men and women into distinct spheres of activity that was seen across Europe, North America, and Australasia, but also by a contemporaneous entrenchment of a particularly Irish version of Roman Catholicism, which often reduced women's role to solely their reproductive functions and denied Irish women the benefits of the contraceptive revolution that would sweep the industrial war in the years after World War I. One aspect of this diminution of women's independence was a movement from paid outside work for women to unpaid labor within the home. By 1900, the rate of female employment outside the home was only two-thirds of the rate in 1880.[22] The masculization of Irish national culture, of which Gaelic sports were a prominent part, eventually pushed Irish women into the home and limited opportunities for independent action in nearly every sphere of life. The games were successful in advertising and propagandizing a masculine worldview for the republican community and in the process mirrored the detrimental effects of androcentrism that were seen throughout the British Empire.

Games for Gaels

The history of hurling stretches back into the time of Irish legend and was intimately connected to warfare and warriors. From the prebattle game played at the first battle of Moytura ca. 2000 B.C. to the specific references in the Brehon Law, hurling had an extended association to violence and predominantly male behavior such as battle. Almost all the great heroes of the Celtic past, including Cahir the Great, Cuchulain, and Fionn Mac Cumhaill, have hurling feats attributed to them. While infinitely safer in its modern form than in its folk and ancient forms, hurling is still perhaps the most hazardous game in the Western world and has been described as "the nearest approach to warfare consistent with peace."[23] The modern game entails 30 men running around swinging heavy, wooden clubs at a small, hard ball flying through the air at distances up to 100 yards. Cusack argued that "The game was invented by the most sublimely energetic and warlike race that the world has ever known ... It teaches the use of arms at close quarters, it gives its votaries that courage which comes from a consciousness of having in one's hand a weapon which may be used with deadly effect."[24] Needless to say, games explicitly developed to be warlike required a certain degree of fearlessness from the men who played them.

This vigorous image of Irish games and men was constantly held up in contrast to the weakened and stunned apathy of the country between the Great Famine of 1845–47 and the founding of the GAA in 1884. Between 1845 and 1850, it is estimated that out of a pre-Famine population of just over eight million, nearly one and a half million people emigrated and over a million died of famine-related disease and starvation. The effects of the Famine were felt for decades after the restoration of the potato crop. The *Celtic Times* reported in 1887 that "it would be idle to deny that a considerable section of Irishmen is thoroughly demoralized."[25] In addition to drawing together the Irish present with a Golden Age of united independence, the promoters of the games also sought to regain the pre-Famine confidence and optimism associated with Daniel O'Connell's movement in the 1840s to repeal the Act of Union between Great Britain and Ireland. The Act of Union of 1800, which was passed in the wake of the United Irishmen Uprising of 1798 and growing strife on the Continent, disbanded the Irish Parliament and made Ireland a nominally equal member of the United Kingdom alongside England, Wales, and Scotland. Ireland was thereafter to be represented in the parliament in Westminster.

The banishment of the image of weak Irish men as produced by the Famine was a prerequisite for national autonomy and the advent of the GAA was the first step in this process for many nationalists. Cusack, it was said, "was content to re-endow his compatriots with the qualities of *Strong-men*, [and] assumed that in God's good time they would reach the status of *Free-men*."[26] In this way, the revival of ancient traditions was in fact part of a modernizing mission to bring Ireland into the community of independent nations.

While discussing every nation's need for a "master fiction" in which political authority can define itself, Clifford Geertz wrote, "Heresy is as much a child of orthodoxy in politics as it is in religion."[27] By creating the GAA, Irish men were performing a deliberate act of heresy in the face of the cultural imperialism and political domination of Great Britain. Rather than standing as an institution against orthodoxy, Gaelic team games came to represent a new orthodoxy. One observer, criticizing half-hearted support of hurling and football, stated that the true Gael "cannot be orthodox today and unfaithful tomorrow: Non-Gaelic on Saturday and Ultra-Gaelic on Sunday."[28] Unlike other peoples in the English Empire, who subverted English sport by beating the British at their own games, the Irish blasphemed in a different manner. By repudiating the central rituals of the British imperial religion, they rejected the tenet that team games were symbolic of the superiority of British manhood. The creation of the "anti-rituals" of their own games became the most visible, viable, and successful pillar of the Irish cultural renaissance.

Gaelic sports were not isolated from the rest of the revival movement; rather GAA promoters surrounded the games with festivals, music, and oratory that explicitly rejected the imperial creed implied in the "foreign" games. During the third quarter of the nineteenth century, the Irish Catholic Church underwent a "Devotional Revolution," which was characterized by a dramatic increase in the number of vocations and the resurrection, accentuation, and reestablishment of many long-forgotten and half-remembered rituals, such as the saying of the rosary and novenas. In the period from 1850 to 1875, the upper clergy of Ireland transformed the casual, personal Catholicism of the pre-Famine era into a highly codified, ritualistic, and institutionally centered religion.[29] The centralization of the Church in these years helped enable the population of Ireland to conceive of themselves in national, rather than parochial terms.[30] In a similar manner, Gaelic games and the Irish language, which had fallen into disuse, were revived and propagated on a national and centralized level. These cultural artifacts were not simply recovered, but reconstructed as well. Both hurling and football needed to be organized and standardized in order to coexist with the self-perception of Irish men as civilized counterparts to their Anglo-Saxon overlords despite British claims to the contrary.

The nationalist community was not monolithic and images of masculinity were not limited to the participants in the Gaelic games.[31] The nationalist movement ranged from radical republicans who sought complete independence to moderate Home Rulers who advocated remaining part of the British Empire but with local self-governance. However, the nationalist movement was, through the sheer number of adherents, the dominant force in Irish life in this period and it was from this community that Gaelic games drew their support. This is the same community that comprised the Gaelic League with its Irish language movement, and the Abbey Theatre of W.B. Yeats, Lady Gregory, and J.M. Synge.[32] In addition to the many shades of independent nationalism, other political ideologies existed and different groups had contrasting conceptions of manhood that were not affected by Gaelic sports, including masculinities molded by English sports then being played in Ireland. Irish members of the Crown Forces offer one example of Irish men who did not hold that participation in Gaelic games was a central requirement for Irish manhood. Soon after its founding, the GAA quickly instituted a policy that came to be known as "The Ban," which for the next 117 years forbade the participation of British soldiers, sailors, and members of the Royal Irish

Constabulary (RIC) in Gaelic games. This policy was in actuality enforced with varying degrees of strictness throughout the period depending on the relative strength of the association.[33] The RIC's organ, *The Constabulary Gazette*, decried the Ban as "outrageous" and "narrow-minded, unsportsmanlike, un-Irish, unmanly . . . The RIC embraces the finest specimens of muscular manhood in or out of Ireland, and they are to a man the product of this country."[34] Despite the fact that the RIC was at this point still comprised overwhelmingly of Irishmen, the GAA would argue that it contained not a single "Gael," and thereby offered nothing to Gaelic games. On the other hand, although the article rejected the Ban and the authority of the GAA to define Irish manhood, its purpose was to encourage the removal of the Ban and allow the subsequent participation of Crown Force members in Gaelic games.

Although the term "Gaelic" can rightfully be applied to numerous Celtic peoples, following the general practice of the nationalist community at the time, within the context of this study "Gael" and "Gaelic" will refer to Irish Catholics who supported the nationalist movement and the cultural renaissance. Implied in this term is a working- or middle-class background, which precluded ever being associated with the landlord class. For example, one pamphlet offered the following appraisal of Charles Stewart Parnell, champion of Irish Home Rule, leader of the Irish Parliamentary Party, founding patron of the GAA and member of the Protestant gentry: "Great Irishman as Parnell was, he could not be claimed as a Gael by any expansion of the term."[35] The GAA's stated aim was to unify the Irish people; however, the organization was in fact exclusionary and divisive. By stressing the concept of the "Gael," those who may have been Irish by birth still might be excluded from the nationalist ranks due to a lack of cultural, political, and sectarian credentials.

Masculinity was connected to Gaelic games in several significant ways. First, there were "civilizing" tendencies, which sought to remove the violence and brutishness inherent in earlier versions of the games. Repeatedly, discipline and control of violent impulses were praised in participants and upheld as a benefit of the games. Here we see that although Gaelic games were a reaction to the British, there were also many areas of overlap between British and Irish games philosophy. Irishmen wanted to demonstrate that they were not naturally unruly and that organized team games did not correspond to British superiority. Simultaneously, they incorporated similar civilizing goals as British games and relied on the imposition of a formal set of rules and regulations to order and enforce these notions of civilization.

Second, in opposition to the civilizing trends and creating a running tension for the games, hurling and football were tied to militarism through descriptive metaphors, the organization of training and tactics, and through a huge overlap in membership between the GAA and the various sectarian militias. These militias, or "Volunteers," were organized to prepare for the seemingly inevitable conflict either between Catholics and Protestants in Ireland or between Irish nationalists and the British. Moreover, in conjunction with the military benefits, the games were a reaction to memories of the physical and moral hardships of the Famine.

Third, the games helped define separate spheres for men and women within the nationalist movement, reserving the most active and prominent duties for the men. In the GAA's *Annual* for 1907–08, the ideal Gael is thus described:

> The Irish Celt is distinguished among the races for height and strength, manly vigour and womanly grace; despite wars and domestic disabilities, the stamina of the race has survived in almost pristine perfection. The ideal Gael is a matchless athlete, sober, pure of mind, speech and deed, self-possessed, self-reliant, self-respecting, loving his religion and his country with a deep restless love, earnest in thought and effective in action.[36]

Hurling and Gaelic football required dedicated men motivated by a republican brotherhood. The games inculcated and cultivated these coveted values whose presence was proven by success. Victorious team members were the pride of Gaeldom and role models for younger men and boys and thus perpetuated both the games, their political ideology, and a Gaelic conception of masculinity.

Irish Exceptionalism

English games, most notably cricket, rugby, and soccer, were actively disseminated throughout the Empire by the hundreds of public school educated teachers, missionaries, and administrators; these games were seen as one of the best ways to transmit the values of British society to the collaborating colonial classes.[37] This was, essentially, an attempt to win hearts and minds, or at least hegemonically engage them, by disciplining colonial bodies. Once hurling and Gaelic football were enlisted to combat that corporeal colonialism, the body became the battle ground for an imperial confrontation. It was not by any means predetermined that the Irish would choose to propagate these "native" games as a means of national reinvigoration. In addition to the British sports, which some Irish men favored adopting as a means of literally beating the English at their own games, there were other options as well, including German-style gymnastics, cycling, baseball, or Australian Rules football, to name just a few. However, it was Gaelic football and hurling which were chosen and which excited massive participation nearly instantaneously; other sports then being played in Ireland did not. Both the games themselves and their accompanying rhetoric welded them to Irish notions of manhood, of the body, of the community, and of their relation to the land. These aspects of Gaelic games made them unique for the Irish.

With a founding motive of improving the musculature of Irish manhood, a nationwide movement was born in 1884, which, by the eve of

World War I, was rivaled only by the Catholic Church as the most powerful organization in the country.[38] As with nearly every modern sport, the spectacle of physical strength, grace, and beauty was central to the success and popularity of Gaelic games; however, a mind/body symbiosis was still held to be of cardinal importance. Watching a game on a typically cold Irish winter day, one priest observed "two or three dozen young fellows with naked arms, naked heads, naked feet, and clad only in a light silken jersey and drawers... Our young men stripped and fought fiercely for victory, utterly heedless of cold or danger."[39] The weekly display of healthy, muscular, and vigorous male bodies provided by hurling and football worked not only to define masculinity, but to illustrate Irish attitudes toward the male body, and to act as propaganda for the Irish-Ireland movement which sought to "de-Anglicize" Ireland.

First, the strength and dominance of rural teams underscored the enduring image of the manly and virile Gaelic body as rooted in a flourishing and fertile rural landscape. Second, the active Gaelic athletes were a reproach to those who were not participating due to their alleged sloth. Third, the will to continue playing despite physical hardships highlighted the manner in which mental and spiritual qualities allowed the men to convert physical ability into victory. Finally, the triumph of the Gaelic athletic movement was viewed as a resounding rebuttal to the anguish caused by the Famine and British policies which protected financial interests of landlords at the cost of the increased suffering of the Irish people. The spiritual aspects of Gaelic games were considered partial compensation for lack of Irish independence in the present, while the physical benefits were viewed as guarantors of that independence in the future.

The GAA produced nothing less than a social revolution in parts of rural Ireland. Many areas had not held games or festivals in over 50 years nor witnessed large crowd gatherings since O'Connell's mass repeal meetings in the 1840s. T.F. O'Sullivan, the first historian of the GAA, believed that the "dull monotony of Irish rural life [had been] dispelled forever [with the advent of the G.A.A.]. A new spirit had been created in the country."[40] *The Democrat* reported in 1893 that before the GAA had revitalized the area, the men spent their time drinking and gambling while "their physique in general had deteriorated and... the young men walked with stooped shoulders and a shambling gait. A couple of years of hurling and football soon changed this and the athleticism which permeated every nook and corner of the South Midlands and the West of Ireland during the years 1886 to 1890 brought forth myriads of athletes."[41] In this way, Gaelic sports fortified the belief that the true Ireland of past greatness was waiting to be resurrected and that nation would rise and take its independence once the men of Ireland recovered their lost physical prowess.

The themes of rebirth and resurrection often enter into commentaries of the Gaelic games revolution. In addition to the revival of ancient and folk games and of community and national morale, there was also the physical regeneration (or cultivation) of the participants. Hurling and football drew their widest support from the countryside where the images of the games, Irish manhood, and the reinvigorated nation flowering after a time of bareness was reminiscent of the way the land had rebounded from the Famine. Repeatedly, the importance of rural support was stressed. Often, city dwellers attempted to claim some connection to the land to distance themselves from the taint of the Anglicized city. *The Gaelic Athletic Annual* described how one successful urban team was in fact composed of men who were raised in the country and that this was, "another argument for those who cry . . . 'Back to the land! Back to the land!' "[42] This fascination with an idealized rural past was witnessed in many emerging urban centers around the world; the increasing rate of urbanization was seen as undermining the physical rural life which was mythologically at the center of the nation leaving only effeminate and sickly urbanized masses.

One report that echoed common sentiments described "country lads overtopping in stature and general physique the rather puny town boys who opposed them."[43] The Irish preoccupation with the land, especially since the Famine, was widespread and came to be embodied by the Land League, which was led by original GAA patron Michael Davitt, who saw landlordism and imperialism as two sides of the same coin. He hoped through the attacks by the Land League on the power of the Irish aristocracy and British political power, to undermine British dominion over the Irish.[44] Although the greater part of the GAA grass roots support came from rural areas, the association's leadership was primarily urban. It was, however, greatly influenced by the same nostalgic and sanitized vision of the rural western peasants as other factions of the Irish-Ireland movement, most notably the Gaelic League and the Abbey Theatre.[45]

In addition to the strong connection to the land, Gaelic games were also intimately tied to Irish-Catholicism both philosophically and through the one-parish-one-club organizational ethos. Gaelic sports complimented their Catholic environment when contrasted with Protestant English games. Unlike many Protestant sects which had stripped their churches of representations of the body, Catholic churches were full of images of embodied religious figures in paintings, statues, and stained glass, suggesting less of a mind/body separation in Irish Catholic corporeality than in Protestant ones. The overemphasis on physicality allegedly propagated by "foreign" games was held up in contrast to the mutuality of mind and body in the Irish case. P.J. Devlin wrote, "The exultation of mere bodily grace and virility is fundamentally pagan, basically carnal and foreign to all our historical conceptions of perfect manhood . . . spiritual qualities long survived the memories of their bodily vigour."[46] Thus, cleverness of play evidenced spiritual advancement by exhibiting the ability of Irishmen to transcend the purely physical and leave the realm of the grossly material behind.

The inherent physical discomfort associated with intense training and the playing of contact games meshed with wider Catholic (and general

Judeo-Christian) teaching on pain, and the salvation brought about through suffering. The image of a healthy male body enduring the agony of crucifixion was one of, if not the primary, shared images of Irish life. Just as the hardship inflicted by a wrathful (male) God will eventually allow the suffering to join that God in the afterlife, the fatigue, pain, and derision inflicted by a (male) coach or captain will eventually enable the beleaguered to win the game, the esteem of their fellow men, the admiration of women, and the independence from oppression. The theme of sacrificing the male body for the salvation of Ireland was shared throughout much of the nationalist community. For example, in Yeats' most famous and popular play *Cathleen ni Houlihan*, the young protagonist Michael forfeits marriage and probably his life in the hope of securing Irish independence. Likewise, Patrick Pearse, one of the leaders of the failed 1916 Easter Rebellion, regularly proclaimed that a "blood sacrifice" of the Irish men was a requisite step in Ireland's march toward independence.[47] For example, the 1916 Rebellion was seen by Pearse as an act of drama, not an effective means of achieving the political goals, but a symbolic sacrifice aimed at motivating others (and in larger numbers) to act.[48] The GAA can be viewed in the same manner; participation in a Gaelic sporting event was as important as a symbol as it was as a practical program for rebellion.

Despite a wariness of overt brutishness, participants in Irish games still came to equate muscularity with manly action and slenderness with neutered apathy. In a scathing attack leveled by the *Celtic Times* at some of the citizenry of Kilkenny, where the GAA had not taken off with the same vigor as in other parts of the country, Cusack contrasted the "fine, strapping men" of the GAA to "a score of pale, emaciated figures, seeming engaged in criticizing the dress and motions of everybody moving past them ... Another crowd of persons, who probably call themselves men, was slothfully reclining with their faces towards the sun."[49] The notion that males who are not part of the movement cannot legitimately be considered "men" is emphasized here, as is the contrast made between the ideal bodies of the Gaels and the undernourished bodies of nonparticipants. In a land haunted by memories of the Famine, laziness and inactivity in the Irish symbolic universe led to emaciation and thinness, not slovenly corpulence as in more affluent societies. The athletic physiques of the GAA men also offered a vivid contrast to the fleshy image of John Bull, who had grown corpulent feasting on profits reaped from the misery of Ireland's poorest. Moreover, in addition to a lack of strength and industry, the highly gendered pastimes of catty gossip mongering and concern with fashion are ascribed to the non-GAA men.

Gaelic games were seen by large numbers of Irishmen as antidotes to the sickly national body. In the article, which officially called for the formation of the GAA, Cusack argued that a "rot" which began in urban centers and had spread across the country could only be remedied by Gaelic games.[50] The organic imagery of a rot spreading visibly across the land clearly equates British culture with the blight, which was responsible for the failure of the potato crop in the 1840s. It was not enough that the games promoted healthy, muscular men, as nearly any sport would have done that. By standing in opposition to Anglican games, Irish nationalists could further nationalist as well as sectarian agendas while creating sports that more closely resembled their concerns and views. Hurling and Gaelic football's success rested in part on their ability to speak to national memories of the pre-Famine era as well as hopes of a post-British future.

Ireland for Irish Men

The widespread support and participation in Gaelic games can be viewed as a discourse on gender differentiation and Irish male fears of the effeminate. The myth of the masculine Anglo-Saxon and effeminate Celt was widespread in Britain in the nineteenth century and the Irish explicitly wanted to counter this.[51] While obviously not everyone in Britain subscribed to this view, Colonial Secretary Joseph Chamberlain is a prime example of one who did not, many other influential figures did, including Lord Salisbury, J.A. Froude, A.J. Balfour, and W. Long.[52] Still, like many European nations, Ireland represented itself and was represented by others in the figure of a woman, although these personifications did not symbolize a unified ideology. British cartoonists depicted a young, beautiful Hibernia being protected from the Fenians by John Bull or Britannia. Yeats's Cathleen ni Houlihan was a haggard old woman beckoning young Irishmen to fight for her. Hibernia and Cathleen ni Houlihan were joined by Erin, Eire, Mother Ireland, the Dark Rosaleen, and the Shan Van Vocht as various female representations of the country.

George Mosse has argued that throughout Europe, "the female embodiments of the nation stood for eternal forces. They looked backward in their ancient armor and medieval dress. Woman as a pre-industrial symbol suggested innocence and chastity, a kind of moral rigor directed against modernity—the pastoral and eternal set against the big city as the nursery of vice."[53] For the Irish, the city and the English were nearly conflated. As part of the national struggle for independence, Gaelic games fit within a long Irish tradition of Irish literature and historiography, which has designated males as active, national subjects and woman as sites of contestation. C.L. Innes has likened the Irish nationalist struggle and even more the historiography of that struggle to the "family romance" of a united band of brothers fighting the imperial father.[54]

The male supporters of Gaelic games often connected images of British men with those of women or neutered men. The effeminization of the enemy here not only displayed male Irish attitudes toward British men, but also toward women and themselves. If the most pejorative label one man can place on another is that he is "emasculated," that is, "made like a woman," the level of equality available to women in that society is necessarily low. Likewise, compliments that stressed manhood by definition demean women and feminize those who do not succeed, thus associating failure with the feminine.

The phrase "worked like men" was often used to describe a particularly diligent side.[55] At times this was in reference to schoolboys, who while male were not adult men; at other times, it was applied to men's teams. Within this context, all males (even all adult males) are not "men" unless they follow certain preordained behavior patterns. It has been argued that "sports suppress natural (sex) similarities, construct differences, and then . . . weave a structure of symbol and interpretation around the differences which naturalizes them."[56] This was clearly the case in Ireland, where the physicality and brutality of the games accentuated differences in favor of adult men and then claimed that artificial advantage as evidence of male superiority.

The concept that men are not always "men" allowed players to step outside their socially dictated roles and behave otherwise at other times. To this end, although they may "work like men" on the field, perhaps they get to "play like boys" at the pub afterward. The increase in traveling and use of the railroads precipitated by the games made many matches holidays in themselves. Although spectators traveled to games, often on specially chartered trains, expenses dictated that usually only the players and perhaps the male supporters would go. Although women often attended matches, it was more likely the men alone who would travel to see the games. For example, *The Gaelic Athletic Annual* of 1910–11 reported "Half the male population of the kingdom [Co. Kerry] must have traveled to Tipperary on that day."[57] The camaraderie generated on trips "with the lads," away from the stresses of work and families included restaurants and pubs with their attendant drunkenness, singing, and gaiety. The games reinforced the image of political unity, namely a brotherhood of Gaels, which, with their women in concomitant subordination, would reclaim their lost nation from a feminized oppressor.

The participants and administrators of the game had little difficulty reconciling the incredible violence involved in hurling and their desire to portray the Irish man as peaceable. *The Gaelic Athletic Annual* stated that "The hurler who would raise a caman to strike another player is unworthy to use it. The caman is not a weapon of offense—amongst Gaels at least . . . [Those who] decry hurling as a dangerous brutal game . . . have acquired the instinctive dread of the 'Anglo-Saxon' for manly vigour."[58] Statements of civilizing nonviolence notwithstanding, the practitioners of the Gaelic games, and especially hurling, clearly associated the games with violence and violence with manhood. Any fear of bodily harm was deemed either as a sign of the encroaching influence of the British or of effeminacy.

The connection between English males and unmanliness dates to the very inauguration of the association. In a letter accepting the invitation to become a patron of the GAA, Archbishop Croke of Cashel penned what was for many years considered the charter of the association. Urging the public to support the new organization, he derided the manner in which along with importing England's manufactured goods, the Irish had also taken to imitating English fashions, mannerisms, accents, and "such other effeminate follies as she may recommend."[59] Croke was not alone in equating English activities and fashions with dandyism and other womanly affectations. Cusack argued in 1887, "that as the courage and honesty and spirit of manhood grow, the hurling steadily advances on the domains of football [soccer]."[60] That is, as the number of Irish males who are truly masculine grows, the unmanly British games will naturally wither away because of lack of participation. Therefore, Cusack argued that by joining a Gaelic sports team, an Irish man not only became more manly, but also contributed to the removal of British domination.

Cultural awareness, anti-Britishness, and fluency in the Irish language were highly regarded nationalist credentials for both sexes in Ireland. Women, as mothers, played an active role in the propagation of a national-ist ideology within the household.[61] As noted earlier, the birth and growth of the GAA coincided between 1890 and 1914 with a widespread exodus of Irish women from the paid workforce in favor of unpaid domestic labor. For example, in 1901 only 430,000 women were employed outside their homes as compared with 641,000, 20 years previously.[62] This trend away from the public sphere in employment matters notwithstanding, middle-class women were increasingly taking a more prominent role in nationalist organizations and in 1902, female members of the Gaelic League devised a less violent version of hurling and called it "camogie."[63] The efforts of these nationalistic women who took to the playing fields with camans in hand were not warmly received by the sporting community and were largely ignored by the press and the GAA despite the fact that traditionally, women participated fully in Irish folk games and faction fights in pre-Famine Ireland. However, by the GAA era, the country's press seemed uninterested in women playing games, Gaelic or otherwise. The perceived newsworthi-ness of sports furthered the gendering of sports and national identity. Evidence of female responses to the game is beyond the scope of this study; however, this remains an area inquiry that would greatly illuminate the rela-tionship between Gaelic games and gender.

Even before the invention of camogie, women were not excluded from the carnival of Gaelic games and their presence was often noted. Before the mid-nineteenth century, folk games of any sort throughout Europe were not events in themselves, but rather were part of festivals and fairs in which whole communities participated. This had changed by the late nineteenth century for most of the world as games became reasons in themselves to gather. For at least their first two decades however, Gaelic games were often surrounded by Gaelic festivals (formal or informal) which included contests or exhibitions of Irish music, dance, and speech-making; all of which involved women in pivotal roles. While describing the spectacle of one day's matches which were preceded by a Mass and a parade, a newspaper praised the young women of the town as "typical

Irish *cailini*, fine Irish speakers, and Irish singers and dancers, and able helpers of the boys, [who] are well worthy of their country too."[64] Although the female participation was welcome and widespread, the gender hierarchy remained firmly in place. Men held center stage while the women were assigned supporting roles of muse-like encouragement. When discussing the sorry state of traditional pastimes in his inaugural letter, Archbishop Croke referred to the "sour humiliation... of every genuine son and daughter of the old land." He went on to discuss the "ball-playing, hurling, football-kicking... and all such favorite exercises and amusements amongst men and boys."[65] Therefore, although the shame of national subjugation was felt by all, only the males were able to avenge this directly. While there were Gaels of both sexes, their paths to that status were defined by the larger bifurcation of Irish society into spheres of activity that overlapped, but were viewed as largely distinct.

While middle-class Irish women were pressing their claims for greater recognition in the public sphere, working-class women were being steadily pushed not only out of the paid workforce, but out of positions of authority in Irish society and culture in general. Socialist Irish revolutionary James Connolly described the life of an Irish working-class woman as being "the slave of the slave."[66] In many ways, the experiences of Irish women under colonialism was more closely analogous to their female counterparts in India, Africa, or the Middle East than to those across St. George's Channel in England. Moreover, as in all the cases of the rest of the Empire, the hopes for equality once the nationalist struggle was won were dashed by patriarchal postcolonial states.[67]

Irish women, finding themselves increasingly superfluous in a homeland socially and economically geared toward men, were regularly being pushed into solo emigration at a rate that was unparalleled in history. Between 1885 and 1920, almost 700,000 Irish women emigrated alone. Whereas before the Famine Irish adult women were co-breadwinners and were generally able to make their own decisions regarding whom they would marry based on popular notions of romantic love, after the Famine this was nearly universally replaced with marriages determined by males based on dowry negotiations. When coupled with women's widespread displacement from the workforce, the options available to Irish women were severely limited. Marriage rates, which before the Famine had reached nearly three quarters of the Irish population, had fallen to below a third by 1881 while the age of marriage steadily rose to the highest average age of marriage in Europe. The growing influence of the Roman Catholic Church in Irish life and the post-Famine emphasis on the repression of sexual activity and expression, created a fairly hostile environment for Irish women.[68]

Both Gaelic masculinity and femininity had the stereotypes of their British and Anglo-Irish counterparts against which to define themselves. The conceptions of British masculinity were applied to British and Anglo-Irish equally, displaying the manner in which a family could have resided in Ireland for 300 years and still be regarded as culturally suspect because of class and religious affiliation. While criticizing the rigid qualifications for amateurism for Irish athletics as governed by loyalists, Cusack stated, "For years...clubs excluded...people who are vulgar enough to be muscular and would give a daddy-long-legs...no chance in the presence of his wasp-waisted sweetheart."[69] Archbishop Croke echoed the popular dichotomy between virile, poor Irishmen and effete, well-off Anglo-Irish, when he contrasted the "youthful athletes...bereft of shoes and coat, and thus prepared to play" to the "degenerate dandies...arrayed in light attire...and racket in hand."[70] The repetitive labeling of the British as effeminate spoke as much to the Irish fear of themselves becoming effeminate as it did to a concern over the status of British men. Distinctions between manly Irish and effeminate British reassured the Irish men that political and economic subjugation did not mean a loss of sexual power. The conception of a feminized oppressor was unusual and represented an inversion of the more common representation of a feminized colonial subject.

Class cannot be separated from the anti-British and anti-loyalist sentiment and perceptions of gender. The gentry of Ireland and the absentee landlords in England were forever tied to Ireland's greatest tragedies, namely Cromwell's brutal conquest of Ireland in the seventeenth century and the Famine, which together were seen as completely robbing the Irish of their own land. The influence and involvement of aristocracy, who previously had sponsored almost all nineteenth-century athletic contests in Ireland in the form of estate cricket and gentlemanly races, were vigorously opposed in Gaelic games.[71] The strict financial and social requirements of much Anglo-Irish sporting activity also contributed to Irish resentment. For example, the Cork Drapers' Association was denied affiliation with the Irish Rugby Union because of their profession.[72] Before the founding of the GAA, the Anglo-Irish run athletic organizations forbade participation to not only those who had competed for money prizes or against professionals, but also to anyone who was a "mechanic, artisan or labourer."[73] In an editorial deriding upper-class women who participated in that most English of sports, foxhunting, a writer asked, "Can anyone even pretend to imagine that such a woman possibly be a good wife or mother, or have sympathy with sorrows and the sufferings of others...How many ladies of rank and leisure and means, either in the city or country, help to teach catechism in our churches on Sunday?"[74] Thus the Gaelic woman was above all a working- or middle-class mate and nurturer who was actively religious and morally unquestionable. Here once again, the valued status of Irish women's reproductive ability is highlighted. Men were consistently defined as independent actors while women were most often defined as relational objects, as the mothers, daughters, sisters, and wives of men. Mosse has contended that, "Nationalism—and the society that identified with it—used the example of the chaste and modest woman to demonstrate its own virtuous aims. In the process, it fortified bourgeois ideals of respectability that penetrated all classes of society during the nineteenth century."[75]

Upper-class women also represented independence of action for women. Women who possessed the free time to go on foxhunts were not working from early morning to late at night running a household. In the same vein, Irish women who strayed beyond the boundaries of the domestic sphere received little encouragement from the sporting community. At one match there were "Several ladies with collecting boxes in aid of the rifle fund for the Irish Volunteers [who] reaped a rich harvest; a strong contrast to the cold reception given to the few ladies soliciting support for the Women's Suffrage cause."[76] This discouragement of women as equal partners by spectators of Gaelic games mirrored their relegation to the background by the games themselves both through the physicality of the games and the symbolism surrounding them, which demarcated the proper roles of the sexes.

The Emergence of "Scientific Play"

The most prominent trend in the evolution of the games themselves in the first three decades of the GAA was the growth of "scientific" play. The term refers to a more open style of play, which relied increasingly on precision passing, accurate shooting, quickness, guile, and teamwork, and less on brute strength. This partiality for "scientific" play was trumpeted ceaselessly by the nationalist community and directly affected their conceptions of masculinity and the sports. The early years of the games had been dominated by sloppy, rough play where "strength" was often the victor over "skill." The standardization of rules engendered by the GAA, which strictly forbade pushing, holding, tripping, and kicking of opponents, represented a move to limit violence in the games. Elias and Dunning have argued that "one of the crucial problems confronting societies in the course of a civilizing process was . . . that of finding a new balance between pleasure and restraint." Gaelic games fall into the sociological category of "mock-battle" and represent the "socially acceptable, ritualized expression of physical violence" that has replaced the more overt, everyday violence that was characteristic of early modern and medieval society that played even more rough-and-tumble folk football and hurling.[77] As the games relied increasingly on skill and maneuver, self-images of the Irish male were further removed from the traditional British view of the strong-but-dumb Paddy. Coinciding with the faster pace, increased scoring, and diminished violence were larger crowds, which were taken by the GAA as evidence of the people's approving attitudes toward the games.

The Irish codes went further than other contact sports at the time in curbing violence, including sending off players for retaliation and allowing replacements for injured players. In contrast, rugby did not permit substitutions for injured players, who were expected to be "hard," conquer their pain and play on, often with serious injuries, to avoid making their teammates play a man short.[78] Those who viewed their own pain as insignificant could easily come to view the pain of others similarly. Gaelic games, in contrast, not only allowed, but also stressed compassion for others; men must play unafraid of injury, but receive prompt and proper treatment if they occur. Despite this, injuries remained common. For example, a letter to a local newspaper sought to explain the Tulla Hurling Club's recent loss by citing the fact that almost two-thirds of the Tulla men were severely wounded during the course of play.[79] The modernization of Gaelic games and the so-called "civilizing" tendencies exhibited affected not so much a reduction in violence but a transformation in the type of violence.

The progressive trend to decrease the number of players on the field from 21 aside to 15 aside worked to heighten the value of quickness and finesse and lessen the worth of brute force.[80] It came to be conventional wisdom that the "thinking" team would always beat a stronger but "unscientific" one. The report of one game stated that the smaller team "made up by science what they lacked in physical strength, and very soon the game was on the side of David against Goliath."[81] The David-over-Goliath theme of course had particular resonance for the nationalist community. The Kerry footballers' decade-long dominance from 1905 to 1914 cemented their version of the game as the standard. In November 1914, the *Freeman's Journal* commented that the "purity of play" exhibited by the Kerry and Wexford teams in one match brought the game to a level of perfection unimaginable even at the turn of the century.[82] Inherent in play which stressed teamwork was the inevitability that in order to succeed, individuals would have to forego opportunities for personal glory to pass the ball to a teammate. This emphasis on the group was reinforced by the refusal of many sports writers to individualize in their reports, choosing instead to compliment the whole side, or both teams in their entirety. When names were singled out, it would not be uncommon to see as many as half of the players on the field mentioned. In this way, the growth of scientific play helped to encourage a model of manliness in which selflessness was deemed the most commendable action.

Discipline was of primary importance to the promoters of the games. In fact, one prominent writer stated his belief that "the creation of proper control was the first and most important task" of the GAA.[83] Few reports passed up the opportunity to comment on the exemplary behavior of the players and crowds. One team was described as having "Celtic faces [which] were the faces of well-schooled, well-disciplined men, full of enthusiasm but also full of self-control. Enthusiasm dominated by self-control!"[84] The unending parade of compliments and emphasis on good behavior would seem almost comic were it not so seriously offered. Rhetoric aside, it seems that as the winning of games became more closely tied to the honor of the parish or county, tempers often did flare. The rough play of one man was blamed for the early termination of a game in 1906, when his use of foul language and deliberate kicking of opponents were described as "ungaelic."[85] In a game in 1889, questionable tactics were derided as "unmanly."[86]

Despite the emphasis on skill on the field, neither the physicality of the players nor the military benefits of disciplined men were ignored. The highly integrated and open playing style forced teams to train more. In this way, the move away from preeminent physicality made ties between the games and military potential paradoxically closer. P.J. Devlin observed that GAA patron and Fenian leader John O'Leary "knew that it was manpower that fought battles, and that only disciplined manpower could win them."[87] As the games evolved, the image of an ideal Gael as a prepared Gael became more axiomatic. However, it was incessantly reiterated that this manly and military vigor must be kept under control. The ritualization of violence surrounding modern Gaelic games was aimed at promoting a martial image. The *Freeman's Journal* described how after one match in 1888 the teams "were marshaled . . . in military fashion [and] ordered to fall into lines." The team "captain" gave the order "Right About!" and the men, victors and vanquished together, paraded through the town.[88] Even though a martial, and therefore inherently violent, performance was enacted, the imitation of the military kept that violence within disciplined ranks. Since controlled and organized violence was, in fact, much more powerful than its disorganized counterpart, the advent of the GAA and modern Gaelic games increased the potential for violence in Irish society. The greater number of men participating in these games enlarged the portion of the population that was directly involved in activities requiring physical force. Here then, we see the transformation rather than reduction of violence that characterized the evolution of modern Irish sport.

The connection between training for sport and training for revolt was not left unstated, but was continually enunciated by players, administrators, and commentators. For example, the caman has long held symbolic value as a substitute for a rifle. The men of the GAA marched at the funerals of prominent statesmen and association figures, most prominently at Parnell's funeral, with camans draped in black and carried on the shoulder in a rifle-like manner, thereby doing little to ease the minds of Dublin Castle, the administrative headquarters of the British government in Ireland, that they were not an army in training.[89] Although maintaining strict neutrality as an organization during the Home Rule Crisis of 1913, the pro–Sinn Féin views of most GAA members were easily discernible and a marked decrease in the number participating ensued as militia ranks swelled.[90] One writer proclaimed that "The Gaelic body, be it club or council, that puts camans into the hands of boys can do as much for a future Ireland of ideal dreams as those who would arm a battalion in the same area."[91] One rally speaker stated that "when the time comes, the hurlers will cast away the caman for the sharp bright steel that will drive the Saxon from our land."[92] The conflation of sport and militarism seemed to suggest that if Gaelic athletes could conquer and defend the borders of the playing fields of Ireland from the imposition of British institutions, surely it was only a matter of time before the same was done for the nation.

The growth of scientific play and the attendant increased importance of discipline had direct and numerous effects on conceptions of masculinity for the Gaelic community. A strict emphasis on discipline from the players allowed teams to play in a more emotionally controlled and analytical manner, thus distinguishing them from women who were viewed as overemotional and irrational. Orderly crowds (which were always the ideal if not always the reality) permitted the games to progress without interruption and displayed to the English that the Irish were a fraternal and peaceable people who were quite capable of governing themselves.[93] Play which favored combination was the perfect metaphor for national unity and the triumph of tactical initiatives over greater strength was a particularly apt analogy for the growing sense of militarization of Irish everyday life. Finally, an emphasis on strategy and artfulness allowed both games to contrast themselves favorably with rugby, where play centered on large packs of brutish men tackling, kicking, and otherwise bloodying one another to determine victory. Even though Gaelic games required strength and included violence within the normal course of play, it was held that the intellectual aspects of the games were paramount. In these ways, the progress of Gaelic football and hurling toward "scientific" play was in many ways symbiotic with the community that fostered them.

Conclusion

Hurling and Gaelic football as propagated by the GAA were instrumental in the restructuring of an Irish nationalist manhood. The power to oppose British games and reclaim independence of action one sphere at a time, marked the first dramatic steps toward greater freedom from English control. Since these endeavors took place within the highly gendered and male-dominated world of sports, they affected the construction of gender roles within the wider community. While masculinity is never a static entity and its characteristics evolve over time, the period from 1884 to 1916 is distinguished by a clear path of development of a distinct conception of masculinity within the Gaelic community, which bound together manhood and nationalism within the context of active participation in Gaelic sports. Being born male in Ireland was not equivalent to being an Irish man, which was the product of a dynamic cultivation of physical and mental qualities that distinguished the Irish man from both women and British men.

The evolution of "scientific" play created a more exciting exhibition for spectators, as well as provided an evolving model of manhood for the Irish nationalist community. The movement toward more scientific play defined Irish men as intelligent, energetic, and progressive. The GAA has mistakenly been described as an "antimodern" force by some historians due to the association's rural base of support and the strictly amateur basis of participation as compared to the creeping professionalization of English football and Northern Union rugby. R.F. Foster, for example, has argued that the GAA "helped focus national feelings and national pride into distinctly non-English, nonmaterialistic and anti-modern activities."[94] While it is certainly true that the GAA endeavored in all ways to be anti-English this cannot necessarily be equated with "anti-modern" unless "Englishness" and "modernity" are conflated.

To be "scientific" was to be part of the future, not the Famine-stricken, politically subjugated, and economically depressed past. The skills, dedication, and physical attributes developed and displayed by these games were the same as those required of a young nation seeking independence. The games uniquely displayed these strengths. A hurling match, with its combination of speed, stamina, skill, and terrifyingly dangerous stickwork, displayed its participants physical stature and grace, fearlessness, and decisiveness. The development of combination-based tactics fostered the attributes desired by the Gaelic community and the games provided the means to propagate these characteristics. The updating of the games, did not in itself, produce a new masculinity. However, in conjunction with other cultural and political factors in the period, masculinity was refashioned and this redefinition was heavily influenced by the GAA-led movement.

The games' dynamic was in large part dominated by tensions that molded and distorted the meanings of the games and their relations to Irish society. The games were characterized by dichotomous conflicts between civilizing tendencies and violent content, between a desire to be viewed as peaceable and disciplined while at the same time presenting an impression of incipient revolution, and finally, between the paramountcy of muscular stature and ascendancy of intellectual control. Like their British counterparts who sought to reconcile Christianity with Social Darwinism, Gaelic sports fed on the tensions produced by these varying objectives competing for dominance. In this way, the games reflect the fortunes of the Irish nationalist movement itself, which wavered between parliamentarism and military defiance and between conciliatory Home Rule and republican separatism. Through the process of revamping the games, new sports were born which shared ideals and goals with the community's conceptions of a nationalist manhood, and which came to symbolize the Irish struggle with the English while simultaneously participating in that struggle.

"As boys we were initiated into the world of sports by men and into the world of men by sports."[95] Irish boys and men were not only trained and initiated into the world of true Gaelic men, but were created by the Gaelic games as the sports themselves were reconstructed. Any process of initiation necessarily involves the crossing of a boundary, whether it be from boyhood to manhood or from outsider to insider. Football and hurling made many of these boundaries formal by providing a forum for the selection of graded levels of competition within clubs and counties and between supporters and outsiders in the country at large. Like every community that aims to unite and include, exclusion of others is a necessary step in that process. The creation of an independent Irish identity was not limited to simply distinguishing Irish from English, but also man from woman, rich from poor, and Catholic from Protestant.

CHAPTER THREE

The King of Sports: Polo in Late Victorian and Edwardian India

During the 1870s and 1880s, the game of polo rose to predominance in India. Initially an Indo-Persian game of ancient origin, elite British men in India reconceptualized and transformed it into a pastime more in line with the ideals of the games revolution then underway at home. A more "scientific" and constrained British game replaced the hurly-burly indigenous one. Polo became a focus of the social life of army officers, a common method of military training, and a locus for social interaction between the leaders of the great princely states and the British establishment. Polo's popularity spread to the point where it would not be an exaggeration to say that in peace time, the main occupation of many officers in India was playing, organizing, training for, and financing their polo.

For the maharajahs and nizams of the larger princely states, polo became an ideal pastime to complement their more traditional leisure activities of pigsticking and hunting.[1] Indian princes took to polo with a keenness that rivaled the army's. The expense of polo made it a useful vehicle for conspicuous consumption and lavish hospitality. In contrast to the local cricketing community, which was dominated by less illustrious Indians, polo was confined to the very upper reaches of Indian society. Consequently, the game provided broad access to and social interaction with the British elite and thus facilitated princely politics and the gamesmanship of Empire. Most importantly, the game fit with princely notions about recreation; namely, it was dangerous, allowed for individual flair, and was prohibitively expensive and elitist. It was not simply a matter of princely states wishing to beat the British, polo was also a way for states to act out rivalries between themselves in a way that was manly, but short of war.

Underlying much British thinking about Indian polo was the belief that elite Indians would absorb discipline, an ethos of sportsmanship, and other characteristically English values. In other words, polo would be a way to make the Indian princes more English. Lawrence James characterized the

British romantic stereotype of the ideal prince as one "whose passionate loyalty to the Crown is matched only by his mania for sport, and whose object in life is to make himself into a benign English aristocrat."[2] However, the princes themselves adopted the game because it reinforced what they saw as their intrinsic qualities while simultaneously proving politically advantageous. For the princes, polo was a means of articulating and displaying their separateness from other Indians as much as their solidarity with the British. If polo was "modern" for the Anglo-Indians, for the princes, polo playing was profoundly conservative. They did not take up (and excel at) polo predominantly because they wanted to be like the British or because the game made them more rational, efficient, or sportsmanlike. Rather, the attraction of polo was that it reaffirmed their distinctiveness, Indianness, and aristocratic traditions that stressed personal valor and equestrian excellence. Likewise, success at polo was a means of winning honors, investment, and British support for an individual state.

Not surprisingly, the game of polo, like other games around the Empire, was on occasion an empty vessel into which a variety of meanings could be poured according to one's outlook and cultural assumptions. Consequently, the British often attributed contradictory and at times opposing meanings to similar practices depending on whether the actor in question was Indian or British. While the exorbitant cost of polo encouraged thrift on the part of British subalterns, it often was said to promote profligacy for the less-restrained (read civilized) princes.

Manliness was the quality at the heart of both the Anglo-Indian and princely devotion to polo; the game and its attendant rituals provided a way to promote specific ideals of masculinity, whether British and "modern" or Indian and "traditional" and it often provided a space in which the various conceptions of what it meant to be a man were put on public display and allowed to compete on more or less equal terms. Despite differing interpretations and shadings, the masculine values thought to be promoted by the game were in large part shared by the officers and the princely nobles and a brotherhood uniting public school old boys and the aristocrats of the so-called "martial races" was frequently evoked by both sides. This declared fraternity could not overcome deeply entrenched British racism and attitudes of cultural superiority, but within the world of polo, there did exist an equality of opportunity and fair competition which would be largely absent from the rest of the imperial sporting world for decades to come. Polo was an important venue for the contestation of masculine ideals amongst and between colonizers and colonized that undergirded the British colonial structure of India.[3] The various overlapping hierarchies of wealth, power, and race that constituted the social structure of the Raj itself were in part created, maintained, and publicly enacted on the polo ground.

A New Game is Born

In December 1898, *The Indian Sportsman* of Calcutta proclaimed, "The ever increasing number of polo tournaments held all over the country under

I.P.A. [India Polo Association] rules, affords striking proof, if indeed such proof were needed, of the hold the game has taken of the affections of Anglo-Indian and native sportsmen. It is as much now the national game of India as cricket is of England."[4] Although Persian and Indian elites had historically engaged in equestrian ball-and-stick games, the practice had been largely forgotten in most of the subcontinent and Middle East for several centuries before the middle of the nineteenth century.[5] However, British planters, after witnessing surviving examples of "folk" polo in the 1860s, reconceived the game and transformed it into a modern sport.

Comparing the "folk" version of the game with the "modern" version, Lord Curzon, the aristocratic viceroy of India (1898–1905), wrote: "Of course, our European game is more orthodox: the ground is more even, the riders are better mounted, the rules more precise, the strokes more scientific, and the play more brilliant."[6] Curzon's "of course" captures an overarching theme of British commentary about polo in India: acknowledgment of Indian origins or Indian greatness at the game did not diminish polo's overwhelmingly British nature. In the unruly indigenous game, an indeterminate number of riders on tiny ponies propelled a ball nearly randomly and generally chaotically around a loosely defined field in the absence of standardized rules or sometimes even goals. In place of this picture of disorder, British polo writers extolled the more inhibited British game to illustrate that the modern game was, above all, British. One reference work on sport argued that "very little beyond the root idea of a game of stick and ball, played on horseback" actually came from the traditional game.[7]

The new creation followed the pattern of other new sports in the era: field dimensions were standardized, written rules were publicized, the number of players was limited, and a hierarchy of governing bodies, official tournaments, and challenge cups was organized. Once established, more refined tactics and strategies developed, orthodoxies evolved and the prominence of the game grew immeasurably.[8] For British writers, polo's development was an apt metaphor for British rule in India. One could "see how the order-loving and disciplined minds of the Westerns have organised a game which was originally a wild helter-skelter into a careful, scientific, and military sport. These things are an allegory, and the polo of East and West may to the careful observer give a suggestion why in war and government the West ever prevails."[9] Brigadier General Robert Lumsden Ricketts (apparently without irony) dismissed the indigenous game as having been merely an "amusement of the ruling classes," although polo could not be considered a game of masses among English devotees either.[10] He nevertheless credited the British with creating a proper game. He argued that "It was not until the game was taken up by the Western races with their more systematic minds and mechanical efficiency that progress in tactical ideas became possible."[11]

Paradoxically, expositions on the necessity of a modern, British mind for the development of proper polo were often found in the same texts that acclaimed individual Indian players' tactical innovations. Ricketts himself noted that in the 1890s, the "Patiala team developed to the highest degree the system of giving the back a clean run-through, perhaps owing to the outstanding genius of Hira Singh, who was head and shoulders above all other players at that time."[12] The history of polo in India is replete with contradictory statements about the skill, contributions, and roles of Indians in the game's development. Individual Indians and particular Indian teams were continually recognized for brilliance, but this brilliance did not reflect on Indians in general. In contrast, when particular British innovators improved the game, it was taken of evidence of the superiority of British intellect, morality, and athleticism as a whole. Polo was clearly not the only part of Indian life where this dynamic was found. Ronald Inden has argued that often for westerners "Indian actions are attributed to social groups—caste, village, linguistic region, religion, and joint family—because there are no individuals in India."[13] Despite the British tendency to generalize among very large groups of Indians, such as "the princes" or "Hindus," the people of the subcontinent saw themselves as varied and diverse. Polo was a way for princes and other elites to illustrate not only their personal individuality and aggrandizement, but also to support of local or state "nationalism."

Polo in the British and Indian Armies

Along with hunting, polo assumed a central position in the daily lives of British officers. Whether in the home or Indian army, polo commonly came to be viewed as essential for teaching horsemanship, tactics and teamwork, for inculcating moral virtues and keeping men's time, energy, and resources focused on a wholesome activity. While it became a truism that the "same qualities which bring a man to the front at polo are required by anyone who aspires to lead men," there were certainly dissenting voices.[14] The cost of a regiment's polo, and especially the cost of supporting the representative team, was often borne by all the officers, whether they played or not. For officers who favored other forms of recreation, the predominance of polo within the military culture of India in this period could be oppressive.

A letter writer in the early 1910s bemoaned what he perceived to be a relative decline in the number of officers wholly focused on polo, a deterioration he attributed to a relaxation of military culture that gave modern junior officers too much freedom and encouraged an overdeveloped love of luxury. He reminisced nostalgically about the 1890s "when a youth who showed a disinclination for horseflesh, often got very roughly handled."[15] Nonetheless, as late as the 1920s, the automatic connection between polo and training military officers in India was largely taken for granted. Edward Miller's *Modern Polo*, which went through six editions between 1896 and 1930, is representative. "To a large section of His Majesty's servants, polo in India is not merely an amusement and a game, but is also a serious occupation, to which a great deal of time, money and trouble are devoted. Polo is now recognized by the majority of our military authorities as one of the most important parts of the training of an officer."[16] Paeans to the invaluable nature of polo to the imperial mission were ubiquitous. Robert Baden-Powell summed up the general tone in his *Indian Memories* when he wrote that polo was "a form of training which appeals to every young officer."[17]

Central to the paramountcy of polo within the army was the widespread assertion that polo was vital for maintaining the manliness of officers in a foreign and eastern land full of temptation. Baden-Powell for instance asserted in 1915 that polo and pigsticking had "completely driven out from the British subaltern the drinking and betting habits of the former generation, and have given him in place of these a healthy exercise which also has its moral attributes in playing the game unselfishly; and above all the practice of quiet, quick decision and dash that are essential to a successful leader of men."[18] In short, polo was the manliest game and those who did not choose to participate were regularly derided as "unsporting, inefficient or effete."[19] This is made explicit in a letter from "Elderly Gentleman" in which he dismissed those who questioned polo's value not just as women, but also as old women. He responded to critics by saying, "My dear old ladies, of both sexes, believe me that the indirect return in kind, not money, is beyond all computation. Polo has, in conjunction with pig-sticking, done more towards teaching our young cavalry officers that dash, nerve, steadiness, seat and discipline, which are the boast and pride of the English nation, than any other pastimes or sport."[20]

The process of buying an untrained horse and transforming it into a successful polo pony was both a way to turn a profit for those subalterns without a generous stipend from home and a means of instilling managerial skills. Breaking the will of a horse while maintaining its competitive spirit was thought to develop skills that would come in handy when dealing with the non-equine beasts of burden in the army, enlisted men.[21] Fame on the polo ground was also decidedly beneficial to an ambitious soldier's career prospects in a military culture that viewed as officer's skill at polo as an important component of his CV and some commanding officers refused to have non-players serve under them.[22] In the Imperial Service Troops, the Indian Army and the Home Regiments stationed in India, skill at polo often led to advancement. Douglas Haig (later Field-Marshall Lord Haig commander in chief of the British forces in the Great War) was an integral part of the success of the 7th Hussars, who dominated Indian polo in the late 1880s.[23] Haig's biographer contended that for Haig and his comrades in the Victorian army, polo was "never just a game, but a test of character" and that the sport provided Haig with "levels of emotional intensity otherwise lacking in a life of restraint."[24] Earl Mountbatten was a world-class polo player and authored, under the pseudonym "Marco," an influential polo book that went through six editions.[25]

Most Indian polo came in the form of "station polo" in which the officers of a given regiment or station played pickup games several afternoons a week. This necessarily involved players of varying levels of proficiency, experience, and seriousness. The polo ground, the practice bowl, and the stables were sites of initiation for new officers assigned to India and it was the uncommonly independent young man who resisted the pressure to play polo, or to at the very least support polo by means of contributing monetarily to the regiments polo fund.[26] This expectation of pecuniary support naturally led to resentment among non-devotees, especially since it was widely agreed that the salary of a junior officer in India was altogether insufficient to support the lifestyle, a remnant of the pre-1870 British army in which younger sons of good families bought their commissions "as part of the natural life of a gentleman."[27] Well-off subalterns received an allowance from home, while those without families of great means often left the British army for the better-paying Indian regiments or lived beneath their station.[28] A young Winston Churchill upon arriving in India as a junior officer promptly employed a dressing boy, a butler, a groom, a bearer, a wet sweeper, and he shared nine other servants with two fellow officers.[29] One officer who had traded the British for the Indian army when his allowance was cut off by his father noted that he was left without a choice "as it was quite impossible to live in British service without assistance."[30]

Beyond station polo, there was the world of tournaments and challenge cups. This level of play was reserved for men with means, as the costs of supporting a proper stable of tournament-grade ponies and transporting them to far-flung contests were prohibitive. The most important tournaments were the Inter-Regimental and the India Polo Association (IPA) Championship tournaments; lesser but still important tournaments included the Golconda Cup, the Subaltern Cup, the Native Cavalry Cup, and the Infantry tournament. The annual Inter-Regimental was the highlight of the military social calendar in India and consequently, players often traveled remarkable distances to play in them.[31] Churchill, the star of the 4th Hussars team which had stunned Indian polo by winning a major tournament within six weeks of landing in India, once traveled from England back to India to play in the Inter-Regimental at Meerut before resigning his commission and proceeding to Egypt to build his career as a writer. The 4th Hussars illustrated one of the fundamental facts of the culture of polo in India: money was the first and most important factor in determining a team's relative success. To be sure, his teammates and he were excellent horsemen and players before coming to India, but the decisive factor in their quick rise to prominence was their ability to afford the massive capital expenditure of purchasing a string of 25, already trained, high-quality polo ponies from the Poona Light Horse, an Indian army regiment permanently stationed in India with Indian sepoys and British officers.[32]

While class differences among the British in India were never wholly erased, they were blurred somewhat by racial solidarity. In Benita Parry's words, "For all white men India brought promotion to membership of a master race."[33] Nonetheless, cavalry officers in home regiments were often aristocratic and/or wealthy and could live lavishly on allowances from home, while British officers in the Indian army were likely to be middle class and dependent on their salaries to support themselves.[34] These differences did not disappear because they played polo together. First, the wealthier one was, the better-trained ponies one could afford. Likewise, players were often given preferential treatment and advanced to regimental teams based on social rather than sporting credentials. Lt. Col. Sir Henry de Beauvoir De Lisle of the Durham Light Infantry, who was deemed one of the great early players, managers, and strategists of the game, wrote in his widely read and widely cited book, *Polo in India*, that social status could distort sporting meritocracy. He noted that were of course "some ambitious beginners who are never content unless they are placed in good games. Such are the greatest trial to a conscientious manger, and if their social standing is high, it is difficult to relegate them to their proper class [of polo]"[35] Still, polo was also a means for Europeans of varying social status to interact in ways which would not have occurred at home.[36] For instance, Edith Glascock, the wife of a police officer at the Delhi Durbar, wrote home to her sister in December 1911: "Saturday was the semi-finals of the polo & their majesties went in state. We all have the entrée to the Royal enclosure and I was all awfully chaffed by the other police ladies as they came and looked at us all."[37] Glascock comments on the novelty of being around so much nobility and royalty. Her husband and she would have undoubtedly run in much more modest social circles in Britain.

If in many ways polo unified disparate elements in the British community, it could also simultaneously be a source of substantial tension in a regiment. Supporting a representative side entailed a tremendous amount of traveling and consequently great expense, which often fell on all the officers, whether they played or not. The enormous expense of polo at any level was a matter of great concern for all but the wealthiest officers. De Lisle reported that "the War Office receives frequent visits from indignant parents whose sons have exceeded their allowance, and who usually attribute the fact to Polo!"[38] Nonetheless, the perceived benefit of the game for the manly development of the officer corps, and consequently for the security of the Empire, was such that grossly unfair practices were countenanced and those who questioned the wisdom of the "polocracy" were marginalized.

That the celebration of polo was not unanimous was often evident in letters to the editor. "A Cavalry Officer" wrote to an Allahabad newspaper mocking the average officer's concern with polo as obsessive and indeed cult-like. He argued that the frequently heard mantra that polo was an essential part of cavalry training neglected to notice that Cromwell, Napoleon, and Frederick the Great, among others, managed to field efficient cavalries trained without polo. The correspondent contended that days without polo were "considered by most votaries as unutterably blank, in which the sun even has lost his shine."[39] Another dissenting officer called on his polo-playing fellow officers to be more tolerant of other sporting endeavors, asking, "Oh! ye slaves of the goddess of Polo! Why do you thus enpinnacle yourselves? Why this lofty supercilious attitude toward the rest of the sporting world? Are you so much superior to other men? Let us cease this intolerance, and agree that all sports are good, which are health-giving and manly. Let us admire a man who strives at his sport no matter what form it takes." However, in the cavalry it is "always polo—incessant, inexorable, inevitable polo."[40] Whether it was described as a cult or a fetish akin to heathen worship of idols, the fervor of players was often compared to uncivilized religion by opponents, in stark contrast to the way in which it was held to be a great marker of British civilization by proponents.

The expense of the game and deleterious effect that this had on junior officers without substantial private resources was a constant topic of debate in the literature of the period. Ideally, each officer needed four ponies, although three would be enough for station games.[41] Each horse would need its own *syce*, or indigenous groom, and one hay-cutter was needed for every two horses. Guidebooks also recommended that officers employ a head groom if two or more ponies were being kept. Newly arrived subalterns were warned that the average "syce is a queer creature, who fancies he knows a great deal more than his master, and at first you may experience some difficulty in getting your orders carried out. The sack of one or two will probably bring the remainder to their senses."[42] Advice books for officers new to Indian polo reinforced the paternalistic tendencies of British officers to treat Indians as children. One remonstrated: "Do not overpay them, but issue them their wages regularly and treat them well, but sternly."[43] Author T. Wilfred Sheppard lamented that although an officer would prefer to take care of his horses himself, it "is not always possible, as after all we are not out in India to play polo only, but to earn enough money to be able to play and keep our ponies and, I suppose, ourselves."[44]

At the Naini Tal station, dissenting officers in 1899 submitted a petition complaining that polo's supremacy at the station was despotic. In response, the Lieutenant-General Commanding issued an order disbanding all station polo clubs in order to stop the "tyranny" of the practice by which all the officers were pressured into paying for the polo of the regimental squads. While acknowledging that polo was indeed, "the most manly of games" the orders decried the "custom" which allowed "the polo player to indulge in the game at the expense of his brother officers." He commented that hunters did not expect fellow officers to subsidize their shooting nor did golfers ask others to purchase their clubs for them, yet "the polo player in some regiments has no such scruples; he expects as a right that any officer in his regiment, whether a polo player or not, is to subscribe to a club to keep him going in ponies and pay his traveling and other expenses whenever the team he belongs to takes part in a polo tournament."[45] This outright attack on the morality of polo financing and the prohibition of clubs at Naini Tal was a rare moment of opposition to the pervasive culture of polo. Clubs continued to exist throughout the subcontinent and peer pressure to contribute was widespread.

The injustice of the system of funding for most regimental polo clubs that amounted to nothing more than a heavy tax on non-playing officers to subsidize the playing officers was defended based on necessity. De Lisle remained "confident that it is impossible for a regiment to compete with success in a first class tournament unless assisted by a polo fund, or unless four players can be found with sufficient means to bring 24 first class tournament ponies into the field."[46] It was not simple hypocrisy that led to this unfairness being tolerated. Rather, it was deemed so vital to regimental honor and standing that the regiment be properly represented on the polo field, that all officers were expected to contribute not for pleasure of the players, but for the glory of the regiment. The intolerance shown to non-players was comparable to the pressure to conform at the public schools that produced most of the officers. The polo-mad regimental culture was often compared to life at school or university. Officers perceived earning a place on a regimental team to be an accomplishment analogous to a schoolboy making his school's XI or a university man earning his varsity colors.[47] For others, that the regiment was simply "an echo of school" meant that it was a life dominated by forced conformity. "The discipline, the regimental customs (especially in matters of dress), the abhorrence of originality—all these are to be found at school." And it was with polo that the "height of intolerance is reached."[48]

The Paramount Power and the Princes

The leaders and noblemen of the larger princely states were the other main supporters of polo in India. Accounting for nearly 40 percent of the land area and perhaps 30 percent of the population of the subcontinent, the princely states were a central component of the British Raj.[49] The aristocrats who ruled these semiautonomous states under the paramountcy of the Crown were the wealthiest and most conservative segment of Indian society.[50] Prior to the Great Rebellion of 1857, the princely states were often discussed in terms of their lingering despotism and oriental excess. However, the value of loyal princes and the dangers inherent in annexationist policies that displaced stable governments were clear to the British after 1857. Consequently, the moral and administrative shortcomings of the princes, which had figured so prominently in British rhetoric in the first half of the nineteenth century, were overlooked in light of the princes' newly recognized political worth and an abrupt sea change in policy ensued.[51]

No longer considered an obstacle to civilization, the British supported the indigenous aristocracy, ushering in a "golden age for the Indian princes" at the end of the nineteenth century.[52] Princely prestige grew in direct proportion to the rise of Indian nationalism in British India. The educated Indian middle classes, which had been created in order to staff the lower rungs of the administrative apparatus of the Empire, "were disowned by the British as being unrepresentative and as claiming rights which were inimical to the interests of the 'real India,' the unchanging India of the rural masses, martial races and the princes."[53] By the late Victorian period, the princes were imagined by the British to be loyal feudatories who could serve as an example to other, less grateful, subjects. The very existence of the Raj came to be seen as resting on the foundation of princely rule as a bulwark against the growing influence of the nationalists.[54]

Nonetheless, the change in policy did not instantly create a seamless working relationship. British commentators frequently officially lauded, while privately doubting, the sincerity of outward manifestations of loyalty and affection by the princes for the Raj. Sir Henry Cotton, Chief Secretary to the Government of Bengal and president of the Indian National Congress, argued that the princes' actions were above all self-serving and "that the real motive power for the outward and visible signs of loyalty which have been so effusively displayed of late is due far less to their love and admiration for the British Government than to the peculiar helplessness of their position, and in no small measure to a keen perception of political opportunity, from which they have not failed to score a diplomatic advantage."[55] *The Contemporary Review* assured its readers in 1895 that a second "mutiny" was impossible "so long as the native princes are loyal." However, it ominously speculated, "The fact that the Government of India is so manifestly anxious to create in England and elsewhere a popular belief in the loyalty of the princes of India gives rise to he suspicion that it is itself considerably disquieted by doubt and distrust."[56]

David Cannadine has posited that the princely presence made India unique and that "analogues of hierarchy" there replaced the absolute hierarchy of elsewhere in the Empire. His contention that the Raj was inclined to treat princes as "social equals" overstates the level of equality between the British and the Indian princes.[57] To be sure, the princes were relied upon as a buttress against disloyalty and Indian nationalism. However, rather than viewing the Indian aristocracy as a parallel and equal hierarchy to the British aristocracy, it would be more accurate to characterize it as being viewed as a mimetic but inferior one. The British publicly proclaimed the sovereignty and glory of the princes while undermining that sovereignty and mocking the pretensions to equality exhibited by most of the princes.[58]

Cannadine sees Lord Curzon's treatment of the princes as emblematic of the general British stance that the chiefs were indeed equal. If an equality existed, it was of a very circumscribed type as defined by Curzon, a man who could hail "leveling down of class distinction" in institutions like Eton, where the children of aristocrats and parvenus alike are at school together and compete on an equal basis.[59] He offers as evidence the high-profile role played by the princes in the 1903 Coronation Durbar for King-Emperor Edward VII, which he views as a great triumph of symbolic unity.[60] However, the contemporary Indian press was less effusive about the role played by the princes. One English language Indian newspaper expressed sympathy for the princes' prescribed role in the festivities. The editorial concluded: "When a number of bejeweled feudatories pass before the representative of the Paramount Power and do homage, while the plebeian spectator holds up his head and looks on as if he were the occupant of a paid-for seat in a circus, it must strike one to ask if the distinction is an unmixed honour."[61] Nor was this solely the view of Indian commentators. One British commentator argued that it was well known in British circles that the princes resented being asked "to play the part of puppets in those Oriental shows" but that it was nonetheless considered salutary on a symbolic level.[62]

Another paper dismissed princely rhetoric of support for the British or language that purportedly recognized the British's high esteem for Indians by stating "Such language in the mouth of a Rajah or his Dewan is one of the commonplaces of Anglo-Indian experience, meaning nothing at all in particular, except that the speakers wants something in the way of titles or extra guns" and it did not preclude the prince from also supporting Indian nationalist causes simultaneously.[63] Likewise, one English author wrote tellingly: "When one hears Sir Civilian Administrator, KCIE or General Sir Indian Army, KCSI, speaking of his dear friend the Rajah of Racepore or Sindar Polo Singh, we need not take their expressions literally but discount them freely, as being evidently tainted with that *official insincerity* (become second nature) which is engendered by and inseparable from the high position he holds or has held in his day. Also when the Rajah or the Sindar alludes to his old and valued friend Sir Civilian Administrator, KCIE or General Sahib, be sure he feels that by this claim he is conferring an honour upon himself."[64] Whether honestly egalitarian social intercourse was possible under the circumstances is hard to determine and notably it was only in the highest strata of Indian society that attempts were even made.[65]

An article in *The Contemporary Review* published in 1895 relayed a story about an agent from the Political Service in India who met "one of the most conspicuously liberal and enlightened of the nobles of India" at a polo tournament in Poonah. They arranged to have dinner that night at one of the military messes. However, when he informed the mess-secretary of his intention to bring a guest, the officer told him that they did not permit Indians to dine there. The agent protested: "But he has dined with the Queen, was the pet of London society at the Jubilee-time, and is a personal friend of the Prince of Wales." To which the mess secretary replied, "All that may be very true, still, being a black man, he cannot dine at our mess."[66] Nor was this an isolated incident. In the first decade of the twentieth century, when Calcutta was at its pinnacle as an imperial city, social interaction between Indians and British officials was severely limited. Indians, regardless of wealth, education, or royal titles, could belong to none of the most prestigious clubs in the city.[67] This was justified as an attempt to spare elite Indians of the "humiliation of being treated as social inferiors."[68] Despite this general climate of segregation, within the boundaries of the game, polo, like pigsticking and hunting, seems to have been a site of genuinely egalitarian interaction for the subcontinent's elites.

Polo and the Princes

Princely devotion to polo quickly equaled that of the army officers. The largest and wealthiest states, or states aspiring to that status, embraced the game and promptly moved to the fore of Indian polo. The major polo-playing states (including most notably, Hyderabad, Patiala, Mysore, Jodhpur, Gwalior, Kashmir, and Cooch Bihar) affiliated with the IPA, participated in and often won major tournaments.[69] Rulers such as the Nizam of Hyderabad, the Maharaja of Jodhpur, and the Maharaja Patiala ("himself a very fine hitter"[70]) assumed a leading role promoting and supporting polo by hosting tournaments, retaining professional coaches, maintaining immaculate grounds, and breeding horses of the highest quality.[71]

The larger princely states had armies to defend their own territory and to assist the British when called upon to do so. These state armies often supported, in essence, professional polo players. Heera Singh of Patiala, declared one of the top three players in India by De Lisle, reportedly rose to the rank of colonel in Patiala's army "chiefly due to his skill as a polo player."[72] The Jodhpur team in 1895 was the best in India and included highly regarded players Heerji Singh and Dhokal Singh, known for their highly efficient team play.[73] It is significant in the literature of imperial sport to find many examples of non-Britons being credited with teamwork, scientific skill, and organization, normally qualities attributed to British—or at least white—sportsmen and teams.

In the extensive coverage of the Coronation Durbar polo tournament of 1911, as was common with all polo coverage in India, racial explanations for style of play or success or failure on the field were rare. Poor teamwork, slow ponies, and bad luck were cited, but were equally distributed across racial lines.[74] This is in stark contrast to the coverage of most interracial sport in Britain. Paul Deslandes has shown how at in the 1890s, critics of foreign (often Indian) students at Cambridge and Oxford often contrasted the athletic prowess of disciplined, British crews with less efficient foreign crews. This, he argues was used as evidence of a perceived "distinction between British efficiency and leadership and perceived foreign deficiencies in these areas."[75] Nationalism, on the other hand, did color the commentary as in the concluding remarks on the polo which noted: "In conclusion it is most gratifying to reflect that in the Durbar Tournament of 1902 no British team even reached the semi-finals, whereas in 1911 the ultimate verdict rested between two British cavalry Regiments."[76]

Racial generalizations were not completely absent from polo commentary; they were simply balanced by frequent compliments of the more cerebral and moral aspects of the game's best Indian players. It would not seem odd to the average British reader that *The Badminton Library of Sports and Pastimes* noted the princes "display the most excellent horsemanship, and all the suppleness that characterises Orientals."[77] Nonetheless, the endless complimenting of individual princes as "sportsmen" by both Indian and British pundits denoted more than just natural, physical skill. The moral uprightness that was thought to go hand in glove with athleticism was also implied. In his 1915 book, *The Ruling Chiefs, Nobles and Zamindars of India*, A. Vadivelu repeatedly used the same term, "keen sportsman" to describe numerous princes. By describing the Maharajah of Alwar as a "very keen sportsman," for example, Vadivelu was laying claim to several overlapping but distinct discourses: Victorian aristocratic manliness of the public schools, a military sense of horsemanship, honor and bravery, and an aristocratic tradition indigenous to Alwar.[78] Likewise, the Nizam of Hyderabad, who ruled over 13 million people and a territory of 83,000 square miles—in other words an area larger than Scotland and England combined—was described in 1915 as a "prince of great enlightenment, a keen sportsman, and a ruler with a high sense of duty."[79]

Princes sought to encompass both the British traits of which they approved while simultaneously maintaining their own traditions. In discussing the Maharajah of Mysore, *The Indian Mirror*, a pro-Indian National Congress newspaper from Calcutta, stated: "He is a model Maharajah. The whole of India may well be proud of him...He is an excellent sportsman and an expert driver."[80] The British often held Mysore, the second largest state in terms of area and with a population in 1915 of some five million people, to be an exemplary state. Notably, Mysore's rulers did not aim to be simply a copy of Britain. "While [Mysore] has adopted most of the ideals of the West in the matter of social and political advancement its innate conservatism, assisted by the rational patriotism of the ruling house and its chief advisors, has preserved for it all that is best in the ancient institutions and practices of orthodox India. Thus in the social and court life of Mysore there meet all the preservative and progressive forces that are at work in this country due to western education and example."[81] This is a theme which permeated princely rhetoric, namely that although allied with the British, the princes were not mere lapdogs, but shrewd rulers who borrowed when advantageous but remained their own men.

The career of Sir Pratap Singh of Jodhpur, one of the most well-known Indians of his day, is instructive. An Indian biographer and contemporary declared him, in 1922, "the great Rajput hero of the twentieth century."[82] Lord Curzon described him as "a gallant Rajput nobleman, a brave warrior, a genuine sportsman, a true gentleman, and a loyal and devoted subject of Her Majesty the Queen."[83] Curzon hoped that "the younger men of India, the Princes and Chiefs, and Nobles of his country, imitate his manly inspiring example."[84] The son of the Maharajah of Jodhpur, a state larger in area than Ireland, Pratap was one of the great princely proponents of polo.

In 1887, he represented Jodhpur at the Jubilee of Victoria, where he was the toast of London and when the riding breeches he wore were dubbed "jodhpurs," a name they retain to this day.[85] Unlike the allegedly effeminate Bengali *babus*, whose English was deemed comical, Pratap's broken English was deemed endearing and was attributed to his desire to entertain British listeners. "No one who had the privilege of knowing Sir Pratap will ever forget the wonderful language . . . his knack of summing up the situation in a most apposite and original phrase of broken English proved so entertaining to his hearers that he clung to it throughout his life."[86] Pratap was famously physically fearless on horseback and in battle, often taking reckless dares at a whim to prove his valor. One British Resident wrote to another that Pratap was "thought in the Army and pretty generally by Europeans to have been knighted for being a good sportsman and jolly fellow."[87] He was also an example of the habit the British had of imagining the princes to be, as Barbara Ramusack has argued, "eccentric preservers of a dramatic past," which enabled the British in India to partake of an "aristocratic way of life that was becoming increasingly remote from daily social reality."[88]

Sir Henry Newbolt penned a famous poem entitled "A Ballad of Sir Pertab [*sic*] Singh" inspired by the events that followed the death of Lt. James Dalmahoy Cadell, Central India Horse.[89] The poem presents an idealized vision of an Indian prince: a chivalric warrior, loyal to the Crown. According to Newbolt, Pratap placed his soldierly fidelity to a British officer over the demands of his caste when he insisted on carrying the coffin of a fallen officer.[90] However, Pratap explained to Major-General Sir Harry Watson that the Rathores were of such exceptionally high caste that they could do whatever they pleased and nothing was beneath them; as a demonstration, he bent down and undid the laces of Watson's boots.[91] The case is illustrative of a common dynamic in India by which the British interpreted Indians' actions in the manner that was most flattering or useful to themselves. Pratap carried a coffin, which the British believed no high caste Hindu could do without losing his caste, therefore Pratap valued his ties to European more than his religion. However, it is clear that even when serving the British, which he did consistently and honorably his whole life, Pratap did so out of a sense of his Indianess, Jodhpurness, Rajputness or Rathoreness.

Pratap rejoiced at the outbreak of the Great War because it offered him a chance to fulfill his destiny as a *Kshatriya*, the warrior caste of Hinduism, and as a Rajput nobleman. He explained, "Religiously, for a Rajput, war is an open door to heaven."[92] Therefore, it was not just that he had a chance to serve the king, but that he had a chance to fight. In other words, although Pratap was a true and sincere Anglophile, he always remained "fiercely Indian."[93] Pandit Shri Dhar Lal wrote: "Sir Pratap's fame as a sportsman will live as long as Polo is played or pigs are hunted and panthers are shot in India. At both games he was in a class by himself, he regarded them as the Rajputs' School for War."[94] Decades before Gandhi captured the imagination of the world with his call to abandon Western dress, Pratap demanded Indian dress in his court, forbidding his officials to wear western designs. "The round-necked Jodhpur coat and jodhpurs for his clansmen and the coat and dhoti for others remained the norm right up to 1949."[95]

It was a desire to assert not only their traditional characteristics but also to accentuate their difference and superiority to other Indians that fed the princely devotion to polo. As cricket swept the entire Empire and took root in much of India, the large, polo-playing princely states generally shunned cricket in favor of polo and pigsticking, sports which were more dangerous than the placid cricket.[96] Polo also had the advantage of being equestrian, which appealed to both princely tradition and a contemporary desire to spend conspicuously; it was likewise more closely and "clearly identified with Indian and English courts than was cricket."[97] Compared with the very real (and at times mortal) dangers involved in the equestrian sports, cricket lacked appeal for many princes, some of whom actively tried to discourage their sons from playing cricket, the great inculcator of English masculinity and school of manhood. From the princely point of view, when compared with the manly and dangerous game of polo, cricket seemed effeminate and dull. Even after the introduction and widespread adoption of cricket in many Indian circles, for many princes, polo retained its rarefied position. Even in smaller states, like Banswara, there is evidence that cricket was frowned upon because it was not deemed "sufficiently manly or chivalrous" and in contrast to polo was a "lazy game and a waste of time."[98]

The house of Patiala was the great exception and excelled at both cricket and polo. Patiala was a middling state of 1.5 million Hindus ruled by a Sikh family. In the 1890s, the Maharajah, Rajendra Singh, propelled Patiala into the limelight of princely politics first by dedicating its resources to polo and later leading Indian cricket.[99] In contrast to the rulers of the larger states, for many middling and minor princes who were not important enough to have a Resident officer in their state, cricket provided an economic way to increase interaction with representatives of the Raj, which in turn could lead to increased investment, the bestowing of increased honors and other benefits for a small state. Keeping a cricket XI and paying for a professional or two from England was much cheaper than maintaining a stable of high-quality, elite ponies. Furthermore, cricket, unlike polo, became a mass spectator sport by the second decade of the twentieth century thereby giving increased fame and notoriety to princes who ruled over small and obscure states.[100]

Social Interaction

The limited opportunity for social intercourse of even a remotely egalitarian nature makes the culture of polo all the more remarkable. Polo was a key forum for the elites of princely India to meet and interact socially, even if it could not erase the reality of power and hierarchy inherent in the colonial context. An etiquette manual for young British officers from 1910 notes Indian fondness for games and reminds young officers "your joining them in such sports will be greatly appreciated." The manual also reiterates several times: "In dealing with Indians show them the treatment which one gentleman usually accords to another"[101] even as it implied that they were not actually gentlemen, and that this indulgence was for British political gain. Sir Francis Younghusband, army officer and noted imperial adventurer, wrote that the loyalty of the Chitralis would have been more certain if the "British Resident had been more prepared to play polo and go shooting with them."[102]

At major tournaments, polo was a mixed affair. Indian teams, Anglo teams, mixed teams competed equally and without distinction. In some mixed teams, Indians captained Anglos, not a common occurrence in the world of imperial sport. For instance, the program of the one tournament from 1905 listed 12 teams; four were regular army, one was Indian army, three were princely teams with Indians and Anglos playing together, one Indian civilian club, one mixed civilian club, one Anglo civilian club, and the vice regal staff team.[103] Of the 13 teams entered in the two-week long Coronation Durbar polo tournament of 1911, six were composed completely of Europeans, five were mixed teams with Indians and Europeans, and two were completely Indians. At least four princes participated including one maharajah, one nawab, and two rajas.

Princes frequently demonstrated their hospitality by hosting elaborate tournaments. Players traveled from all over India to be pampered at the princes' expense. At the 1885 nizam-sponsored Hyderabad Polo Tournament, for example, the winning team was presented with a cup worth Rs. 1,000 and each member of the winning team was given a commemorative cup as well. Newspapers reported these tournaments and often extolled the generosity and accommodations provided by the princes, publicity which contributed directly to princely prestige. John Campbell Oman, a professor of science in the Government College Lahore, wrote that the princes "make it a practice to extend magnificent hospitality to European gentlemen and ladies perhaps a week at a time once or twice a year. Nothing that money can provide or courtesy dictate is wanting on such occasions for the entertainment and comfort of the guests."[104]

Princely support, while welcomed, was also a source of jealousy for less wealthy British officers. Comments made in passing about the "unlimited purses" of the princes were common.[105] Implications that the wealth of the princes provided an unfair advantage often undercut complimentary coverage of Indian polo success. One British memoirist wrote that Kishangarh was "the best Indian team in the country at that time" and included both the Maharajah of Kishangarh and the Maharajah of Rutlam. While acknowledging that both princes were first-class players, he concluded his report by adding "needless to say, their team was very well-mounted."[106] Likewise, it was noted that Patiala had, "like all [princely] State teams, command of an almost unlimited number of polo ponies."[107] To be fair, it is not that the wealth of the princes was not a factor; indeed it was. It was also, however, a factor in the success of any polo team. Nonetheless, the successes of British teams with spectacular mounts were not qualified in a similar fashion.

Even when in the presence of princes who possessed vast riches and ruled autocratically over perhaps millions of people, many officers maintained their sense of British superiority by categorizing princely rule as primitive, atavistic, decadent, and exotic, if nonetheless politically expedient. Frequently, in correspondence both official and private, English officers and agents snidely commented in passing on relative size of a raja's drink bill, harem, or expenditures. Sir Philip Crawford Vickery, Indian Police 1909–47, in describing his duties at the Delhi Durbar of 1911, wrote of the Maharajah of Orcha: "His manners are rather native also, as he once left us walking down to spit at the side of the platform! Of course one pretends not to notice these minor details."[108] In recalling his time as a Resident Officer of three small states, Younghusband lamented that "The incompetence, the corruption, the slackness to which a Resident has to turn a blind eye and a deaf ear would drive any thoroughgoing British Minister wild."[109] More commonly, British writers frequently noted that respectable Indian women were excluded from social interaction with foreigners. One etiquette manual for new officers explicitly reminded British officers neither to mention this fact nor to inquire about the ladies of the house.[110] Indeed, the fact that Indians and the English had differing conceptions about the probity of public social interaction between the sexes was frequently invoked by English commentators as a way of proving that Indians, regardless of education, remained uncivilized to a degree.[111] Similarly, behavior of the princes that did not fit with English sensibilities, colored characterizations of all princely rulers regardless of the degree of education or Westernization of the individual.

In other words, playing with the princes and being invited to their tournaments raised the officers' social status in many ways; yet, the exoticism of the princely states still allowed them to see themselves as superior than the princes. Like an organ-grinder's monkey in a suit, it was the juxtaposition of the pedestrian and the exotic that aroused the British imagination. Baden-Powell recounted one maharajah who had covered the walls of his audience chamber with nonworking clocks and kept a room full of unopened packages from an English hardware store "which had been bought up by a previous maharajah when on a visit to England... by way of impressing the shopkeeper with his rank and dignity."[112] Princely devotion to polo became the stuff of legend which often reinforced stereotypes of the princes as amiable if eccentric oriental oddities. Tales relating how the Maharaja of Rewa allegedly gave his favorite pony a state funeral or how Jay Singh of Alwar had his favorite pony publicly immolated after it threw him, must be placed beside other stories that caricature the princes as only semicivilized.[113]

At the core of polo's popularity for both princes and officers was the game's perceived relationship to issues of masculine power. Importantly, the game did not equate with a single vision of masculinity, nor were competing visions of manly perfection always even internally consistent. Nonetheless, polo was time and again used as a public and easily understood way of defining, displaying, promoting, and policing gender norms and drawing lines of inclusion and exclusion between competing groups of men whether they be aristocratic and middle-class officers, Britons and Indians, princes and nationalists, or martial races and Bengalis.

For British disciples, the battle to promote the manly qualities of polo in the face of other ideals was fought on two fronts. First, they needed to convince (or silence) compatriot critics of the sport. Second, there was the thorny issue of negotiating the relationship with the princes and Indian players. On the one hand, it was necessary and desirable to forge strong links with the princely elite and there seems to have been a genuine meeting of gender ideals in the public school/martial races relationship. On the other hand, if the game was a true meritocracy and a true barometer of manliness, then Indian success would have put Indian men on an equal footing with British men, a politically unacceptable outcome in the wider imperial context. Thus, British rhetoric qualified, justified, and trivialized non-British success in a variety of ways even while claiming meritocracy. This is a problem which British sporting propagandists would increasingly encounter as nonwhite and interracial participation in sport grew in the twentieth century. However, unlike later sporting contexts in which power differentials "beyond the boundary" seeped into the games themselves and were made manifest in unequal opportunity to compete on the field, Britons and Indians of means competed at polo without equal regard to race, even while off-field inequities may have mocked the ideals of egalitarianism on the polo ground.

It is one of the most paradoxical aspects of polo in India that the perception of the value of polo as an inculcator of manly restraint was vastly different depending on the player's ethnicity. The considerable costs of maintaining polo for British officers was seen as having a salutary effect. It limited their ability to waste time or money on less wholesome pastimes and taught them thriftiness. In contrast, British observers of Indian polo expenditures often implied that it was improvident and irresponsible to spend such money on polo and polo playing princes' natural decadence was evident in their management of polo. Echoing a common theme in the literature, a guide to polo in India advised young officers that polo encouraged healthy, moral living. Reportedly, the "polo players of the regiment often had no drinks at all at polo, and after the game, ran home to get their wind in order, and several cut their drinks and smokes in mess so as to allow the keep of an extra pony. By exercising such self-control they proved themselves to be men and soldiers, and the formation of the fund had much to do with it."[114] In fact, polo was a way to save the impressionable junior officer from falling victim to the temptations of the East; polo "had done its share preserving from decadence those who might easily have fallen victim to sloth or mere self-indulgence."[115] A 1902 review of Anglo-Indian novels, entitled "The Romance of India" defended social segregation as a necessary means of "self-preservation" upon which the Empire depended. The author concluded "The English in India are wise to surround themselves, as far as they can, with English atmosphere, and to defend themselves from the magic of the land by sport, games, clubs and the chatter of fresh-imported girls, and by fairly regular attendance at Church."[116] Advising a young officer new to India, one writer cautioned "that while refusing to admit that the cost of polo is any way prohibitive for those with moderate allowances . . . still the game makes sufficiently stringent demands on the pocket to call for very careful living, and . . . [one] must be prepared to forgo many of the flesh-pots of this life."[117]

While polo was considered an important way of keeping British officers on the straight and narrow, it was frequently mentioned as a source of excessive spending and irresponsibility on the part of the princes. William Barton, a Resident in Mysore, wrote: "There are Indian States where tigers are more important than blue-books: where first-class polo ponies threaten budget stability: where a pretty face may be a passport to political influence: where the polo player who hits the winning goal may be rewarded by a week's tenure of the office of Chancellor of the Exchequer. Indian India is indeed a country of lights and shades, and of many of the courts, small and great, tales might be told which would rival the *Arabian Nights* in vividness."[118]

The lingering, albeit often unstated, belief in the inherently decadent nature of the princes was seen in the fact that British observers constantly questioned whether the public school training being promoted around the Empire as the ultimate inculcator of manliness would be enough to overcome centuries of princely hedonism. For example, at the investiture of the Raja of Pudukotta, Lord Wenlock, the Governor of the Madras Presidency, noted his pleasure at the young Raja's love of sport but he ominously added that these games should not obscure the fact that his duties as a ruler took precedence.[119] It was explicitly and repeatedly made clear that the purpose of the Chiefs Colleges and the Imperial Cadet Corps was to create better, more manly princes through instruction in British learning and sports.[120] Policy makers believed that British education and sport would offset the deleterious effects that the *Pax Britannica* had wrought on the martial races. In the words of Curzon, the martial races had traditionally been hardened by the ordeal of war, but with the coming of the British-imposed peace "could aspire to no higher ambition than the idleness and intrigues of the zenana," that is, the part of an Indian home which was reserved for the women of the family.[121] Polo was seen as a constructive pastime which would teach manliness to the princes as war had previously.

Orientalist myths continue to influence historical treatments of the princes and India. The *Oxford History of India (fourth edition)* reiterates the same highly gendered reading of the princes and recreates the British imperial rhetoric that claimed to acknowledge the limits of the civilizing mission in those in whom debauchery was so deeply engrained. It argues that before the founding of the colleges produced a new (and improved) prince, "The old type of prince, nurtured in the zenana and softened by traditional vices without being tempered by the traditional hazards of war and politics, gave place in many cases to the man of modern outlook regarding his domains as an estate to be improved. Princely modernism might be vicious as well as benevolent, leading to Parisian nightclubs rather than the administrator's desk; sometimes it did both. But a new class of men was to be found among the princes just as a new spirit was to be found in the states themselves."[122] British stereotypes such of this were widespread and they continue to color modern historiography. In response, princes consistently stressed their own conceptions of virile masculinity when commenting on polo and other equestrian sport.

Conclusion

J.A. Mangan has written that "within imperial sport racism, sexism and imperialism were as valid a Trinity as athleticism, militarism and imperialism. To a considerable extreme imperial sport was a favored means of creating, maintaining and ensuring the survival of dominant male elites."[123] Moreover, such was the case with polo in India as well. However, the sport did not simply define and prop up British, elite masculine power. Polo's various supporters poured tremendous resources into the game for a variety of reasons, some of which were in line with British claims of superiority and others that were not. Nonetheless, in general, the princes were not interested in opposing British political or sporting hegemony as such. In fact, they used sport in ways not unlike the British: as a marker of inclusion and exclusion and of superiority and sub-servience. The difference between the British and the princes was largely about interpretations about where each fit into the hierarchy and whose values were being inculcated by the game of polo.

Long-standing stereotypes aside, there did exist a brotherhood of sorts between polo-playing princes and officers based on shared conceptions of masculinity and manliness and tied to a military and public school ethos. The princes and the martial races were repeatedly pronounced Indian versions of English public schoolboys, were often credited with, and claimed, the same characteristics of pluck and honor so familiar in English sporting discourses. Writers were eager to point out the connec-tions between soldiers of the martial races and their British commanding officers were built on affection and respect for one another. In his exam-ination of representations of "The Gurkha" in British military writings, Lionel Caplan argued that "in the way he is portrayed the Gurkha reminds us of nothing so much as a British public schoolboy."[124] The willingness of the Sikhs to fight for the English in 1857 was viewed as sporting and manly: good losers who recognized the superiority of their conquerors. In contrast, the mutineers were seen as ungrateful blacks who had disloyally turned on their benevolent imperial masters.[125]

Like the relationship between the martial races in general and the British, the cultivation of a sense of unity with the princes allowed both the princes and the British to distinguish and differentiate themselves from other Indians. Competition between the princes' teams and the army officers strengthened the British claim that manly martial races and Indian princes represented the truest face of India, as opposed to the increasingly bothersome, National Congress supporters who were deemed effeminate. Educated non-princely Indians were derided as "miserable weeds of clerkly sons" who needed to be led for their own good by both the British and the more masculine Indians.[126] Author Mihir Bose described this dynamic, stating that "Quite soon after the Raj had been established, Indians were divided between on the one hand, the ugly, deceitful Bengalis who, finding the Raj's liberal education inadequate, created the first nationalist movement; and, on the other, the good Indians: the tall, upright, uncomplicated, martial races of the north, who were credited with manliness and a certain Indian version of public schoolboy comradeship and trust."[127] Subhas Bose, the great anticolonialist leader, rejected the British and the gendered sexualized hierarchy of Indian manhood that accompanied British rule. He refuted the common characterization of the "manly princes" and "martial races" and stated, "Those who are considered good boys in the society are in fact nothing but eunuchs."[128]

Regardless of one's point of view, the relative masculinity of competing groups in Victorian and Edwardian India was perceived to be a matter of some significance for contemporaries. For the elites of the princely states and the British military establishment in India, the game of polo developed into a central marker of the masculine ethos thought to be necessary to defend the imperial status quo in the face of increasingly strident calls for reform and independence. For historians of India in this period, the fascination of British and princely elites with the game of polo illustrates the complex and overlapping layers of power and causation affecting political alliances within imperial politics. Although the princes were the Crown's staunchest allies in India from the military to the ceremonial to the sporting realms, the history of polo demonstrates that this was, from the princes' point of view at least, more than a simple case of loyal devotion to the Empire and a desire to ingratiate themselves with the paramount power. Rather, while the overwhelming difference in power between the Raj and the princes certainly constrained the range of possible decisions a prince could make, they nonetheless continued to lay claim to independence of action and thought based on their own traditional principles and customs in an effort to distinguish themselves from the British as much as to copy them.

CHAPTER FOUR

May the Best White Man Win: Boxing, Race, and Masculinity

He never had any science, but his success was nevertheless amazing owing to his magnificent fighting spirit and his superb physique. It is men such as Goddard that make one realize the splendour and excellence of this great land of ours. An Australian born and bred, all that Goddard had was what his native land had given him—the might of his arm, the toughness of bone and sinew, unconquerableness of spirit—those things could be gained in no college or gymnasium.

> —Australian boxer W.J. Doherty on his countryman
> Joe Goddard[1]

Of the brutality of old-time prize fighting there could be no doubt, yet, a fair stand-up contest, with man's natural weapons—his fists—was infinitely preferable in the matter of settling a dispute to the free use of the knife and stiletto in Europe, the cunning usage of the poisoned phial in Asia, or the still worse misuse of the revolver in America. We still have something to be thankful for that British boys, who ever will be boys, have still that pretty knack of properly defending themselves and settling their petty differences and bickerings in a characteristically British manner.

> —"Boxing as a Clean Sport," an unsigned article in
> Baily's Magazine, 1909[2]

During the reign of Queen Victoria, many popular amusements, from fighting to football, were organized, standardized, and regulated. The games and activities, formerly arranged on a local or ad hoc basis, increasingly came under the control of national and international governing bodies with the majority of participants adhering to a single set of written rules. Not all popular recreations underwent this process. Some pastimes simply became obsolete because they no longer fit with a changing society's self-perceptions; others were marginalized by being relegated to the province of children. For example, at the same time that various forms of "folk football" were being codified into the modern sports of soccer, rugby and Australian Rules, animal blood sports such as bull baiting, cockfighting, and ratting were being banned and/or discouraged by a society which had come to view such activities as uncivilized. Likewise, chasing greased pigs and other pastimes formerly enjoyed at country fairs by all age groups were increasingly deemed appropriate only for child's play. Finally, some pastimes like rounders, an antecedent of baseball, were gendered and deemed fit only for schoolgirls.

Fighting with one's fists was among the last common popular amusements to make the transition to organized modern sports. Its atavistic violence made it a bridge between the two worlds of modern and premodern sport. Whereas bare-knuckled prize fighting had been the pursuit of the Regency "fancy," gamblers and lowlifes, by the late nineteenth century, pugilism had been transformed in a typically Victorian way. Like so much in Victorian society, rationalization, standardization, classification, and bourgeoisification of institutions and manners characterized organized fighting. Previously, contests had arisen out of personal challenges and were organized in secluded places, beyond the ken of the law, for a motley collection of aristocrats and gamblers. These rough-and-tumble battles were transformed into a sport with standardized weight classes and widely accepted rules, a transformation that permitted the sport to gain respectability despite the general rejection of overt violence in Victorian society.[3]

Even with changes in the structure of boxing, the sport would not have survived as a lawful pastime without the support of English society's elites, particularly the aristocracy, whose active championing of boxing and participation in the sport's rituals prevented it from being outlawed by a government interested in upholding bourgeois respectability. In the face of rising international tension and an increasingly volatile racial climate in the first decade and a half of the twentieth century, the gentlemen of the National Sporting Club (NSC) viewed the right of English men to participate and watch boxing contests as central to the maintenance of British manhood. It provided a space in which the tensions between Britain and her various rivals, whether it be the United States, Australia, or the subjects of color within the Empire, could be played out in a genteel manner.

Boxing in the late Victorian and Edwardian periods was closely associated with issues of masculinity, especially the relationship between the fitness of a nation's men and the nation's preparedness for war. The sport provided the British Empire with a distinct version of masculinity which differed in many ways from masculinity as promoted by boxing's predecessor, bare-knuckle fighting; likewise, it differed from other masculinities being produced by disparate currents in society, such as the movement toward bourgeois respectability and Christian gentlemanliness. Boxing, with its unique spectatorship, participation, and violence, produced divergent discourses of masculinity than might be found in other sports then played in the British Empire: polo, cricket, rugby football, golf, tennis, or soccer for example.

60   *May the Best Man Win*

The same period which saw the standardization of boxing under bourgeois-influenced rules and the ardent defense of the sport as a necessary engine for the creation of British men, also saw the birth of the "New Woman," who boldly sought new prerogatives for women in all spheres of life. In this period, British women took increasingly to vigorous physical activities—bicycling, hiking, gymnastics, tennis, golf—and simultaneously demanded political, educational, and reproductive rights.[4] Female assertiveness did not necessarily produce a "crisis of masculinity," but it did create a need for some British and Australian men to defend their visions of manhood against what they viewed to be corrupting influences. Men of color particularly concerned white men in the British Empire in this period. Since the boxing ring was one of the few places where men of different races met in open competition, the sport became a lightning rod for fears of the degeneration of white manhood and the threat of black masculinity.

Boxing differed from other sports for three main reasons. Most importantly, participation in boxing was severely and strictly circumscribed by class and gender. While women sometimes played soccer or cricket and many regularly played golf or tennis, they did not box. Furthermore, social elites participated in boxing in two forms only: occasionally as fighters in amateur competitions with other members of their class, and more often as spectators and gamblers backing and betting on working-class boxers. Second, the near-naked appearance of the male body highlighted not only the strength and physiques of professional boxers, but also their skin tone. Finally, the nature of the sport, while in many ways as ritualized and symbolic in its violence as any other, promoted the appearance of primal aggression and violence, which lent the sport an air of atavism and authenticity lacking in apparently more "artificial" or contrived sports. This "authenticity" was juxtaposed with a predominant discourse regarding the need to be "scientific" in training and tactics in order to be successful. Thus, boxing allowed civilized English and Australian men to compete with American fighters or fighters of color regardless of nationality and demonstrate not only their capacity for utilizing violence to achieve their goals, but also display their superior technical skills by virtue of their systematic training and fighting methods. These differences, in conjunction with issues of imperial and racial rivalry, made boxing an important arena of the contestation for the meaning of manhood in the late Victorian and Edwardian eras.

The Culture of Boxing

By the turn of the twentieth century, a culture of boxing was firmly established in the United Kingdom, the "white" Dominions, and the United States. The sport's widespread popularity, coupled with fighting's very nature, made it an obvious touchstone for observers concerned with the state of manhood in the various countries. Unlike other prominent sports in Britain and the Empire, the United States played a major role in the boxing world and as a result, the dynamic was different from that found in cricket, rugby, or soccer, which were played largely among subjects of the Crown. In every country where boxing was practiced, the relative quality of elite boxers vis-à-vis elite boxers of other nations was held up as emblematic of the nation's preparedness for war and the general Darwinian struggle for world power. The question of the worth of nations' men as displayed in the boxing ring was greatly complicated by the presence of numerous elite boxers of color, who upset racial hierarchies and easy distinctions and associations between national strength and an individual. For example, was a black Australian boxer illustrative of Australian might and know-how or the rising threat of black masses on the character of white Australia? Debates over such points made boxing into a prime signifier of national belonging and exclusion.

While boxing certainly had friends in high and often noble places, the sport belonged to the masses. Boxing referee Eugene Corri recalled in 1927 that when Robert Fitzsimmons fought the American James Corbett in Carson City, Nevada in 1897, "Evening papers sold in Fleet Street as when great victories were announced during the war."[5] With the advent of motion pictures, growing media coverage and lucrative music hall engagements for winners, paydays in Australia and America rose enormously and crowded smaller English venues out of the market for championship fights. This did not, however, limit the sport's appeal in Britain. As the stakes and paydays increased, public attention to championship fights increased correspondingly.

Modern professional boxing provides an interesting counterpoint to the team games that were the hallmark of the games revolution. Unlike national cricket, rugby, and Olympic teams—or in the case of Gaelic or Australian football, games that were played only in one country—professional boxers went forth as individuals. However, they also inevitably came to be seen as representing their country in an era of extreme nationalism. The nationality of various fighters was often the subject of intense debate. For example, Cornish-born, New Zealand-raised, Australian-trained, naturalized American Robert Fitzsimmons was claimed as an "English champion" by the English, and an Australian, New Zealand, and American champion by the other countries respectively. One London newspaper expressed disbelief that American newspapers were claiming Fitzsimmons as an American. The *Licensed Victualler's Mirror* reported that "a great controversy has been existing between Various American and English papers as to the nationality of Fitzsimmons, the champion of the world...how the Americans can lay claim to him is beyond belief."[6] Despite the sometimes confusing and changing national identifications of certain individual boxers, boxing occupied a special place in the world of imperial sport as a marker of national conceptions of masculinity.

Although other athletic activities—football, polo, horse racing, cricket— could result in serious injuries or death for participants, generally these injuries were accidental and incidental to the course of play. In boxing however, hurting your opponent was the main objective even while boxing also retained symbolic importance. Walter Ong has argued that in pugilism "the objective was not to kill, as it well can be in fights between human beings, but to be known as the victor by performing certain viscous but also symbolic action."[7] Boxing was the most obvious throwback to the pregames revolution era when popular recreations incorporated violence in more open and less circumscribed ways. Perhaps the question which comes to mind most readily when studying boxing at the turn of the century is why this pastime had not gone the way of cockfighting, bullbaiting, and ratting; that is, why had boxing not been abandoned or at least pushed into the shadows of disrespectability by a people who considered themselves the apex of world civilization?

Despite attempts to outlaw boxing and recurrent bids to prosecute organizers for deaths that occurred in the ring, the sport not only flourished, but came to represent the epitome of modern manhood for many. That boxing was not banned and organizers of fights were not jailed for manslaughter after deaths in the ring was due to the identification of national conceptions of manhood with boxing and the common belief that the nation benefited from having the contests take place. In describing Fitzsimmons toward the end of the Corbett fight, *The Mirror of Life* opined: "If ever a man displayed the proverbial qualities of the Englishman that man was Fitzsimmons."[8] It was commonly held that examples of "true manliness," like Fitzsimmons, were indispensable to the fate of the nation.

Unlike team sports, which generally drew supporters to their national teams, boxing fans' allegiance switched often, as hopefuls quickly became challengers and then just as quickly became has-beens. This common progression from the bottom of society to the pinnacle of fistic success to either complacent publican, a common post-boxing career choice, or washed-up degenerate seemed to be needed or desired by many upper- and middle-class commentators. They did not wish to see the class status quo disturbed by newly wealthy social inferiors trying to climb above their station, especially when a successful fighter was black. Fighters were almost expected by elite followers to lose everything and return to their appropriate social position. One commentator complained about *nouveau riche* American boxers (or those imitating Americans) for spending lavishly. The author conceded that money fairly earned could be spent however a person desired, however he held that such expenditures were "a sad buffoonery."[9] Black fighters were held to be especially prone to flashy displays of newfound wealth. Despite the fact that amateur boxing was practiced and taught in public schools and elite universities, there were no professional boxers of note who came from more than modest means. Boxing has always been a poor man's career choice because of the inherent potential for life threatening violence makes it largely unattractive to men with other viable career options.

The fact that only working class and nonwhite men were liable to reach to the top of the professional boxing world created a problem for elite English men when it came to the issue of representing manliness. How could boxing be held up to represent a national ideal of masculinity if it was largely the province of the lower classes and nonwhites? This was accomplished largely by retreating to the world of literature and fantasy on the one hand, and through the participation of social elites as organizers, patrons and most importantly, gamblers.

Although class considerations kept gentleman out of the professional ring in reality, they were not exempt from conquering it in the world of fiction. In boxing novels, socially elite men ventured where they dared not in real life; alternately, working-class heroes of the novels were co-opted into a respectable worldview. Numerous boxing novels, such as the famous Aldine Boxing Series, appeared in the first three decades of the twentieth century and were aimed at young males. These books followed the adventures of fictional British boxers who were either from the middle class or who, despite being from the respectable working class, behaved in ways remarkably similar to middle-class ideals of working-class behavior. For example, in the first Aldine Series installment, British boys read about Lorry Derrick, "an untamed colt" and Cambridge man, who was forced to leave Cambridge due to his wild yet wholesome hijinks. Upon reaching the City of London and being hired by the knighted father of his old roommate, he is thrust into the boxing ring at the NSC as a last minute replacement for a sick boxer. After impressing the gentlemen of the NSC, Lorry fights in a series of matches, culminating in a battle with an American Indian named "Reckless Red," that prove he is capable of regaining for England "those highest laurels of the ring which, for so long, had rested abroad," the heavy weight championship. Before the novel ends, Lorry has also won the Grand National, destroyed a spy ring trying to smuggle British industrial secrets out of the country, fallen in love, and enthralled English audiences, who "were moved by the sight of this gallant young Englishman who was showing that the breed of fighting men had not quite died out in this little sea-girt isle which had first produced the great game of the ring." Not only are class enemies firmly put in their place in novels such as these, but race foes and national rivals are as well. The chapter in which the white Lorry beats the Indian Reckless Red is entitled "England versus the U.S.A."[10]

British commentators made unceasing claims that race was not important in Britain as it was in America, South Africa, and Australia. Nonetheless, race came to play an important role in the history of imperial boxing. Fights between blacks and whites aroused great interest among the populace, the sporting press, and at times the government, which went to extraordinary lengths to prevent interracial fights between top boxers from taking place in Britain. Nonetheless, interracial fights between non-contenders constantly took place up and down the length of Britain. However, the British government and high-ranking members of the boxing establishment, most prominently Lord Lonsdale, felt it was not in the best interest of the country to allow high-profile interracial

fights to go on, regardless of the inherently unsporting nature of preventing a contest from taking place just because the probable winner would
be distasteful to some. By the turn of the twentieth century, the issues of
race and manhood had become inseparable, particularly in Great Britain,
where fighting was long considered the national sport. However, it was
also true in Australia, where the need to be as strong as the British was a
prime motivation in society.

   The creation and growth in popularity of modern boxing is emblematic of the manner in which sports both worked to spread middle- and
upper-class values and ways in which this diffusion had unintended and
often undesired consequences. Elite amateur boxing in England, while
representing the minority of the boxing taking place in the country, also
most closely adhered to the ideals of the games revolution. The values of
Muscular Christianity infused these competitions. Sportsmanship and
chivalry were high on the menu and brutality and knockouts were rare.
If professional boxing was about masculine national power, amateur boxing was about character building.

   In a book called *The Complete Amateur Boxer*, J.G.B. Bohun Lynch wrote
that boxing training was very good for teaching a lesson to lower-class ruffians who might be mistreating a woman, child, or animal. However, the
author did offer the caveat that a gentleman must be cognizant of the fact
that chivalry had its risks; unlike ladies of class, women of the lower orders
knew the value of the efficacious use of a bonnet pin. He stated, "Women
of the class referred to cannot endure the least interference with their concern; and after all, a fight with your husband is quite a private and familiar
matter. Moreover, women of this kind are usually well able to take care of
themselves."[11] Furthermore, there was also the possibility that a gentleman
would have to defend his person against attacks from thieves and muggers
and therefore the Noble Art taught the necessary skills and values for such
eventualities in a way that team sports did not. All representations of the
ability of elite men to defend themselves however were not complimentary.
The Referee of London argued that the men of the great English universities had become by 1910, "enfeebled, debilitated, and effeminate, with the
ever-growing magnetism of luxury" and that the quality of boxers produced there was lacking and "inconsistent with their tradition, their
endowments, and their opportunities."[12] Boxing was seen as an antidote to
this degeneration.

   Unlike today in which amateur boxing serves as an apprenticeship for
an aspiring professional boxer, the two worlds were completely separate at
the turn of the century in Britain. Class expectations dictated that a
middle-class man would never fight for a living. The transformation of
organized fighting from a semi-legal activity conducted outdoors and in
remote places in the early nineteenth century to a largely respectable spectator sport which was primarily urban in nature by the end of the century
required a comparable transformation of the men who fought for the
entertainment of their social superiors. While professional boxers never

reached the social level of professional cricketers, they generally were much more bourgeois in styles and affectations than their predecessors from the bare-knuckle prize ring were. While Edwardian commentators infinitely preferred the sportsmanship displayed by the modern boxer, a sense of something lost also lingered. For example, in the introduction to Joe Palmer's *Recollections of a Boxing Referee*, Lynch contrasted the clean-living professional of the twentieth century with the bare-knuckle bruiser of the nineteenth. He wrote:

> the professional athlete of to-day . . . who lives the life of an anchorite when training, never goes out of training to any alarming extent, cunning, calculating and cold, devotes himself to physical fitness, is a tee-totaler, a non-smoker, invests his prodigious takings wisely, is seen at flash restaurants with a gorgeously appareled wife, read Shelley after lunch, and has learned not to wear too many diamond rings—such a man as he is no doubt a "better" man than the old-time bruiser who always had to start training with a violent purge, alternated hard work with debauchery, and generally died before he was thirty-five, but I am not quite sure that he is a better sportsmen, nor that in the vitiated atmosphere in which the bygone pub lived the greater human qualities of mercy, tolerance, enthusiasm, and courage did no more richly thrive.[13]

Objectively speaking, the transformation of fighters from drunken ruffians to civilized, poetry reading athletes should have been hailed as a great example of the progressive and "civilizing" benefits of modern sport. However, not all commentators welcomed these changes because they simultaneously threatened the class and racial status quo.

The role of the spectator in the history of boxing is of vital importance, for this is the manner in which the most important advocates for boxing were involved. In contrast, socially elite cricketers played on the same field with their class inferiors (albeit in a supervisory capacity) and rugby union limited involvement by class. Likewise, national games like Australian Rules football, Gaelic football, and hurling, cut across class boundaries in a way that no English sport did. It has been argued that in boxing, the spectator/gambler is actually the main figure in the event. By wagering, the bettor equates his own risk-taking with that of the combatants.[14] J. Nelson Fraser writing in 1903 saw risk as the central element of sport. "The element of personal risk, as we have said, is essential in sport, and where the sportsman is a mere on-looker himself, this has to be artificially supplied by betting. If the sportsman does not risk his person, he risks his money, and this saves him from degenerating into a mere spectator."[15] In contrast, a large part of the transformation of cricket from pastime of the aristocratically idle to a respectable engine for the creation of middle-class Christian gentlemen was the removal of betting from English ovals. In fact, the Australian and West Indian practices of betting on cricket were often criticized by English elites as being emblematic of the failure of non-English sportsmen to fully capture the essence of athleticism.

While other sports, especially cricket, often took place with few spectators, this is almost unheard of in boxing, where the presence of a crowd is essential. The centrality of spectators in boxing sheds a great deal of light on the symbol nature of the sport. It is not enough in boxing to have to male bodies struggle, they must be watched struggling because they then can come to represent the struggle of imperial or national masculinity. It is only in the mass nature of the event that the actions take on meaning.

The Black Threat

In 1914, the British Empire spanned twelve million miles and had a population of over 430 million people, of whom the United Kingdom and the white self-governing Dominions made up a mere 70 million. Anglo-Saxonism was a form of racism that held that by divine providence, the British and their white-skinned Protestant brethren in the colonies were destined to rule over the degenerate and dying races found throughout the Empire. Anglo-Saxonism also held that the British Empire was the apex of civilization. This was the ideology of Thomas Carlyle, Matthew Arnold, Sir Edward Bulwer-Lytton, Charles Dilke, Charles Kingsley, and Cecil Rhodes.[16]

During the first 20 years of the twentieth century, there were several efforts by the British government to prevent high-profile fights between black and white fighters from taking place because it was feared that such bouts would disturb both the local and imperial peace. This trend intensified after black American Jack Johnson won the heavy weight championship of the world in Australia in 1908 and then successfully defended it against Jim Jeffries in 1910. The latter fight set off rioting across America, which resulted in 18 dead and at least 100 injured, mostly black men who were attacked by whites angered by black victory celebrations. Despite the fact that high-profile interracial fights were being prevented form taking place, at the lower echelons of the fight game, men of different races battled one another frequently without arousing government intervention.

The governments of Australia and Britain, like that of the United States, were not particularly interested in protecting actual white male bodies, especially not working-class white male bodies. Rather, their concerns lay in protecting the metaphorical white male body that represented the patriarchal nation. Therefore, away from national and international press coverage, black men could beat white men in the ring with impunity. However, when such fights became the center of media attention, they were then stopped. Like their counterparts in Australia and the United States, British officials wished to keep championship titles, and especially heavy weight championship titles, in the hands of white fighters for symbolic reasons which were thought important to the larger Social Darwinian struggle between nations and races. In October 1909, a British minister, Rev. J. Hirts Hollowell, wrote to the editor of *Boxing* magazine in London to counter the recent criticisms of boxing. He expressed common sentiments when he argued: "Man is a fighting animal. He always has been and always will be. Let him once cease to fight and he will be crushed out of existence by other and more ruthless orders of creation."[17] Hollowell concluded his letter by warning that if the white man, "wishes to remain extant he must keep a firm grip on the World's Championship."[18]

Racism permeated British society in the early decades of the twentieth century despite recurrent British assertions that race mattered less there than in Australia, South Africa, and the United States. For example, after the Jeffries–Johnson fight, *The Referee* wrote, "Of course there is not the antipathy to the black man in England that exists in other places where they see much of him; but it is useless to deny that a certain—or uncertain—amount of prejudice does prevail."[19] However, despite frequent British claims of unfamiliarity with black-skinned people and their relative neutrality toward them, blackness in British society was designated and perceived as a symbol of moral, intellectual, and cultural inferiority.

J.A. Mangan argues that in their ongoing endeavor for gentility, the Victorian and Edwardian British middle classes often equated race with class, and this led to the middle-class desire to exclude those of questionable status. He writes: "As a rationalization for the domination of 'inferior' peoples, imperialist discourse is inevitably racist; it treats class and race terminology as covertly interchangeable or at least analogous."[20] Anne McClintock contends similarly that the "invention of race" was of pivotal importance in the British and imperial middle-class process of self-definition. Moreover, she contends that race worked as policing mechanism to keep the "dangerous classes" in line. In this case, the dangerous classes included among others, the working classes, the Irish, Jews in addition to people of color.[21]

British newspapers and magazines did not refrain from using terms like "nigger," "coon," "darky," and the like, to describe boxers of color. In describing a fight between Jack Johnson and Al Kaufmann, *Boxing* wrote that it had been a "poor showing by the nigger" and that Johnson had fought a better opponent, "the coon" would not have fared as well. In the same issue, the paper commented on a match between "East London favourite Curly Watson and the nigger, Bob Scanlon" of New York.[22] Both Australian and British promoters frequently paired a black and a white boxer in order to generate greater public interest. Even the venerable NSC was not above playing on color prejudice to hype a fight. One paper reported: "Long before the lights were turned up considerably more than average attendance of members at the National Sporting Club had taken their seats to view the contest, which partook an international character. Charley Rowles, of Wood Green, who had yet to taste defeat was set to try his skill in eight rounds against the latest importation from American in the person of Jack Lewis (coloured)."[23] Although the governments were not interested in stopping interracial fights on an everyday basis, these fights did arouse popular tensions and prejudices. By the second decade of the twentieth century however, the NSC, which viewed itself as the guardian of British boxing, took it upon itself to not hold interracial fights.

Nor were color prejudices confined to England in the British Isles. Eugene Corri, a prominent English referee recounts a time he was watching a fight in Dublin between Irish champion Jim Roach and Frank "Coffee Cooler" Craig, a black fighter with a fine reputation as a fighter and sportsman. Allegedly, after the Irishman was knocked down, the referee, a compatriot of his, counted him out as such:

> One!—what the devil are ye' doin' down there? For the love of Ireland, get up.
> Two!—think of your ancestors; lovely people. There's yer dear father in front over there. Do you want 'im to think you're a coward?
> Three!—will ye listen to me? All ye have to do is to get up and hit 'im in the stomach with your left hand and cross him with yer right. I tell ye, ye can do it.

At that point, Roach got up and knocked down Craig (the "nigger" in Corri's terminology), who was quickly counted out.[24] Attitudes like Corri's were common and openly expressed along side assertions that for all intents and purposes, the British boxing establishment was largely color blind. The essence of organized sport is that all participants follow all the rules and officials fairly and uniformly sanction transgressions against those rules. However, often referees and time keepers were biased against a fighter because of his color and thereby denied some fighters a fair chance to succeed, while maintaining that success was evidence of innate superiority as a man.

The 1913 *Boxing New Year's Annual* included an article headlined "Penny Plain & Twopence Coloured: The Sensitive Nature of Certain Professional Boxers" which discussed how black boxers purportedly become overly sensitive once they were dressed up in (what they considered to be) the style of a gentlemen, but which was normally a gaudy and laughable imitation thereof. The article held up the example of a boxer called "Pluto," whose real name was probably Joseph Dudley Brown. Describing a charity ball that Brown attended, the boxer was telling the author that a black friend of his was not allowed to enter because of his skin color. "It took me all my time to restrain my laughter, and it was only a knowledge of Pluto's abnormal vanity that kept me from remarking that, if anything, he was several shades darker than the aforesaid friend."[25] Throughout the British and Australian press, blackness was criticized and whiteness was held up as the standard of civilization. For example, in answering charges that fellow boxer Joe Goddard was uncouth, uncivilized, and a simple bruiser, Doherty wrote: "I found Goddard to be a white man and a gentleman in all our associations."[26]

From the 1890s onward, as racial tensions increased in Britain and the Empire, many white champions "drew the color line" for years on end and refused to fight black men. By the turn of the twentieth century, although many tried, it was becoming more difficult for white fighters to easily maintain the color bar and refuse to fight highly regarded contenders simply because they were not white. Some commentators felt that a refusal to fight the best contenders eroded the value of the championship and the attendant claim to be the best man.

When Doherty beat Mick Dooley for the heavyweight belt of Australia, Dooley left him with the plea "keep the championship white!" Despite his foe's pleas, Doherty went on to fight West Indian-born black Peter Felix who was widely despised in Australia because of the allegedly flashy arrogance he displayed by his dress and boastfulness. Doherty explained that being black alone was not enough to make a fighter unpopular and cited the popularity of black Australian Peter Jackson, whom Doherty described as the "whitest black man that ever lived."[27] Jackson was the most popular and well-known black athlete of his day. His fight against Frank "Paddy" Slavin at the NSC in 1892 was attended by England's elite, including the Prince of Wales, later Edward VII. Edward Scobie argues that Jackson's contemporaries held that "his main assets were his excellent behavior and his sportsmanlike qualities—The fact that he did not marry a white woman or consort openly with white women was also a point in his favor."[28]

Felix, on the other hand, refused however to play the part of a non-threatening black man the way Jackson had and consequently earned the hatred of much of the white population of Australia. Doherty believed that he could have pursued any means, legal or otherwise, to beat Felix and still maintained the support of the white crowd. This is despite the fact that Felix had fought, in Doherty's opinion "fairly, cleverly, and gallantly." Doherty concluded that the crowd simply hated him and wanted him beaten no matter the means.[29] This is a far way from the sportsmanship ideal that was purported to be at the base of the British and Australian sporting tradition and the hallmark of imperial manliness.

The personification of the black threat was American Jack Johnson, whose rise to preeminence was met with anger by much of white Australia, Britain, and the United States. Johnson took the title from the white Canadian Tommy Burns in a fight in Sydney that electrified Australia for at least six months before the fight and was followed closely throughout the world. Coverage everywhere had focused heavily on the fight as an indicator of the relative value of white and black manhood. In general, white observers seemed to believe that the innate qualities of white men would enable the smaller, slower, weaker Burns to defeat the stronger, larger, more skilled Johnson. Former English champion Jem Mace reportedly favored Burns, "on the theory that, other things being nearly equal, a white man ought to beat a black because he is a quicker thinker."[30] Unfortunately for Burns's supporters, other things were not at all equal in the fight.

Mace was not the only one to base his predictions of the fight on racial stereotypes. J.G.B. Bohun Lynch echoed many popularly held beliefs when he wrote that while black men often were good fighters, they were inherently different than white men, primarily because blacks were less sensitive to punches than whites. However, Lynch noted that "in some cases a negro's weakness in the stomach countervails the hardness of his head, but not always."[31] Physical differences aside, Lynch continued that the temperaments of the two races were just as unequal as the physiques. Incorporating the standard evolutionary theory that blacks were merely children compared to white, Lynch claims that the average black fighter "behaves like a spoiled child, which is just what he is." The greatest danger in the fight according to Lynch is that if the black man should win, "the nigger becomes an appalling creature, a devil. His insolence knows no bounds. His preposterous swagger excites the passionate hatred of ignorant white men, the disgust of their betters. There is no holding him until his money has run out, or he transgresses the law."[32] Johnson epitomized the arrogant black man who flaunted his wealth, strength, and sexual and fistic prowess in the face of white men; he consequently earned the hatred of a good portion of the white boxing world. His presence in the 1910s in Britain and the Empire raises many important issues regarding sport, racism, and contemporary images of masculinity.

Johnson Versus Burns in Australia

The *Sydney Morning Herald* reported on December 28, 1908 that between 15,000 and 20,000 paid to see the Johnson versus Burns fight and an equal number who could not get tickets were in the vicinity. While noting that interest in the fight was not based solely on its sporting criteria, the paper agreed with British assessments of comparative race relations when they stated that Australians were more concerned about the "colour question" than they would be in Britain, where "the only feeling would probably be that the better man should win," but less than in America. Furthermore, it was argued that although most Australians favored the white Burns, this was not because of racial considerations, it was only because they dislike the arrogant behavior of Johnson, as opposed to Peter Jackson, who was perennially held up as the model of a "good black."[33]

Johnson's insolence, which had so irritated the Australian public in the months leading up to the fight, came to the fore from the very beginning of the fight. *The Age* of Melbourne reported that Johnson knew that he was the better fighter from the start and quickly took to mocking his opponent. They wrote: "He became offensive and flash, taunted his game little antagonist, and riled him to rush into close quarters, where Johnson was able to hold and beat him as he pleased." His derisive behavior was not saved for Burns alone. He also poked fun at the crowd's anger as well. When an irate spectator screamed that Burns would "knock that smile off you directly, you flash nigger," Johnson reportedly replied, "But I can't help but smilin'. He's ticklin' me to death!" Likewise, Johnson took time during the fight to blow kisses to the movie cameras.[34] *The Observer* of Adelaide reported that despite his overall mastery from the start, hopeful members of the crowd were still taking 2 to 1 on Burns up until the beginning of the eighth round, when the only hope being commonly expressed was that Johnson finish his opponent off quickly and be merciful.[35]

In seven full columns, nearly two pages, of coverage of the fight the *Tasmanian Mail* reported that a large crowd of people waited outside the telegram office in Hobart, where round by round reports of the fight were being received. These reports were then immediately relayed around Tasmania in order to quench the thirst for information about the fight. The paper concluded that "it was an ethnological study as well as a box-ing contest. The 'white man's burden' was too great for Burns to carry."[36] The reactions of the public were often contradictory and ambiguous. Despite giving lavish and daily coverage to the fight, the *Sydney Morning Herald* called for the government to stop more contests of this sort before they have a deleterious effect on the general tone of the community. The paper argued:

> To say that they are "sport," in any decent meaning of that term, is flatly untrue. To claim that they have a tonic effect upon the "manly" quali-ties of the race is the sheerest hypocrisy They give no more stimulus to "manly" qualities than do the sanguinary bull-fights of Madrid to the effeminate who watch them. But they do is to stimulate the brute not only in those who actually witness them—for a large proportion of these are animated by nothing more than a passing curiosity—but upon that unfortunately all too numerous class at the bottom of soci-ety, to whom the mere "bruiser" is ever the supreme type of hero. The effect is to glorify brutish practices in quarters where the brutish instinct is already an anti-social force.[37]

Despite some elite views pressing for the abandonment of fights like this, the public showed no such desire. Two days after the fight, 7,000 people paid to see the fight films.[38]

The *Sydney Morning Herald* editorial came in for widespread criticism by its letter-writing readers. Many letters and opposing editorials criticized clergymen and religious people who opposed the fight. *Punch* of Melbourne wrote that "good, easy, comfortable men who eat too much, whose skins are too white, whose flesh is too soft, whose stomachs assume bow window proportions, are not fit people to judge a boxing match, or to arrive at a reasonable conclusion concerning it" because they are unaccus-tomed to a physical life and therefore overestimate boxing's brutality. *Punch* continued: "The opponent of boxing is headstrong, conceited, hysterical, determined on making out a case, and quite unscrupulous in dishing up his evidence, although, poor little creature, he does not realise his own unscrupulousness, and fondly believes he is guided by providence." Finally, the magazine noted the connection between boxers and the much vaunted fighting spirit of Australian troops: "If you have a nation of soldierly young men, their fighting spirit must express itself in contests, and boxing contests are the natural expression of that spirit and the best demonstration of it."[39] This view closely echoed similar pronouncements in the British media.

One author argued that the fight was important because it would highlight the threat posed to white Australia by the dark-skinned races. This letter felt that effeminate clergymen and newspaper editors need not tell Australian men what to think about the fight since "thanks to our splendid supply of national education, men are now able to think for themselves." He viewed the fight as a call to arms to uphold the white Australian state.[40] Other letters also connected the need to defend Australia, both figuratively and militarily, with importance of staging prize fights. One correspondent stated that as war was but an inevitability and England would not be able to maintain her position as guardian of Australia's rich continent, thus making the latter a prime invasion site. Since a standing army of sufficient size was not practical, the best thing is to have a healthy strong male population ready. "These boxing contests, in the normal man, appeal to that bulldog nature—that desire to be on top, that in our forebears has paced the Anglo-Saxon race in the pre-eminent position that it occupies to-day. To keep this position in the struggle for existence these instincts must be fostered. Real war is a merciless game, and to the strong in mind and body is given the victory."[41] Another letter writer chastised his countrymen for being upset that the black man had won. "Let us be sportsmen, let us cultivate the manly arts, let us not grow faint at the sight of blood . . . let our youths not be weaklings, let them remember how the Japanese bullies, by reason of their superior art, were able to treat the poor Koreans, let us have our contests at the Stadium, and rather than stop the game, let us see if we cannot do something to reverse last Saturday's defeat and prepare for the bigger fight that is to come."[42]

At the heart of much of public opinion was the question of whether Australian manhood was prepared to defend their country in times of war. A letter signed from "A Manly Australian" argued that the authorities should try to fight the immorality in Sydney, not the wholesome sport of boxing. The author asked, "If the late fight creates a boom in boxing in New South Wales, will it not tend to do away with the feminine, cigarette-smoking weaklings into which many of our young men are degenerating who ought to be full-chested and well developed instead of wearing corsets, having pale faces, and stooping noticeably? . . . Boxing is for manly men (may we have more of them), not for ladies, nor for effeminate degenerates."[43] Although most of the discussion of the fight and its effect on Australia centered on men, they were not the only ones interested in the spectacle. An "Australian girl" also wrote to the paper, arguing "It is good for us, a young country (who will so soon need all the strength, skill and defense our men can give) to have our fighting instinct awakened, our boys urged to train and make themselves strong, our girls, too, to develop their bodies and minds, leading clean, healthy lives that they my be worthy to be the mothers of fighters. It was our misfortune Saturday last that the black man proved the stronger, and I only hope a white man will arise and show the coloured one that he is the better man."[44]

Melbourne *Punch* reported that despite a general prohibition against the admission of women, some notable women were allowed in dressed normally, in petticoats and the like; for example, Mrs. Jack London sat next to her husband at ringside. Other women who did not have recourse to a famous husband were forced to sneak in dressed as men. *Punch* opined that this development was an unwelcome import from America, Thankfully, however, the magazine believed that although Australia was the most politically egalitarian nation in the world since Australian women voted, on the whole, those women did not aspire to such unfeminine activities as attending prize fights with their men. "If they did, they would probably get there in defiance of his efforts to check them, but they don't, and we're glad of it, for although boxing may not be the brutal thing some moralists find it, it caters for mean's taste and encourages qualities of character that are purely masculine, the quality of the soldier. As we do not want to make fighters of our women, we do not want them to cultivate a taste for fighting, and the practice of excluding females from such displays should be enforced."[45]

Not all opinion was focused on whether the fight was worthwhile or not. The American Jack London wrote the lead article on the fight for *The Argus* in which he concluded, "Personally, I was with Burns all the way. He is a white man, and so am I. Naturally, I wanted to see the white man win.... Because a white man wishes the white man to win should not prevent him from giving absolute credit to the best man, who did win, even when that man was black."[46] Likewise, Australian boxing great and the nation's preeminent boxing instructor, Larry Foley was interviewed and had only praise for Johnson, albeit while downplaying the significance of beating Burns. "The big fellow was too clever, too wise. However, Tommy showed great pluck. He took punishment like a man, all right. It's funny that a fighter as poor as Tommy could ever have been champion of the world. He struck a barren spot in the history of the boxing, when there weren't many good men about."[47]

In England, the *Sporting Life* of London published a special edition of the *Sporting Life* as soon as telegraph news of the Burns–Johnson came through. "His [Burns] antipathies were few, but they included coloured men. We in England cannot understand the racial hatred that consumed Burns. We do not believe that Johnson feels the racial flame so keenly as does Burns."[48] Many champions before Burns had drawn the color line and simply refused to fight black men regardless of challenger's qualifications. Burns abandoned this long-held practice out of a mixture of financial considerations and pridefulness. The *Sporting Life* praised Burn's decision not to hide behind the color line and argued in December 1908 that "it will ever stand to [Burn's] credit that he played the man's part, even against the advice of his friends, and in revolt of the teachings of a country where in racial feeling is very pronounced."[49]

Jack Johnson, Heavyweight Champion of the World

After Johnson defeated Burns, there arose a cry for a white man to take the championship belt back for the white race. Retired since 1905, former heavyweight champion, Jim Jeffries answered the call and was entrusted with the hopes of whites around the Anglophone world. For almost an entire year before the Johnson–Jeffries fight, American, British, and Australian newspapers wrote about it with eager anticipation. Many papers sent their own correspondents to Reno for the fight rather than being forced to rely on general wire reports. Much of the commentary focused on racial qualities and divisions. *The Sports Times* of Bristol wrote:

> Niggers are often honest, faithful, kindly, brave; we have all read about the ardent devotion with which multitudes of them used to serve their masters and mistresses in the Southern States, and in innumerable cases do so now; but, through no fault of his own, a nigger is a nigger, and when it comes to a fight between one of them and a white man, those of us who do not wear the butchered livery of the sun want to see the white man win.[50]

The common narrative of much English press coverage of the fight was that the "American public" demanded a champion to face Johnson. Despite the fact that he was born and raised in the United States, Johnson was always "the negro" or "the black," and was usually opposed to the "Americans" who wanted to see him defeated. For example, *Boxing* wrote that "confronted with the lamentable fact that they ['Americans'] possessed no modern heavyweight capable of even extending the new champion" Jeffries had been forced out of retirement by his countrymen.[51] Clearly then, Americans were white to the British and Australian newspapers.

Once Jack Johnson had won the heavyweight title and successfully defended it against Jeffries, the boxing world began its search for a "Great White Hope." Johnson would be harassed and hounded out of the United States by the federal government. Johnson had crossed state lines with a white woman who was not his wife (although she later became his wife) and was duly charged him with violating the Mann Act, a law created to stop "white slavery" and commercial prostitution. After his arrest and arraignment, Johnson was tacitly encouraged to jump bail and flee the country. His victory over Jeffries not only led to the banning of fight films in various parts of the world, including the United States and South Africa, but also led to Johnson's virtual banishment from the United States.

A week after the Johnson victory, the issue of showing fight films in Britain was raised in the British House of Commons. Sir Howell Davies asked the Home Secretary Winston Churchill if the government had the power to prohibit the showing of the films of the "the recent prize fighting America ... in the interest of public decency." Churchill replied only that it was not in his power to ban those films. One member quickly pointed out that the essence of the Sir Howell's complaint was not the fight film per se, but a fight film in which a black man beat a white man. Mr. W. Thorne, MP asked: "Does the right hon. Gentleman think that, in connection with the talk which has been going on all last week with regard to this prize fight, if Jeffries had knocked out Johnson there would have been so much of this slobber talk at the present time?"[52] In South Africa where racial tensions ran higher, the government banned movies of the fight from being shown. Despite the British parliamentary concern over whether the films should be shown, proprietors of music halls and cinemas were clamoring for the chance to show the films. The representatives in London of the Vitagraph Company, who owned the rights to the film, received over 400 requests for them in the days immediately after the fight.[53]

The reaction to the Johnson victory over Jeffries was varied yet substantial in Britain. For the most part, the English press admitted that the better man had won the fight, but proceeded to question Jeffries's fitness and to speculate on the possible international consequences of his failure. *The Referee* of London wrote: "No doubt Johnson's strength and ability had been underrated. It is unfortunate, because the victory of Johnson was certain to make men of his colour disgustingly bumptious, and some black idiots will believe that their prayers were answered, that the blasphemous petitions to Heaven affected the result. Nevertheless it is to be regretted that after the fight, as before, Jeffries would not shake hands."[54] The paper sadly concluded that every Englishman "wanted a fair fight and no favour, to see the best man win; only we wanted him to be a white man."[55] The article, which discussed the fight and its reception in America, failed to mention the widespread rioting, choosing instead to report on the fighters' earnings for the fight. Jeffries received £20,000 for losing, while Johnson got £27,000 for winning. Significantly, such was the public fascination with champion fighters that there would also be a nearly unlimited run of music hall engagements for the winner, who would earn an extra £300 a week for running through some sparring drills and exercises for a paid audience in any major city in the United States or in London.[56]

Boxing magazine criticized the white American public for pressuring a no longer fit Jeffries into fighting. The magazine contended that while the motive of putting the black races in their place was good one, the choice of an unfit Jeffries as the standard bearer for the white race was ill founded. The magazine argued that "had their desire been directed solely to the exaltation of the negro, they could not have selected a more certain and sure method of procedure."[57] Jeffries, and the whole of the white race, had been humbled. Much to the magazine's dismay, it reported that there was not a single white man capable of taking the title back. The *Boxing World and Athletic Chronicle* agreed that the future outlook for white boxers was bleak and, by extension, perhaps the future of the white race was shakier than had previously been thought. "That Jim Jeffries, the champion of champions, should have gone down to defeat without extending the coloured boxer, has been a sad eye-opener to all who depended on him to prove the superiority of the Caucasian race."[58] The paper concluded that "one of the results of the a battle for the championship has been the lamentable outburst of racial feeling in the United States, and in a more modified degree in every English-speaking country where there is an admixture of the white and coloured races."[59]

Fears of the sexual prowess of black men contributed to the desire to ban interracial fights or films. Over the course of the second half of the nineteenth century when cultural and religious racism was increasingly transplanted by scientific racism, there was a contemporaneous heightening of fear about black men's sexuality on the part of white society. There had long been a fear that the sexuality of black men was by definition predatory in nature toward white women. This predatory nature was held to be greatly increased when the black man in question was deemed "primitive" either due to culture, such as the great mass of men of color in the Empire, or his ability to physically beat white opponents in any endeavor. This was nothing new in the second decade of the twentieth century in Britain. In 1889 for example, at the Earl's Court Exhibition in London, a "Kaffir Kraal" was erected and populated with Africans, which English people could pay to see. The press was horrified by the fact that the exhibition became a huge success with English women who purportedly went to fawn and "hustle each other in their rivalry to obtain personal association with the Matabele and other colored men on view... The Kaffir Exhibition at Earl's Court has in fact degenerated into an exhibition of white women visitors, and a very disgusting exhibition it is. These raw, hulking and untamed men-animals are being unwillingly and utterly corrupted by unseemly attention from English girls."[60]

Black boxers were inherently sexualized beings in the eyes of the white citizenry of the British Empire. Edward Scobie in his study of blacks in the Empire argued that the fact that Peter Jackson neither married nor openly consorted with white women was as important to his widespread popularity as were his excellent boxing skills and exemplary sportsmanship.[61] In contrast, Jack Johnson flaunted his sexuality and played on white fears of black prowess. Gail Bederman has written that Johnson consciously toyed with the white American's public's stereotypes of black sexuality and used his claim to bodily strength and vigor, both in the ring and sexually with white women, to make a claim to public power. Bederman writes that "during his public sparring matches, Johnson actually wrapped his penis in gauze to enhance its size. Clad only in his boxing shorts, he would stroll the ring, flaunting his genital endowment for all to admire, displaying his superior body to demonstrate his superior manhood."[62]

If Johnson's desire was to raise the white public's ire, he certainly succeeded. Although he attempted on numerous occasions to arrange fights in Britain, especially against English fan favorite Bombardier Billy Wells, Johnson was not permitted to ply his trade in Britain for fear of the consequences on public order and imperial peace. On July 15, 1911, a year after Jeffries had been defeated, Johnson signed to meet the British heavyweight champion Wells in October at Earl's Court. The announcement of the fight sparked off a campaign to have the fight banned. Rev. F. B. Meyer led the most organized effort and earned the animosity of fight promoter John W. White. After suggesting numerous ways in which the public could be assured, including extra police presence around the grounds, bonds placed with the police and a public hearing composed equally of sportsmen and clergy, White came to the conclusion that Meyer was unbending in his opposition to the fight taking place and no compromise was possible. In a letter from White to Meyer, which had been copied to the police, White concluded that Meyer's opposition must be taken to be mere "self-glorification or persecution of one who has used every available means to furnish you with the best guarantee that this contest was arranged and will be conducted under the highest traditions of sport."[63] Meyers apparently would have welcomed the banning of all professional boxing matches in England, and perhaps viewed the Johnson–Wells fight as a case around which he could rally support for the eventual prohibition of an activity he viewed as immoral.

Despite White's attempt to secure the support of the police, it appears that they were not his main foe. In a long series of urgent letters, a resident of nearby West Kensington, Mr. John Butson, was gravely concerned about the effect that the fight would have on both Earl's Court and on the country and Empire at large. His letter-writing campaign warned "that such a performance would be a disgrace in this country and a return to the old Brutal Days and I further say there is bound to be some *outrageous* conduct by some of the class that are sure to be sightseen and most probably result in loss of life."[64] In general, the police treated Buston as a bit of a crackpot and made repeated statements that nothing could be done unless some crime had been committed. In a report compiled regarding Buston's numerous letters, the officer in charge concluded by saying that he could "safely say that nothing takes place in the Exhibition Grounds that any reasonable minded person could take exception to, and writer as no foundation to his complaint."[65]

If opponents to the fight were not prominent in the police, they were in the Home Office. In a memo from the Undersecretary of State regarding the campaign to end the fight before it started, the Home Office argued:

The racial element which enters into this contest is also a question which calls for special consideration from the point of view of public policy. I may add that in addition to the agitators which are appearing in the public press, I am in receipt of representations urging that the contest be stopped, and the Secretary of State may think fit, in circumstances which are so exceptional, to obtain the opinion of the Law Officers of the Crown as to whether any steps can be taken to prevent the contest being held.[66]

In a memo to Home Secretary Winston Churchill a few weeks before the proposed fight, a barrister, Sir John Simon, outlined the legal ways in which the fight could be stopped if it was so desired. These included a number of options including simply refusing Johnson permission to enter the country. The object was not just to keep the peace, but to "preventing a meeting of the Prize Ring of a black and a white man in the Capital of the Empire."[67] Shortly before the fight, White was informed that the Home Office had decided that the fight was illegal and was therefore prohibited.[68]

The Wells–Johnson case came to act as a precedent for the Home Office and was used in the years to come to ban any high-profile fight between white and nonwhite fighters. When a fight between Louis Phal, a black French Senegalese fighter popularly known as "Battling Siki," and a white Englishman named Joe Beckett, was under review for possible prohibition, a series of memos and letters were sent to and from the Home Office, by Lord Lonsdale a strong opponent of interracial fights and a prominent figure in British boxing. In a 1923 letter from Lonsdale to Mr. Bridgeman at the Home Office, Lonsdale stated that he and "all the leading men" whom he had approached, were of the opinion that "a definite decision should be given that no coloured men, (no matter what their weight, size of qualifications may be) should compete with white men."[69]

Lonsdale's friend, Arnold Wilson, wrote him a letter that Lonsdale then passed on to the Home Office with his own marginalia added. Arnold argued that banning the fight would be an insult to the French and to all black subjects of the British Empire. Furthermore, he continued that black and white fights were constantly being held in Britain. Plaintively, Arnold asked: "Surely if these men were fitted to take a chance with us in the War, then they are fitted to take part in our sports." He also argued that the Johnson–Wells fight had been stopped not because of race but because of the fact that Wells had absolutely no chance whatsoever of beating Johnson. Lonsdale wrote in the margin regarding this last accusation: "This is not so. It was stopped by order of the Home Office owing to the fact that they considered fights of this class between black and white as detrimental to the interests of the nation."[70]

The Siki–Beckett fight was banned, as was a proposed fight on the island of Jersey between Siki and French champion Georges Carpentier. In the latter case, the Home Office sent a letter to the Lieutenant Governor of Jersey, who had sought their advice, stating that the fight should not be allowed. The letter stated:

> The Secretary of State recently took steps to prevent a similar contest in this country between Siki and Beckett, and in 1911 his predecessor did the like in the case of a proposed contest between Johnson and Wells. The grounds for this action were the same in both instances, namely, the grave objection to a contest of this character between a black and a white in view of the danger that it should stimulate race jealousy between white and coloured wherever the races are in contact.[71]

The fear that boxing exhibitions in the capital of the Empire would ignite uprisings on the part of black subjects of the Crown does seem far-fetched. However, Lonsdale and the Home Office were unwilling to risk anything that could possibly increase the confidence of the King's dark-skinned subjects or which might erode the mythology of British superiority at home or abroad. By the 1920s, the British were still reeling from war and some Englishmen must have been wondering if the victory over Germany had indeed been a Pyrrhic one. Though nominally aggrandized by the League of Nations protectorates they were given and reparations that should have been coming, Britain's position in the world was seriously weakened vis-à-vis the Americans and the Empire.

Conclusion

Australian and British boxing from the 1890s through the 1910s provide historians with a unique vision of national identity formation and its relationship to national images of masculinity. At the heart of this process was a fear that British and Australian men were not as masculine as they had once been in the past. Whether it was looking back on a pastoral idyll, which freed men from the taint of urban living, or to a period of time in the past when dark-skinned peoples did not seem as threatening to white hegemony, the sport of boxing provided Australian and British men with a visceral exhibition of what was considered masculinity stripped to its core. For the British, it harkened back to a time when fighting with fists was both a national sport and held to be particularly British in the early nineteenth century.

From the vantage point of the 1910s, the early nineteenth century was seen as a simpler time during which Britain's position in the world seemed more secure, especially after Wellington's victory over Napoleon. In 1810, the English champion Tom Cribb met and defeated, albeit with the help of a crooked referee, the American born, former slave Tom Molineaux. A century later, the political, racial, and international climate convinced the Home Secretary that the possible repercussions from the defeat of a white champion by a black man dictated that no such fights take place again. The reality of championship boxing in the twentieth century was that the best man, as often as not, was a man of color. This truth was too unpalatable for the British, who preferred the nostalgia of reliving bouts from the past and hoping for a white deliverer in the future. The alleged revulsion at the brutality of the Prize Ring did not prevent newspapers from discussing the good old "Dark Ages" of bare-knuckle fights. Sporting papers regularly carried long and detailed histories of fights that had taken place in the late eighteenth and early nineteenth centuries.[72] In some ways, boxing in Britain at the dawn of the twentieth was as much a pastoral myth as the more commonly thought of cricket.

For Australia before World War I, the strength of its boxers stood along side the prowess of its cricketers as personifications of an Australian masculine ideal. As the inevitability of war seemed more and more certain after federation, the violent nature of boxing seemed to propel the sport into the limelight. This of course would eventually be replaced in the national psyche with the myths of Gallipoli and the ANZACs. However, before the war, Australian boxers were deemed representative of a young, but virile race, which sought its place on the world stage and would fight if necessary to defend itself. As boxing became more respectable, press coverage increased. This coincided with the advent of the mass production of the motion picture camera, which enabled substantially more people to view fights. The money that the films brought to the fight game increased its importance and became a self-reinforcing spiral of publicity based on large purses which generated more money and permitted organizers to offer more astronomical purses ad infinitum. All of this in turn fed on white male fears of black men and national degeneration. As a result, during this period, the display of muscular male bodies enduring pain and physically dominating other men came to occupy a central place in the national imaginations of white Britain and Australia.

CHAPTER FIVE

Defending White Manhood: The Bodyline Affair in England and Australia

Life is short, but cricket is long. We live in a world which shakes on its foundations. We have seen stable things totter and fall before our eyes. Great empires have passed away, great kings and Churches have fallen in ruin. American prosperity, the faith of the naïf, has shown itself the plaything of time. Even the pound sterling, the rock of ages, has crumbled in our sight. Darwin has disturbed our pride, and Galileo has undermined our fables. Einstein has upturned our calculations, and Freud our notions of morality. The stable things are shaky things, no match in their pretentiousness for time and tide. The simple things outlive them. After all successive ruins we still find the sand, the grass, life, and human impulse, much as they were before. Because of this nexus with simple things, none of the shakers has been able to shake our English soul and spirit which takes its form in cricket.

—"Gryllus," *Homage to Cricket*, 1933[1]

Ludus enim genuit trepidum certamen et iram;
Ira truces inimicitias et funebre bellum!
("A game may beget dreadful strife and wrath,
and from wrath may spring savage enmities and murderous war.")
—Mr. Reginald Carter, letter to *The Times*, January 26, 1933[2]

In the Australian summer of 1932–33, a cricket team sponsored by the Marleybone Cricket Club (MCC) and representing England was placed under the command of a dour Scotsman named Douglas Jardine and sent to Australia to avenge their humiliating defeat at the hands of the Australians in the English summer of 1930. Hoping to curtail the prolific scoring of a young New South Welsh batsman named Don Bradman, who had embarrassingly dominated the English in 1930, Jardine devised an arguably novel form of bowling attack which eventually came to be referred to as "Bodyline," or as many English commentators preferred, "fast leg-theory." Bodyline involved the highly dangerous and ethically dubious practice of bowling fast, high-bouncing balls at or near the upper-body and head of the batsman while a semicircle of fielders was menacingly placed within yards of the wicket. This left the batsman no sporting chance of success and a great likelihood of sustaining an injury.[3] This would all be unremarkable except for the fact that the Australian furor in response to this bowling attack, coupled with the English refusal to abandon it, led to a scandal which shook the imperial sporting world; it led to a significant loss of prestige for the English in the eyes of many in the Empire and opened the door for a variety of challenges to English preeminence in imperial culture. The game, which had previously been viewed, as illustrated above in Gryllus's *Homage to Cricket*, as more stable than any other institution, had succumbed to the turbulence of the twentieth century. Furthermore, the controversy provided an empire-wide stage for a prolonged debate between England, Australia, and the West Indies over what values should be emblematic of true manhood. Notions of class and race prevalent at that time strongly influenced this debate.

Richard Holt has written that the Bodyline affair was "probably the best-researched controversy in the history of sport." The controversy excited not only an outpouring of literature at the time, but has continued to interest historians ever since.[4] While the contemporary books and articles largely either chose sides in order to assign blame or attempted to point a way out of the imperial quagmire, secondary sources have tended to give causal significance to nationalistic feelings. However, nationalism alone cannot explain the significance attached to the incident at the time. Class, race, and gender considerations were equally to blame for the passions stirred by a simple dispute over a game. For many white Britons and Australians, defending their respective visions of cricket became nothing less than the defense of their visions of white manhood, an undertaking made all the more urgent by the floundering economies ineffectively coping with the Great Depression and sapping national morale.

The determination to win that the English took to Australia in 1932 and the subsequent support that the English public gave its team and captain in the face of all logic and tradition leads one to the conclusion that much more was at stake than a mere desire to avenge a series loss in 1930. The English had lost series numerous times before and did not resort to questionable tactics to restore their athletic pride. Of course, part of their resolve to stop the Australians can be traced to the unprecedented debut of Bradman who presented the possibility of stymieing the British for the next 15 years. However, it would appear that this alone was not sufficient to account for the English acceptance of the turmoil that ensued. Rather, the perception of crises of masculinities in both Australia and England set the stage for an imperial conflict that would be hard to imagine in any other time.

Ric Sissons and Brian Stoddart argue that "while political and economic tensions might strain good will in restricted circles, cricket was general currency... [the Bodyline affair] might be equated with the damage done to British prestige at the popular level by the supposed inefficiencies in its generals' disposition of Australian troops during the First World War."[5] Interest in the tour was widespread and went far beyond the restricted cricketing community that followed English county cricket, the nominally premier domestic county cricket competition.[6] The public fascination with international Tests between England and Australia dwarfed the attention given to domestic games to the extent that the biannual Ashes tours went a long way toward subsidizing the regular season county matches. Newspapers devoted extensive coverage to the tour, its buildup, and its aftermath. Newspapers from England, Scotland, Wales, Australia, and the West Indies all placed tour news in the main news section rather than with the other sports. Furthermore, even many papers that did not normally cover cricket, like the *Football Post* of Nottingham, for example, placed tour information and Bodyline-related stories as lead news items. Reporters cabled over 300,000 words, a small fortune in telegraph charges, out of Adelaide during the five days of the third Test to all parts of the Empire.[7]

In his seminal autobiography-cum-cricket book, *Beyond a Boundary*, the great West Indian intellectual and cricket writer for the *Manchester Guardian* C.L.R. James wrote about Bodyline in a chapter entitled "Decline of the West." He described the affair as "the blow from which 'It isn't cricket' never recovered."[8] Although Jardine comes in for particular criticism, James viewed the controversy as something much larger than clash between a handful of personalities. Rather, James wrote, "Body-line was not an incident, it was not an accident, it was not a temporary aberration. It was the violence and ferocity of our age expressing itself in cricket... It began in World War I. Exhaustion and a fictitious prosperity in the late 1920s delayed its maturity. It came into its own in 1929. Cricket could no more resist than other organizations and values of the nineteenth century were able to resist."[9]

It is undoubtedly true that cricket was not immune to the changing world in which it existed. It should perhaps have been expected that public school boys who viewed the war in 1914 as a great game, would eventually come to view their games as war in the aftermath. Nonetheless, the controversy cannot be reduced solely to a reflection of the violence of World War I. Bodyline was the product of a specific historical moment in which economic, social, and gender tensions explosively combined for a brief period that forever changed the institution of cricket and in the process enflamed a generation of men for whom the game was a significant building block in their self-perceptions as men.

Cricket in the Interwar Empire

In the midst of the Great Depression and struggling with calls for the devolution of imperial power, the British Empire, which had seemed unshakable to much of the world in the three decades before the Great War, was increasingly unstable in 1933. The British Parliament passed the Statute of Westminster, which gave legislative independence to the parliaments of New Zealand, Canada, Newfoundland, the Union of South Africa, the Irish Free State, and Australia, in 1931. In India, the independence movement was in full swing. In addition to the ongoing transformation from Empire to the Commonwealth of Nations, Britain was also experiencing a period of notable flux in gender relations in the interwar years.

The aftershocks of the Great War had left the national psyche of Britain badly scarred and the gender status quo shaken. The psychological and demographic disruptions did not end overnight; in 1933 there were still 8.7 percent more females in England and Wales than males, which fed concerns of gender imbalance.[10] Elite British manhood was particularly unstable. University and public school educated upper-middle-class men were the most likely to have been front-line junior officers, and consequently suffered the greatest proportional losses during the war. Men of this class, like Siegfried Sassoon, Robert Graves, and Edmund Blunden, produced most of the published war poetry and memoirs that helped to shape and articulate English memories of the war and helped cement the myth of the "Lost Generation," which referred not to the mass of British dead—Britain suffered proportionately smaller losses than Germany or France—but rather to the loss of the upper echelon of British manhood. That so many young men from the relatively small, cohesive English elite died or were psychologically or physically wounded, produced a mass trauma and cult of the dead for the country's leadership. The interwar period was infused with the popular myth that the cream of England's youth had been killed in the war, murdered not so much by the Germans, but by an older generation of their own countrymen.[11] War poems such as Wilfred Owen's "Parable of the Old Man and the Young," which concluded that the older generation had ignored God's will and sent "half the seed of Europe, one by one" to slaughter, dramatized this intergenerational conflict.[12] Although the trauma was indeed great, one should not exaggerate the extent to which the generation and its successors turned their backs on the Victorian and Edwardian world. England in 1919 was after all more similar than dissimilar to England in 1914. However, a break with the past had occurred, and Victorian ideals were dramatically opened to criticism and revision by the postwar generation.

The class that formed the basis of the Lost Generation myth was the same class that dominated the cricketing establishment of England. The gentleman amateurs, who were the backbone of English county and Test cricket in the 1930s, were the younger brothers of the war generation. Jardine, for example, was born in 1900, and was too young to serve in the war but old enough to live through the aftermath and for a time be the *ex officio* standard bearer of his class's manhood. The tenacity with which the English defenders of the Bodyline tactics argued their case could be attributed to a siege mentality engendered by the horrific losses of the war and the destabilized position of the public school elite in British society.

Joanna Bourke has argued that the interwar years saw the emergence of new masculinities or new masculine ideals "as a response to the perceived need to reassert manliness in a society undergoing rapid change."[13] One of these responses was the attempt by the MCC to reestablish English cricketing superiority, and by extension the control and superiority of the MCC-led elite; however they pursued these ends with the adoption of unprecedented means, namely Bodyline.

While the war had disrupted and tarnished old expressions of manliness, English men still looked to the past for guidance in their attempts to remake their world. This nostalgic yearning took many forms: the pressure on women to leave the workforce, animosity toward flappers and New Women, the reassertion of traditional maternal and domestic roles, and fanatical attachment to English victory over Australia at cricket.[14] They simultaneously reached back to the past for comforting images of docile women, pastoral games, and Victorian certainty, while grasping with the other hand for the future that would help them forget the horrors of the war. This desire to reassert the old by resorting to new tactics would come to a head in the Bodyline series. The humiliating loss to the Australians in 1930 came directly on the heels of the great outpouring of war memoirs in 1929 and their renunciation of pre-1914 ideals of valor and honor, which had led so many public school Old Boys to enlist enthusiastically in 1914.

The economy of Great Britain was another obvious concern that shook the English elite and masses alike. The Depression was severely affecting the entire Empire; unemployment in Britain was hovering around 20 percent and between 29 and 34 percent in Australia. British exports had dropped by almost 70 percent between 1920 and 1933.[15] In Australia, there was a widespread belief that the Australian government's decision to follow the advice of the Bank of England to cut expenditures and continue paying debts owed to English banks had worsened the Depression.[16] For example, in 1913, 9.5 percent of Australian export earnings went to repay overseas debt; that figured had climbed to 25.8 percent in 1931 and to a full third by 1933.[17] Australia had become legislatively independent, strategically irrelevant to imperial defense, and economically remote from British interests, but British culture remained one of the prime bonds of Empire. Although the homogeneity and unity of such a far-flung Empire have often been overdrawn, it has been argued that the common ideological beliefs, most notably the tenets of the "civilizing mission" bound the Empire together.[18]

Within the British context, perhaps no institution characterized or proselytized the ideological underpinnings of British rule across its diverse collection of colonial possessions more than the sport of cricket. Robert Graves and Alan Hodge wrote that after the Crown, a common Anglo-Australian devotion to cricket "was the chief sentimental link that bound the two countries together."[19] The game of cricket was central to the training and worldviews of British and colonial elites and was seen to embody the masculine values that had created the Empire. Harold Larwood, the English fast bowler at the center of the controversy, wrote that any attempt to curtail Bodyline bowling would "make of cricket a less manly game. That would be an Imperial disaster."[20] A belief that any alteration to the game of cricket would have imperial consequences was such a widespread elite sentiment in the Victorian and Edwardian Empire that Altham and Swanton in their *A History of Cricket* (1938) could state without hyperbole that cricket was "simply the most catholic and diffused, the most innocent, kindly, and manly of popular pleasures. It is a liberal education in itself, and demands temper and justice and perseverance. There is more teaching in the playground than in the school rooms, and a lesson better worth learning very often."[21] Specifically, these were the values thought to be necessary to make men out of the boys, both British and colonial, who would eventually run the Empire. English control of the organization and administration of the game at the international level was complete until the Australians protested the lack of sportsmanship in the bowling tactics endorsed by Jardine. By questioning the ethical limits of the English pursuit of victory and the right of the MCC to dictate the laws of cricket, their Australian opponents challenged the prevailing English hegemony in sport and culture, and metaphorically, imperial relations in general.

In the 1930s, the exclusive MCC, which is headquartered in St. John's Wood, London, controlled and administered English and imperial cricket. The MCC began sending representative teams of "English" cricketers abroad in the 1870s.[22] When a nation had developed a sufficient standard of play in the MCC's opinion, the MCC awarded that country "test" status, a term, which refers to an official match between the representative teams of two nations. This normative concept of competence, and by extension "civilization," was applied to white settler colonies, India, and tropical dependencies alike. However, it was hardly applied consistently, as white colonies achieved Test status much more easily than did colonies dominated by people of color. Australia was the first nation to participate in official Test matches, followed by South Africa, New Zealand, Canada, India, and the West Indies. Test matches were, as a matter of course, held up to be a bond of Empire; likewise they retained an air of tutelage in which the English passed on behavioral norms to the colonies and dominions.[23] The Anglo-Australian cricket rivalry was by far the most intense and the most important to both nations. Altham and Swanton argued that with the proliferation of Test nations, "Nearly every county team contains several England blazers. Test finery is cheap, yet to have played against Australia remains, as, perhaps it will always remain, the hall-mark of English cricketing ability."[24]

By the interwar period, the English and Australians had developed a standard schedule of alternating tours every other year or so. The touring sides usually played five Test matches and between two and three-dozen matches against county and benefit teams. Victory in the Anglo-Australian

Test series was and is known as the "Ashes," a term that originated after the first Australian Test victory on English soil in 1882.[25] The 1930 Ashes tour was particularly devastating for the English, as the Australians unveiled the young batting prodigy (later Sir) Donald Bradman, who remains to this day arguably the best batsman of all time.

It has become a truism that by the interwar period, cricket was an "imperial religion." This religion was complete with rituals and relics. For English cricketers going out to the colonies, tours resembled a missionary society executive reviewing the work of his missionaries in a semicivilized society. For the Australians, the trip "Home" was more of a pilgrimage to the Holy Land, the originative sites of the religion. The ceremonies associated with this imperial religion were as choreographed and unalterable as a Roman Catholic mass. The tour included civic welcomes, games with tea and luncheon breaks, post-game dinners with good fellowship, toasts and paeans to imperial vigor and unity. The rites of a first-class cricket tour did not, until 1932–33, include adopting a hostile and physically dangerous tactics and ignoring the protests of your honorable opponents. This deviation from tradition was partly at the root of the vehemence of the Australian outcry over Bodyline.

Although the Bodyline scandal was initially an Anglo-Australian dispute, the West Indies came to play an important role in the unfolding affair, which was far from settled when the West Indies team toured England in the northern hemisphere spring and summer of 1933 (see chapter four). The presence on the West Indies team of several extraordinary black cricketers, and their willingness to "follow the English example" and employ tactics of disputed ethical character not only induced the English to ban the tactics, but also foregrounded issues of race and gender in the world of imperial sport.

At the root of the controversy was an international debate over the relative strength of manhood of the English, Australian, and West Indian nations.[26] Through several different, and at times contradictory, discourses including "manliness," "civilization," "athleticism," and "good form," the debate surrounding Bodyline and nationalism came to encompass not only gender but race and class as well. The scandal marked the end of the golden age of imperial sporting relations and the end of the dominance of the English sporting ethic, which never recovered from the controversy.

Cricket fans and historians have endlessly debated the technical and tactical aspects of Bodyline, the repercussions of this technique for the sport, and some of the wider implications of the affair. However, that the cricketing establishments in England and Australia, but not the West Indies, eventually renounced the practice has been largely ignored. This is not an insignificant development, as the West Indian refusal to renounce these tactics and the Anglo-Australian abandonment of them were at the root of their relative claims of superior manhood with regard to cricket.

On a purely cricketing level, there were supporters throughout the Empire of all points of view as to whether this was a legitimate tactic or not. However, events which call into question the relative manliness of two nations are rarely evaluated on a rational and objective level. Generally, regardless of an individual's personal views on the merits of Bodyline as a tactic, in the first few months of the controversy, there were few Englishmen who publicly disowned Jardine and Larwood for unsportsmanlike behavior and even fewer Australians who publicly sided with the English. One contemporary account noted that "though now and then an Australian was found to criticize the resource if not the courage of their batsmen, the cricketers of that country were as a whole absolutely united in its denunciation."[27] In contrast, *The Times* could argue unequivocally in January 1933 that "there was nothing unfair or unsportsmanlike or contrary to the spirit of the game in the tactic of the English captain and his men."[28]

The Australians claimed that the English team was not playing fair and had disgraced the game by adopting these tactics, which in their opinion were clearly not ethical or sporting. In contrast, the English initially claimed that the Australians were simply squealing effeminately and behaving like petulant schoolboys and poor losers. English commentators often blamed Australian "democracy" for contributing to both Australian effeminacy and juvenility. After the English unilaterally decided in late 1933 that this form of attack would not be allowed in cricket, the majority of English commentators began to argue that it was fair but aesthetically unpleasant and therefore not in the best interests of the game. Meanwhile, the only group, which did not reject the tactics in principle, were the West Indians, who maintained that bowling fast bumpers inside the leg stump was standard practice in the West Indies and that the others were simply afraid of injury.

The Controversy Erupts

Although the component parts of Bodyline were in themselves nothing new, their combination produced a novel bowling attack that was effective, nearly unplayable when bowled at the velocity of a Larwood or Bill Voce, England's main fast bowlers, and ethically questionable. Bodyline consisted of fast, short-pitched balls (called "bumpers" or "bouncers") bowled often at chest-to-head height, on or inside the leg stump while the field was set with up to five men crowding around the batsman on the leg side with two more on the leg side boundary. This, in short, left the batsman with no real shot to play and therein lies the essentially unsporting character of the tactic. The pace of the English bowling limited the batsmen to a split second decision whether they should duck, be hit, or play defensively, and risk being caught by the array of close fielders. While the English did not bowl this form of attack constantly, they bowled it enough to unsettle the Australian batsmen and in the end, easily won the Ashes back. The question being asked around the Empire was, "At what cost?"

With the series tied at one match apiece, the teams met at Adelaide on January 13, 1933 for what would turn out to be the fateful third Test. *The Times* described the Test as "the most disagreeable match that has been played since the game began."[29] During play, English bowlers hit and injured two Australian batsmen, including a fractured skull for Australian wicket keeper Bert Oldfield. Incidentally, neither batsman was injured while Bodyline was being bowled, but the fact that Jardine and Larwood switched to a Bodyline field placement directly after Australian captain W.M. Woodfull was "struck over the heart" (as it was always reported) infuriated the Australian spectators.[30] *The Australian Worker* commented that "among Australian cricketers there is an unwritten law not to take advantage of an injury which a player may sustain. Evidently it has no place in English cricket ethics."[31] The ferocity of the crowd's response to Jardine's tactics led the members of the Australian Board of Control (ABC) present at Adelaide to decide that some action was necessary to curtail the bowling tactics, which were enflaming the Australian crowds and causing widespread fear of violence. The situation worsened when the Australian press, thanks to a leak in Australian dressing room, reported that the Australian captain Woodfull rebuffed the English manager Pelham Warner when the latter came to inquire after the injured Australian. Woodfull declined to converse with Warner telling him that there were two teams out on the field and only one was endeavoring to play cricket.

In what can at best be described as a less than diplomatic or even realistic protest, although one widely supported in Australia, the ABC cabled the MCC protesting that the English tactics were unsportsmanlike and that Bodyline bowling threatened the heretofore good relations between Australia and England. The MCC had neither seen the bowling nor ever heard of the term "Bodyline," which had only recently been coined in Australia. Consequently, they had no real option but to support their managers, captain, and team fully and express their disgust at the charge of unsportsmanlike behavior.[32] This began the confrontation that would be fought over the telegraph lines as much as on the field of play for most of 1933. Once the Australians explicitly stated that they considered the English team's actions, and by extension the English team, to be unsportsmanlike, all possibility of a quick and simple solution vanished.[33] The English would not continue the series until the charge had been withdrawn, which it diplomatically was by the ABC. However, it was difficult for the Australians to make their case to the English, when the latter had through years of convention circumscribed what language could be employed and still permit dialogue to continue. On the surface of the matter, as far as the English were concerned, this was an argument over language.

The press took considerable interest in and hotly debated the nomenclature used to technically describe the tactics. What was simply an abbreviation for "bowling in the line of the body" invented by an Australian journalist hoping to save cable charges, was viewed by most English commentators as a deliberate Australian plot to mislead and incite an Australian mob into intimidating the English team into acquiescence. Larwood wrote in his autobiography that the term Bodyline "was maliciously coined by a cute Australian journalist for the express purpose of misleading, and for obscuring the issue, which it did with great success. The mere use of the word 'Body' was meant to damn me, and damn me it did."[34] The English term, "fast leg theory," inaccurately implied that this form of attack was simply a variation of an older and vastly more benign bowling attack which included balls bowled inside the leg stump, but without the pace, distance, and field setting of Bodyline. English journalist Bruce Harris reduced the difference in terminology to simply a matter of manners. He referred to what was "politely described as 'leg theory' and impolitely as 'body line.' "[35] However, accuracy, rather than etiquette, dictates the use of the term "Bodyline."

An exchange of cables between the MCC and the ABC ensued and the teams concluded the series under an uneasy truce, but not before the English threatened to cancel the tour and the Australians threatened to break off cricket relations with England. On the field, the English won the series easily. The question of the legitimacy of the tactic was not decided finally for eight more months until a West Indies team, featuring fast bowlers E.A. Martindale and Learie Constantine, came and bowled Bodyline against the English at Old Trafford. Although this display was only a pale imitation of Larwood due to the slowness of the Manchester pitch, the heavier atmosphere in England and the fact that the West Indian bowlers were slightly slower than Larwood, it was still an effective enough display to change the minds of many English commentators who had until then been perfectly in favor of these tactics despite never having seen them in person. Shortly after the Old Trafford Test, the MCC, who still maintained that these tactics were completely fair, decided that they were not in the best interests of the game and should therefore be banned from cricket.

The Men who Made the Controversy

Many English commentators before and after the 1932–33 Ashes campaign have denigrated the Australian Bradman's achievements by arguing, as F.J.C. Gustard did in his book previewing the 1934 Ashes tour, that "[Bradman] is the greatest run-getter in the history of the game, an expression which is not necessarily synonymous with the greatest batsman."[36] C.L.R. James, mocked this (usually English) stance by writing that Bradman "has been blamed for machine-like play. He has been blamed for the ruthlessness with which he piled up big scores. This is absurd . . . people speak of Sir Donald's heavy scoring as if each and every great batsman was able to do the same but refrained for aesthetic or chivalrous reasons which Sir Donald ignored."[37] Bradman's average over a 21-year career was 95.14 runs per innings in first-class cricket (and 99.94 in Test matches).[38]

The next closest is V.M. Merchant with 71.22 in first-class cricket. Only three other players in history have averages over 60 and two of them, W.H. Ponsford and W.M. Woodfull, played with Bradman for Australia in 1932–33.[39] This gives some indication of how innovative and unplayable Jardine's Bodyline tactics were to render these great batsmen impotent as happened during the tour; Bradman averaged a full 44 runs below his career average during the 1932–33 Ashes campaign.

Bradman's scorching performance and Australia's resounding victory in the 1930 series had encouraged the English selectors to attempt to recapture the Ashes by any means necessary. This mercenary determination to win led to the selection of Jardine as captain.[40] Jardine was a grim barrister of Scotch–Indian descent, who played with a professional's intensity despite his gentlemanly amateur status. On the previous English tour to Australia in 1928–29, Jardine had come to detest Australian crowd behavior, which was notably more boisterous than the austere behavior in first-class English ovals. There are two often-repeated stories about the severe skipper. The first is a remark made by the West Indian-born manager of the 1932–33 English team, Pelham Warner, who believed that "when [Jardine] sees a cricket field with an Australian on it, he goes mad."[41] The second, which may be more myth than reality, relates that upon learning that the MCC had selected Jardine captain of England, an old schoolmaster of his at Winchester remarked, "Well, we shall win the Ashes—but we may lose a Dominion."[42]

Despite the apocryphal foresight of this caustic remark, it does illustrate the nature of the man, as well as the fact that the selection of a skipper who forthrightly eschewed the traditional diplomatic and ambassadorial duties of the English captaincy, was a significant departure from tradition in the pursuit of revenge and would result in almost destroying the sporting relations with England's closest dominion. His selection may also be indicative of the growing insecurity of the imperial edifice and the public school Old Boy elite which constructed and maintained it. By the interwar period, as the economic and political dominance of Great Britain became more precarious, many in Britain attached increasing significance to victory in Test matches, rather than just participation. Previously, a cricketing tour for the English was viewed somewhat as a long holiday filled with leisurely cruises and dinners, pleasantly interrupted by cricket matches played against members of a colonial elite. Normally there would be a good deal of fellowship and camaraderie, or at least civility, between the opposing players. Bradman bemoaned the fact that the friendliness of previous and later tours was completely absent during the acrimonious Bodyline tour. In his autobiography he recounted how by the middle of the tour, "Players of both sides got to passing each other without a word of greeting . . . Oh, that cricket should ever have got to that."[43]

The Board of the MCC chose the captain of the English cricket team and this selection was traditionally determined in equal measure by a candidate's cricketing, social, and class qualifications. Superb strategic or batting acumen were by no means sufficient to earn one the position of the captaincy. Jardine's batting form in 1932 was outstanding and he should certainly have been included in the team for his batting alone. However, it was his appointment as captain that should and did raise eyebrows in English cricketing circles. The first qualification necessary was the appropriate class status proven largely by one's public school education and amateur status. English cricketers were divided into two categories: gentlemen and players. The former were nominal amateurs who officially were only reimbursed for travel expenses incurred while playing for a county or England side. "Amateur" did not denote an inferior level of play necessarily, but rather signified that the player was wealthy enough to play for the love of the game without being paid. Some amateurs had professions; Jardine was a barrister for example, while others like A.W. Carr were full-time gentlemen.

Iftikhar Ali Khan, the Nawab of Pataudi (who was known as "Pat" to his teammates and Australian barrackers alike), was an Indian prince, graduate of Balliol College Oxford, and member of the English side. As such, he occupied a unique position on the English side; elevated because of his wealth and amateur status, but somewhat subordinate because of his being Indian. Despite hitting a century in his Test debut in Sydney, he only appeared in one other Test for the remainder of the tour. Although it has been argued that he was dropped because of the incredibly slow pace of his innings, more commonly, it is attributed to his resistance to support Jardine's Bodyline tactics. In the Melbourne Test, Pataudi refused to move from the off to the legside and take up a Bodyline fielding position, at which Jardine reportedly remarked, "I see His Highness is a conscientious objector today."[44]

In contrast to the Gentlemen, were the professionals who were paid on a per-game or per-tour basis and who were known as "Players." The amateur–professional divide was pronounced. Professionals and amateurs on the same team dressed in different changing rooms, entered the pitch from different gates, and ate lunch separately. Likewise, English amateurs were referred to as "Mr." on the scoreboard and in programs and the professionals were addressed simply by their initials. This split remained in effect in English cricket until 1962 when repeated failures to field a competitive amateur side in the annual Gentlemen versus Players match led to the abandonment of the system. Despite this, it was not until 1968 that *The Times*, the clearinghouse for all-important discussion about cricket in England, deigned to publish a letter from an acknowledged professional cricketer.[45] All Australian visitors, although officially "honoured guests," were listed only with their initials, like English professionals.

Patsy Hendren, a well-regarded professional batsman from the 1920s and 1930s, wrote in 1934 that there had been "one man who might have captained England for the past twenty years—who should certainly have captained England often. I refer to Jack Hobbs. But he was a 'pro' and I take it that on this account he was never even considered as a possible."[46]

It is conceivable that some of the more liberal amateurs might have accepted Hobbs as captain; however it is unthinkable that the administrators of English cricket would have countenanced a professional captain. A.W. Carr, English gentleman and captain of Nottingham at the time of Bodyline, gave English professionals a backhanded compliment in the process of criticizing the Australians:

> It is all very regrettable in a lot of ways, but there it is and despite the democracy of Australia socially many of their so-called amateur cricketers cannot compare with many of our English paid players. I know plenty of professionals whom I would delight to have as guests in my own home, but I am afraid I cannot say the same thing about most of the Australians whom I have met. But the Australians when they come here are made a great fuss of and given privileges which are denied to our own professionals.[47]

The treatment of working class and lower-middle-class Australians as equals to English amateurs galled Carr, as it did many upper middle-class and aristocratic Englishmen. For English amateurs, professionals were a necessary tool for winning, but certainly not to be confused with the gentlemen anymore than one would confuse a landlord who owned 50,000 acres in Kent with the people who picked the hops.

Throughout the Bodyline Affair, there was a perception that the egalitarianism of the Australians was at the root of all the trouble. Bruce Harris, the correspondent covering the tour for the London *Evening Standard* and author of a book defending the English tactics, echoed a common establishment sentiment when he stated that the English amateurs should not be expected to put up with Australian barrackers.[48] He warned that "the time may come when English cricketers—and especially amateurs financially independent of cricket tours—will quite reasonably decline to face the raucous music... Conceivably it may be necessary eventually to send out a team under a professional captain. His will be a difficult task, for necessarily he will not possess the independence which fortifies an amateur leader."[49] The English cricketing establishment generally considered amateur leadership essential for English cricket.

This phenomenon was mirrored in the colonies of India, where princely leadership was standard and unquestioned for decades, and the West Indies, where a white man skippered the side until the C.L.R. James-led campaign for a black captain resulted in (later Sir) Frank Worrell being appointed West Indies captain in 1960. While Australian teams were more egalitarian in class terms, there was for many decades sectarian discrimination in the selection of a captain. The preferred criteria for an Australian captain for many years were that a candidate be Protestant and a Mason. Despite the large number of Catholics playing elite Australian cricket at the time, there were no Catholic captains between 1888 and 1951.[50] The importance attached to amateur leadership in England, princely leadership in India, white leadership in the West Indies, and to a somewhat lesser degree Protestant leadership in Australia is indicative of national conceptions of masculinity as well. All men were clearly not created equal, or at least the cricketing establishments would not allow all men to be seen as equal. A cricket captain was allegedly the best man on the team *ex officio* and the cricketing establishments were not about to allow that position of prominence to go to a person from an undesirable class, race, religion, or caste as the case may be.

English captains had important diplomatic and social obligations that were deemed central to a tour's success. These duties included civic welcomes, teas, balls, and dinners, all of which required speeches by the captain and the manager. As a result, the tour captain regardless of nationality was traditionally a hail-fellow-well-met sort who could rattle off a few humorous remarks and praise the Empire and the good sportsmanship and hospitality of the hosts endlessly. Jardine, unlike previous captains such as his most recent predecessor Percy Chapman, did not fit this mold whatsoever as long as he was in Australia. Interestingly, during a post-Australian tour of New Zealand, Jardine proved to be a jovial and gracious guest, albeit only when the outcome of the series was secure. Upon reaching New Zealand, Jardine commented, "We have just come from a country where our parentage was regarded as doubtful, but our ultimate destination absolutely certain"; thereby filling the traditional role of a captain more in one sentence in New Zealand than he had in five months in Australia.[51]

After the controversial third Test in Adelaide, the post-game remarks of the two captains highlight the irregular nature of a Jardine-led English team. Woodfull, the Australian captain and one of the injured players, spoke in the normal and accepted manner of the imperial unity engendered by the game and the importance of sportsmanship. Jardine, on the other hand, commented only that the crowd had gotten what they had paid for. This commercial attitude was in direct contradistinction of decades of cricketing rhetoric. These remarks also highlight the different attitudes toward manhood informing the two captains' approaches to the series. Woodfull, ever the gentleman, was referring to Victorian manliness with its attendant moral values and obligations. Jardine, by commenting explicitly on the commercial imperative and alluding to the voyeuristic delight the crowd had taken in the display of violence, was speaking not of a moral ideal, but rather of what was seen as the gritty reality of modern masculinity.

The incongruities within the ever-mutating discourses of manhood in Britain and the Empire made the debate surrounding Bodyline possible. The Victorian conception of an "English gentleman" possessed many traits which had increasingly come to be viewed as effeminate; thus what in the nineteenth century was considered "manly," losing gracefully and with humility, for example, did not always sit well with twentieth-century conceptions of virile masculinity, such as the dogged pursuit of victory at any cost and the acceptance of "primitive" violence. Likewise, other attributes associated with an English gentleman, such as effeteness, attention to dress, and dandyism in general, had increasingly become associated with homosexuality and womanliness. The growing dominance of a masculinity which encompassed acceptance of previously working-class traits like violence and ruthlessness, opened the door for upper- and middle-class men to embrace "beastliness" or "savagery" associated with less "civilized" men in certain circumstances. This acceptance of the "uncivilized" was also a trait of artistic modernism as well. Within the furor over Bodyline, different groups of West Indians, Englishmen, and Australians employed different and often opposing attributes that were considered "masculine" and/or "manly" to justify their actions.

A leading English cricket authority at the time, Neville Cardus, wrote,

the Australian plays cricket to win . . . One summer we decided in this simple old land to put an end to all that. We decided to have for our captain a man who had a rare capacity for unsentimental leadership. Jardine will go down in the history of the game as one of the strongest and sternest and most realistic of all English captains . . . For my part I admire Jardine beyond words. I dislike his view of cricket. I believe that the qualities of character he possesses would suit better a leader of armies than a leader of cricketers . . . his influence on modern cricket has been sanitary; he has cleared away the cant. To the Australians he has returned tit for tat.[52]

Of course, Jardine is first a Scot, and during the after-game speeches in Adelaide it was the Australian Woodfull who made the Empire-binding speech and Jardine who crassly spoke of money. In addition to being factually questionable, Cardus' statement is a significant departure from a "traditional," that is, pre-1914, view of cricket. It would have been logically impossible for an adherent of the ethos of sportsmanship in the nineteenth-century tradition to admire a man whose view of cricket one detested, as the latter was seen as entirely representative of his worldview and morality. It is this newly found ability to rationalize transgressions against their own code, which opened the English up for criticism from the West Indians and the Australians.

Cowardice, Effeminacy, and Childishness in Bodyline

Throughout Bodyline, the English claimed that they were the best men due to their success as cricketers and due to their willingness to employ hard-nosed tactics to win regardless of the popularity of those tactics. Herbert Sutcliffe, a professional batsman on the England side summed up the lesson he took from the tour as follows: "I learned that Jardine was one of the greatest men I have ever met. A stern master but every inch a man and as straight as they make 'em. Jardine had the courage of his convictions; it was unfortunate for him that they did not meet with general approval, but that did not alter his outlook."[53] In contrast, the English nearly universally derided the Australian players and public as "squealers" for not accepting their defeat with dignity; the fans were criticized for barracking the English players, and the batsmen were ridiculed for being afraid of injury. Carr, in discussing the intimidating nature of the Australian J.M. Gregory's bowling in the 1920s, wrote: "It needed a lot of 'guts' to stand up to Gregory; and I often wonder what the Australians would have said about him if he had happened to be an Englishman . . . Lord! what a row there would have been if Gregory and [E.A.] McDonald had been on our side instead of theirs! The trouble about Larwood was, of course, that he was the right bowler on the wrong side."[54]

"Squealing," which was the most frequent charge leveled against the Australians, was deemed terrible form and its existence could only be explained, according to the English, by a decidedly deficient sense of honor and manliness on the part of the Australians, who would rather blame someone else for their shortcomings than own up to them. Carr believed that the Australians lacked a sufficient sense of gentlemanliness and had a mercenary approach to cricket; he commented: "My own experience of the Australians is that if they cannot win they will not stand to be beaten if they can help or avoid it. They will go to almost any length to dodge defeat. I am perfectly sure that I can say that this is also the opinion of a very great many people in this country. To the Australians cricket is a business almost pure and simple—a matter of money—and success is all that matters to them. We have a different view of things; to most Englishmen it is primarily a game."[55] The British press ceaselessly leveled the charge that the Australians simply did not want to accept being beaten. The *Morning Post* posited that it would have been more efficient and straightforward if the Australian cricket authorities simply proposed an "Act in the Australian Legislature rendering any English bowler who hit an Australian's batsman's wicket without the latter's written consent liable to instant deportation."[56]

In rebuttal, one Australian expatriate in England suggested that "cricketing traditions are nothing here [in England]. I find it a land as unsportsmanlike as possible . . . The Aussie is first a man. He demands what he pays for—sport. The present English team has given him other than sport. It was not a beating he feared."[57] Being given to excessive complaining, or in Australian parlance, being a "whinger," is particularly hated among Australians. That Australian men found themselves openly and unabashedly (and perhaps not unfairly) charged with being whingers, was certainly extremely irksome to them, as much as being called unsportsmanlike was to the English. This may have contributed to the Australian resolve to resist compromise with the English.

Fear of injury was at the heart of the Bodyline claims of effeminacy. The English, and later the West Indians, insisted that the Australians (and later the English) were simply afraid of getting hurt. This charge was usually followed by the claim that in the past the accuser had played bumpers without fear or complaint. In innumerable letters to the press and in articles and memoirs the accusation repeatedly was one of Australian fearfulness. The great English batsman Jack Hobbs, who was on tour as a journalist, managed to insult Bradman's bravery while nominally complementing him for his sensible thinking and willingness to "courageously" admit that he was not as much of a man as his English adversary, Larwood. In his book about the tour, *Fight for the Ashes*, Hobbs wrote,

> It looked to me as if Bradman had a little inquest in his mind, and returned this verdict: "If am hit by a ball traveling as fast as Larwood can make it travel my career may be finished. That isn't going to happen." The outcome was that Don played a gamblers' innings ... He took not the faintest risk of injury, and, in view of his slight physique, I do not blame him. But there were times when he need not have surrendered quite so wholeheartedly as he did ... I want to pay a tribute to him, because he had the courage to follow his convictions. It could not have been easy for Don to give in to Harold Larwood, especially as he had such a big reputation. But, having made up his mind not to get injured, he stuck to and followed out his view, a procedure requiring great moral courage, especially as his own supporters, those how made him an national idol, called him very hard names.[58]

This commentary was particularly strange since Hobbs had been the center of a small controversy the previous season when he was roundly criticized for complaining that a bowler was bowling short in a county match.

In response to English charges of cowardice, the Australians asserted endlessly that they were not afraid, but affronted by the attack's lack of sportsmanship. It would seem to a neutral observer, that of course part of the issue was fear of injury, especially a debilitating injury that might end a career. After all, Oldfield did have his skull fractured, which can hardly be dismissed as a minor injury, and broken arms are not uncommon in cricket even when the batsmen are not explicit targets. With that said, it is likely that the Australians would have been just as outraged had it come out that the English had illegally doctored the ball to obtain an advantage. However, what is interesting in the context of this discussion is the absolute urgency to deny fearfulness that all parties demonstrated. That is, even though clearly part of the animosity engendered by the English tactic was based on the fear of severe injury, no one arguing in Australia's defense would admit that the possibility existed that Australian batsmen were afraid of being hurt. Except for Englishman Patsy Hendren, who despite heavy criticism donned a prototypical batting helmet when he faced the fast bowling West Indians, not a single batsman admitted that he was afraid of injury. Indeed, Jack Fingleton, Australia's opening batsman in the first three Tests, was well-regarded by Australians for his stoic masculinity in the face of Bodyline bowling which left him bruised and battered, but unbowed. The only explanation for this insistence was that the imagery of masculinity was at stake in this imperial confrontation.

The British press and public commentators used both the trope of civilized manliness (i.e., that they were the keepers of the traditions of gentlemanly manliness) and that of virile masculinity simultaneously in criticizing the Australians, who allegedly were not brave enough to stand up to fast bowling the way the English had to J.M. Gregory and E.A. McDonald and then were so puerile as to blame others for their failures. When Jardine made this point, he also managed to allude to the suspiciously Irish character of Australia, by stating:

> Unlike most Englishmen, the Australian, while impatient of criticism from without, is not given to criticizing either himself or his country. He reserves his criticisms for direction against other countries and their inhabitants. His general attitude is too frequently that of the Irishman who said 'My mother, right or wrong; my wife, drunk or sober'—Australia can do no wrong in his eyes.[59]

The alleged effeminacy of the Australian response was highlighted in many English comments. For example, one letter to the *Manchester Guardian* captured the mood of many when the author suggested the following: "Roll, Bowl, or Pitch, a proprietor of a coconut-shy booth and therefore a sportsman, has always recognised the 'fair and weaker' sex by letting them throw from half way. Surely the same concession can be adopted when we are batting in the Tests and so prevent this feeling of unfairness that the Australian Board of Control is displaying."[60] A similar attitude was displayed in a cartoon published in the *South Wales Football Echo and Express*, a paper that normally did not even cover cricket. The cartoon depicts a rustic village cricket match; the wicketkeeper asks the batsman why he is wearing his wife's frock, to which the batsman replied, "Our side do tell me that there leg theory bowler of yours is going to bowl at my legs, so I'm not going to show them!"[61]

For their part, the Australians insisted that they were the true gentlemen because they were not willing to contravene the spirit of cricket for the mere pursuit of victory, which traditionally was ancillary to participation. For example, in a letter to *The Advertiser* of Adelaide, one Australian wrote, " I like many others, for a brief period, thought that Woodfull should introduce reprisals against the Englishmen by giving them some of their own medicine, but am thankful to say that the thought was only temporary, and that Woodfull's gentlemanly attitude is absolutely in keeping with what we believe to be the glorious traditions so long attached to cricket. What a fine example he is setting the rising generation to 'play the game,' however great the sacrifice."[62] Moreover, Australians viewed the eventual English reversal on the matter of Bodyline as hypocritical, thus further evidencing the alleged English abandonment of gentlemanliness.

In the imperial lexicon, the phrase "not cricket" denoted far more than extralegal practices. Rather, "not cricket" encompassed any action on the field or off that was unethical, devious, cowardly, unmanly, and perhaps above all, un-English. Indeed, Pelham Warner stated that cricket was "a name synonymous with all that is fair, and kindly noble, and upright."[63] As the arbiters of Anglo-Saxonism and ethics, for the English to be accused of unsportsmanlike behavior and to admit eventually, albeit tacitly, that their actions were indeed "not cricket" was highly significant for it represented a colonial challenge to the very core of the English right to impose behavioral standards on the colonies and dominions. For example, Jardine suggested that the "Australians . . . would do well to remember sometimes that there are other standards of behaviour besides their own, and that it is possible that there is much to be said in favour of those other standards."[64] Of course, that the English might follow this admonition clearly did not occur to Jardine, or many other Englishmen for that matter, since the English positioned themselves as the sole arbiters of civilized behavior.

Continually, the English stated or implied that the whole problem with Australians was that they were simply not manly enough to take what they had so freely dealt out in the past. Manliness is usually contrasted with either womanliness or alternately childishness; both implications are present in many attacks on the Australians. Larwood claimed, "If certain critics had not made such an effeminate outcry about it during and after the third Test the whole bother would be too childishly ludicrous to merit further consideration by grown-up men."[65] Likewise, Carr reminded his English readers, "You cannot play cricket with a soft ball or without taking some sort of physical risk. The game was never intended for namby-pambies."[66] In a line of argument that was typical of the general English tone of reporting, one columnist asked, "Would they have us believe that the manly game of cricket must, to suit their taste, be mutilated to be fit for eunuchs, not men?"[67]

These attacks on Australian manhood came at a time when the national morale regarding manhood was low and many commentators were particularly sensitive to charges of emasculation. The Depression had caused high unemployment and had pushed many men on to the dole while increasing the number of women who were the main breadwinners for their families. Patricia Grimshaw writes that "Unemployment and receipt of the dole were experienced by many men as emasculating. Equality, independence, and activity—the attributes of men—has been ignominiously snatched away and they felt keenly their sudden inferiority [to those with employment]."[68] This dynamic was not unheard of in Britain of course and it affected perceptions of manhood there as well. Joanna Bourke has argued that while employment levels were high, such as was the norm between 1870–1914, wage earning was the primary basis for gauging masculinity for working-class British males. However, once the economic downturn came and unemployment rose, the connection between masculinity and physical strength became increasingly more important.[69] Attendance at sporting events was seen by many as an escape from the grim realities of life, thereby explaining why cricket attendance went up in the Depression years despite the lack of disposable income many experienced. However, when the sporting event becomes simply a reminder of the inequities and shortcomings of everyday life, this is distressing for many.

Along with the common discussion and charges of effeminacy, there was also a widespread discourse of youth and age. John Gillis, in talking about young nations and old nations, has posited that "youth" was seen as the antidote to decrepitness, which could come to plague nations that rested on their laurels and did not actively renew themselves. He writes: "The myth of progress, which endowed each [nation] with a glorious past and a great future ... at the same time utterly denied the possibility of degeneration or death that its own understanding of itself as a living body implied." For European nations, it was not enough to have a future, but a nation also needed a bright future.[70] The English obviously had no diffi-culty drawing on a past full of glorious achievements, but their belief in a glorious future was much less tenable. Bodyline and the victory over their youthful dominion were one way in which they could reassert the strength of their past while nominally utilizing the attitudes and determi-nation of the modern age. The Australian attitude seemed to naturally focus more on the future than on the past, but they still resented charges of infantilism. Where the English tended to write of the Australians as will-ful and difficult children or young adolescents, the Australians spoke of their nation as a young, full-grown man with a bright future and the capacities to fulfill his potential. J.C. Davis, an Australian journalist writing in *The Referee* hypothesized that "if Wilhelm Hohenzoller were still Kaiser, he might interpret these things to mean that the British Empire was at war with itself, tearing out its own vitals, that Australia, the independent youngster, was at the throat of Old Mother-land, and that now was the time to strike across the Channel, strike boldly and hotly."[71]

According to Alistair Thomson, the "test of Australian manhood" at Gallipoli during World War I, not the official transfer of power in 1901, marked the maturation and realization of the Australian nation. Australian war correspondent Charles Bean was instrumental in spreading a vision of the campaign and the Australian soldiers which came to be taken as emblematic of all true Australian men: loyal, cheerfully cheeky, and irrev-erent when out of the line, courageous, resourceful, and independent. Thomson contends: "These qualities, fostered in the Australian bush, dis-covered and immortalized in war, were said to typify Australians and Australian society, a frontier land of equal opportunity in which enter-prising people could make good. This was the nation which 'came of age' at Gallipoli."[72] Thomson concludes that while class differences between Australians was often noted in memorials to the Australia New Zealand

Army Corps (ANZACs), it was only in the context of heralding the union between all Australian men against a common enemy. As far as the myths of the ANZAC legend go, the common class enemies of all Australians were the British generals who had been cavalier with Australian lives.[73]

Jardine also evoked the imagery of adulthood and childishness when he stated that any attempt on the part of the MCC to dictate tactics to a cricket captain was unthinkable for a true man. Perhaps the Australians thought it was proper to direct play from the boardroom, but Jardine refused to acknowledge this as a possibility. He wrote: "It is all very well for school boys to have their bowling changes dictated from the pavilion, but it is hard to imagine this type of control being exercised in international cricket."[74] More often, however, the Australians claimed to find themselves being treated like school children. Bill O'Reilly, the great slow bowler for the Australians in the 1930s, argued that "the M.C.C. had assumed the righteous attitude of a worthless headmaster dealing with a school scene about which he had taken not the slightest trouble to become conversant."[75] A letter to the *Liverpool Post & Mercury* stated: "A number of urchins playing cricket with a box as a wicket and any old piece of wood as a bat, may squeal when they miss a ball on the leg side with the bat and top it with their anatomy, but the squeal is frequently a threat as to what will happen to the next ball so pitched. One can get a good deal of amusement out of this. But the squeals from Australia are getting on people's nerves."[76] In other words, even British children, as members of an ancient race, were more adult than grown Australians as members of an infant nation. Similarly, one letter to *The Morning Post* stated that the Australians "must learn to accept defeat in a more sporting spirit, and that dreadful barracking should be sternly discouraged. The only excuse is that Australia is a young country, she has not the splendid traditions that England has behind her."[77] Likewise, a letter to the editor of the *Liverpool Post and Mercury* argued that "it is not what the Australians have said, but the time chosen to say it (in the middle of a series of Test matches), which seems to me so nervy and childish."[78] The recurrent reference to childishness became even more pronounced when it came to English attitudes toward the black cricketers from the West Indies.

While the Australians seemed to resent being compared to willful children, they displayed no real yearning to be an "old country" like England. Their strength and vitality came from their youth and their golden era was the present and future, unlike the British who were seen as slightly past their prime. The rough egalitarianism and refusal to bow to many older forms of etiquette set Australians apart from Britain and of this they were justifiably proud. *The Referee* of Sydney defended the Australian departure from staid tradition, contending that it was less than manly to follow tradition for tradition's sake when there were more important matters at hand. "Many have criticised the Board of Control for the use of undiplomatic terms in its message to the M.C.C.," argued the lead article on February 1, 1933. "There are times for the exercise of the most delicate diplomacy. But, delicacy even in diplomacy may become effeminate, or it may become a vice by clothing the false of the sinister with the garb of the truth. Diplomacy, by reason of its delicacy, its lack of honest outspokenness, helped to create the cataclysm into which the world fell in 1914, and from which it is still struggling to rise."[79]

Elite Englishmen, like elite Europeans generally, often claimed that issues of character, and not race or class, were at the root of the exalted status of Europeans and colonial elites.[80] However, in imperial cricket, character was assessed not by some objective standard but by the degree of Englishness and whiteness. Even after colonial cricketers had achieved apparent parity on the scoreboard by beating British or producing outstanding individual players, the English simply emphasized a different aspect of their tradition and claimed colonial deficiencies, whether it be in behavior, tactics, or dress. This is illustrated by English charges of misbehavior by Australian crowds and by English critiques of West Indian cricketing brilliance being too sporadic, undisciplined, and overly emotional to match in innate quality that of the English. Not coincidentally, the inconsistency, irrationality, and over-emotionality ascribed to the West Indian cricketers are also character traits associated with women in this period, furthering the process of effeminization of colonial subjects by the dominant power as a justification for continued subjugation.

Class and Bodyline

Much English criticism of the Australians, while purportedly based on national distinctions, was in fact based on class divisions. The cricketing establishment of England abhorred the disregard with which most Australians treated class distinctions that were deemed sacrosanct by middle-class Englishmen. Furthermore, it is possible that domestic English class tensions were being displaced on to the Australians, who could possibly serve as a dangerous model for the English working class. As stated earlier, cricket in Australia was infinitely more egalitarian than English cricket. However, even as the Australians subverted the class-based nature of cricket by doing away with the gentleman/player divide and other overt class markers, they still supported the wider public school ethos that had permeated the English middle- and upper-classes worldviews since the mid-Victorian era. The ideal of being a "good sport" and showing "good form" was instilled through games as boys and came to be seen as required for all phases of life from warfare to gambling to cricket to parliamentary politics. This sporting ethos, which grew out of the games revolution, was founded on the creation, stabilization, and maintenance of hierarchical relations of power.[81] The games at the center of public school education endeavored to separate men from women, strong from weak, rich from poor, and British from colonial. Not only were many imperial administrators trained on the cricket and rugby pitches of

Eton and Harrow and the other public schools of England, but also imperialism was in part justified by the values inculcated on the playing fields. These values included honesty, fair play, fearlessness, unflappability, quick wittedness, and observance of hierarchies based on strength.

The German "rape of Belgium" in 1914 was, for example, seen as an outrage by the British because it broke the rules of war and was therefore not "sporting." The imagery of an unsporting Germany was prevalent in Australia as well; J.C. Davis in *The Referee* wrote:

> Real action must be taken by real fighting men to preserve the game's pleasant, personal and international relationships from utter discord, if not utter disruption . . . the feeling is that the English tactics in this direction are what Britishers often described the German tactics in the war. Those tactics, in the end, helped to defeat those who used them. It will be the same in this cricket business, but the effects will last for generations, and the men responsible will not be held up as paragons in pushing their game forward as a great Empire-builder.[82]

The public school ethos was encapsulated in the notion and term, "good form," which was, at its most basic level, a worldview encompassing the intertwined ideals of masculinity, class, and race. Good form was defined as the accepted behavior for English middle-class white males who were educated at a public school and/or university. In the case of the socially inferior professional cricketers, good form manifested itself as the willingness to know one's place and act accordingly. Normally, the working classes did not have to worry about the concept of good form, but since working-class professional cricketers were in such close contact with their social betters, a manner of good form developed. According to their beliefs, the English should have been the arbiters and exemplars of good form, and therefore by extension the exemplars of manliness, but their old ideals were no longer sufficient to achieve their desired ends. This realization that their so-called social inferiors had better form than they, created a crisis of sorts for the English and opened the possibility for an Empire-wide debate of what constituted manliness and "cricket."

What the English found most distasteful about Australians and about playing cricket in Australia was largely the Australians' disregard for class conventions which for the most part remained widely accepted in England. Australians lacked any distinction between "gentlemen" and "players"; the players were all paid small sums for play above a certain level but few if any did not have another career at the same time. The easy familiarity common in Australian society, founded as it was, on a myth of universal egalitarianism, led to the complete disregard of a professional–amateur divide. Despite widespread social inequality throughout Australian society, the Pacific nation was still dangerously classless for many English commentators. For example, Harris described Australia as a place where "free-and-easiness runs riot."[83] However, it was this democratic streak in the Australian character which Australians perceived to be the strength of their cricket teams, and by extension their nation. *The Argus* of Melbourne argued that the reported dissension on the English team was due to class divisions; the paper argued "as long as the wide margin between amateur and professional continues no team will be a happy family. Can anyone imagine one of our Australians who always calls his captain 'Bill' daring to disobey him on tour? It would be preposterous to think of it."[84]

The purportedly ill-bred nature of Australians manifested itself most dramatically in their proclivity for "barracking," or yelling, often vulgarly, at the players on the pitch. This was not confined simply to the cheap seats; rather the members (i.e., the wealthier section of the crowd) also barracked. For the English, this was conclusive evidence, even to a former professional like Hobbs that the democratic nature of Australia was at the root of all of its problems. Hobbs described the manner in which "Sometimes the Australian club members joined in the barracking, and I thought that was discreditable. In England, we do not expect this, even if the crowd shows displeasure. . . . The average Australian is far more partisan and antagonistic to opponents than the average Englishman."[85] *The New Statesman* described "the tedium [for the English players] inspired by the raucous jests of the barrackers. The whole atmosphere must be intolerable to a civilised man."[86] The debate surrounding Bodyline allowed the English finally (and angrily) to vent their frustrations with what were seen as decades of Australian misbehavior, which was often described as insolence or cockiness thereby reinforcing the supposed hierarchy of the mother country and the former colony, since only an inferior could be insolent. Every Australian protest regarding Bodyline was countered with an English charge of poor behavior or poor form on the part of the Australians.

One journalist who traveled with the English team asked of the Board of Control's cable, "Could anything be more tactless than this blunt and clumsy challenge? Accuse any Englishman of being impolite, dishonest, even immoral, and he may hold in his anger. Accuse him of being unsportsmanlike and you wound his deepest susceptibilities."[87] Likewise, Jardine stated, "It is often suggested in Australia that . . . every free-born Australian has an absolute and inalienable right to self-expression. Whether one subscribes to this Article of Faith is not of much importance. My objection is limited to the hostility and lack of taste to which this self-assumed license gives rise."[88] "Taste" is of course decided by its relative proximity to middle–class English mores. In an article in *The Argus* Pelham Warner while discussing barracking condescendingly and patronizingly asked the Australians if they wouldn't be happier if they behaved the way the English do. He stated, "I am not criticising, but I am speaking for the good of the game, and I ask again 'Do you think the greatest match in the world should be interrupted by a lot of noise?' "[89]

Likewise, Jardine expounded more fully on a widely held English attitude toward the Australian practice of barracking.

> No doubt a lot of barracking is thoughtless, nor is it to be expected that Australia should appreciate the Imperial responsibilities of cricket as deeply as we do at home; but a consideration of these responsibilities should prove a great incentive to action on the part of those who are determined that their painful exhibitions of hooliganism shall be suppressed. It is only too seldom appreciated in England, let alone Australia, that there are millions of British citizens throughout the world who take their cue, so far as behaviour at cricket matches is concerned, from Test Matches between England and Australia— matches which have so much in their part history to appeal to all of us, irrespective of colour, creed, or race.[90]

The Australians opposed these claims of bad behavior at every opportunity. In one letter from an Australian reader of a London paper, the letter writer stated: "I have seen cricket both here [in England] and there, and defend the Australian barracker. He is clever, witty, alive, smart, manly, and extremely fair. He is not dull. He does not sit through a match puffing a pipe and grumbling his dissent. A game of cricket without him is a dull affair."[91] Although many women attended cricket matches (especially, it was noted, when the heart-throb Bradman was due to bat), the public activity of barracking was a male domain.[92] The papers often mocked women for being at the matches for social rather than sporting reasons.[93] It is doubtful of course that the men were only interested in the game and not the excitement of a day out and the camaraderie evinced by a day at the cricket. In fact, men were often at the games for a variety of reasons in addition to the sport, such as interacting with other spectators, picnicking, drinking, and relaxing. Ironically, despite the often derogatory nature of comments regarding heavily female crowds, *The Referee* of Sydney argued that the only thing that saved Adelaide from having a riot the day Woodfull and Oldfield were felled by Larwood was that there had been a great proportion of women at the match.[94] This might have been as much an excuse for Australian lack of action, as a statement of relief.

The description of a pipe-smoking English observer would most likely be happily accepted by many English men as appropriate behavior for a cricket fan; however it only describes a middle-class, county cricket fan, not the lower-class Lancashire League cricket fans of the North nor the fans of local cricket in mining villages and collieries throughout the midlands and north of England. In the North, cricket was generally more rough and tumble as discussed earlier. Jim Bullock wrote that in mining village cricket fierce fast bowling was the order of the day and that slow bowling was dismissed as an old man's necessity. He recalled: "The young men tried constantly to increase their bowling speed, but not much attention was paid to length, variation, or swing. Speed was the thing that mattered."[95] Not coincidentally, mining village cricket produced some of the nation's most ferocious fast bowlers, like Larwood, who had been a miner when young.

Likewise, most first-class cricket spectators would also quickly distinguish themselves from their working-class brethren who followed football. One prominent sportswriter argued, "The two publics [i.e., football fans and cricket fans] are not comparable. The football public is a cloth-capped, fried-fish lot, and why some newspapers give more space to football than to cricket I cannot understand. The cricket public is on an altogether higher plane. Cricket attracts the intelligentsia—a word which I hate, but I cannot think of another."[96] In elite English eyes, Australians of all walks of life would more closely resemble the English working class in manners, sporting ethics, dress, and worldview.

Despite the claim by the English to a higher standard of spectatorship, by defending the ideal that cricket is not war, it was the Australians who seized the moral high ground from the English beginning with the opening salvos fired by Woodfull after the third Test. Australians, for the most part, resented the widespread and pronounced snobbery of the English. One English expatriate who lived in Australia believed that class differences were at the base of Australian anger over Bodyline. He reminded English readers that "as long as Englishmen take to Australia that public school manner which has rightly earned reprobation in other countries the present hostility will remain."[97] Throughout the tour, the outstanding emblem of English aristocratic disdain for Australian democracy was Jardine's multicolored Harlequin cap, which caused fetishistic hatred among the Australian public. For many Australians "Jardine in his harlequin cap and his ever-present silk neck-choker" was the embodiment of the English establishment and therefore an object of derision.[98] In a similar manner to the way in which a Wilhelmine spiked army helmet seemed to sum up all that was both wrong and quintessentially Teutonic about Germans in English eyes, so the Harlequin cap was an instantly recognizable icon of aristocratic English disdain for Australians and simultaneously for English effeminacy. In a letter to *The Times* about the Ashes campaign, the children's author and war poet A.A. Milne called for calm heads to consider the English tactics since the "bitter feeling already aroused by the colour of Mr. Jardine's cap has been so intensified by the direction of Mr. Larwood's bowling as to impair friendly relations between England and Australia."[99] According to Larwood, Jardine donned this multihued hat just to annoy the Australian crowds.[100]

A small, but vocal minority of English commentary on the subject, while stopping short of supporting the Australians, found the whole controversy distasteful and beneath the dignity of English cricket. One letter that is representative of this view was printed in the *Morning Post* and stated that the English should not "worry about what Australia did in 1921. If one side or another thinks that the tactics of its opponents are 'not cricket' in any sense of the word, that should be quite sufficient for those tactics to be dropped. After all, cricket is a game, and while it remains a game it does not matter who wins."[101] The quintessential stiff-upper-lipped Englishman should have been above squabbling over a cricket result. While the game and its cherished traditions were perhaps worth going to war over, a simple result, even of an international match or series, should never be worth even raising one's voice. In its review of Jardine's first book on the tour, *In Quest of the Ashes*, the *Daily Telegraph* wrote: "To go to the root of the matter, cricket ceases to be a game when players have to write books in order to explain their tactics on the field."[102] This view, despite being the quintessence of good form, did not win widespread support in England. Similarly, those Australians who felt that the country was embarrassing itself by complaining did not win far-reaching support in Australia.

Finally, many English critics based their arguments on the premise that it is inconceivable for the tactics to be unsportsmanlike simply because they have been used by an English captain, which in the minds of many English, by definition made them fair. Larwood argued that if he was not a fair bowler then the MCC would not have selected him and his captain would not have continued to play him.[103] Likewise, general English opinion held that the English bowlers must have bowled at the stumps and not at the man (as was alleged by the Australians) or else Jardine would have taken them off. Likewise, P.G.H. Fender, former Surrey captain and England batsman, argued: "Neither facts nor the imagination can substantiate any charge that bowlers . . . bowl with the intent to maim. The bowlers are men, and their captains cannot be charged with permitting such methods. Such inventions are mischievous."[104] That an English captain would employ unfair tactics did not seem to enter their realm of possibilities. In their history of Great Britain between the wars, Robert Graves and Alan Hodge put an interesting, if erroneous, twist on Bodyline by blaming ruthless professionalism among the English "Players" for the emergence of the tactic, as if the bowler could have employed Bodyline of his own volition.

Even the Australians were not immune to the traditional truism that an English cricket team was the embodiment of sportsmanship; a fact that accounts for the widespread sense of betrayal displayed by the Australians. In December 1932, after the English bowled a version of Bodyline against the Australians but before its full force was brought to bear, even many Australians refused to believe that the English would resort to unsportsmanlike conduct. In response to initial grumblings in the Australian press that the glimpses they had seen of Bodyline had been unfair, *The Advertiser* editorialized that "The Englishmen have the reputation, and deservedly so, of being true sportsmen, and would not adopt what are not sporting methods."[105] For the Australians and other cricketers from around the Empire however, English underhandedness was a distinct possibility from this point forward.

For all the English charges that the Australians were simply squealing or were acting hysterically, the Australian response was as a rule well considered and fair. Apart from that is, the Board of Control's first rash

telegram and the more radical writers who called for Australia to with-
draw from the Commonwealth in protest. Despite their fairness, the
Australian response was vehement, as in an article in *The Referee* that was
headlined "Australians are not Squealing! They Want Cricket to Live!"
That article quotes an English newspaper that asked: "What kind of
effeminacy has entered Australian cricket that relations are supposed to be
jeopardised by such trivialities?" In response, the Australian wrote that the
English attitude is "suggestive of a bitter bigotry that condemns itself. If
he thinks that Oldfield's battered temple is a trivial injury, one would like
to know what particular stuff his own head is composed of."[106]

For the most part, the Australian outcry was that the English were simply not playing in the spirit of the game that they had given to the world.
Overall, the Australians positioned themselves as the true bearers of the
ideals of sportsmanship, and by extension Anglo-Saxonism, which had
degenerated in Europe. O'Reilly remarked that Woodfull's decision to
continue batting after being struck "was the stuff that Empires were made
of ... [and] Woodfull knew, and through him we knew, that we were
being called upon to make a colossal sacrifice for the good of the
game."[107]

Australian Test player Alan Kippax took a very reasonable view of the
affair which made the Australian case without descending to mere name-
calling as so much of the English criticism did. This does not seem to be
posturing; rather, it appears to be a sincerely widely held belief on the
part of the Australians. In his book, *Anti-Bodyline*, Kippax diplomatically
wrote: "I don't think any reasonable person, however partisan, has in cold
blood accused either bowler, or Jardine, of wishing to injure a batsman.
Such a suggestion is unthinkable; but I state without reservation that I
believe that the campaign was from the first one of intimidation, aimed
in the first place at Bradman and Woodfull, and, secondly, when it began
to prove successful, at all the recognized Australian batsmen."[108] Kippax
took a remarkably longsighted view of the affair and argued that it is possible for two sportsmanlike parties to disagree on whether a tactic is
sportsmanlike or not. If, after a debate it is deemed unsportsmanlike,
the original practitioners should not necessarily be condemned.
He wrote: "Sportsmanship is not a strictly defined and absolute code ...
It is, in fact, a convention, established by public opinion as a result of
experience. Occasionally there crops up in the arena of sport something
new, something which public opinion has not yet been able to
label."[109]

Conclusion

In the end the nations settled the dispute with a gentleman's agreement
which stated that the "the type of bowling in Australia to which exception
had been taken by Australia" was not in the best interest of the game and
would not be used against the Australians in the future. The MCC banned

"direct attack" bowling, which was defined as "persistent and systematic bowling of fast, short-pitched balls at the batsman standing clear of his wicket." The MCC statement continued, "The M.C.C. Committee have always considered this type of bowling to be unfair, and that it must be eliminated from the game. Umpires are the sole judges of fair and unfair play... and are therefore empowered to deal with 'direct attack.'"[110]

Jardine never captained an Ashes campaign again and Larwood never bowled for an English representative cricket team again. After the English had seen a West Indian simulation of what the Australians had faced and the excitement over the charges of unsportsmanlike conduct had died down, the Australians and the English were in broad general agreement on the matter. While most commentators in both countries agreed that bowling at the body, while technically within the laws of the game, was contrary to the spirit of the game, this does not mean that the English people renounced it. Moreover, Larwood and Jardine continued to receive widespread support and acclaim nationally for their unrepentant stances. The English refusal to admit their own bad form (i.e., to admit publicly that they had been unsportsmanlike) led them to in effect ban Jardine and Larwood, the two English players most responsible for the Ashes victory regardless of Bodyline, and lose the Ashes in 1934. Perhaps most damaging to their reputation was that they behaved in a blatantly hypocritical manner just to keep up the pretense that they had acted appropriately.

Ashis Nandy argued in his book *The Tao of Cricket* that "Imperial Britain... judged itself on the norms of cricket and the colonies by their actual ways of life, exactly the way it judged Western Christianity by its philosophy and Hinduism or Islam by the way real life Hindus or Muslims lived."[111] Bodyline could be seen as the moment when the underside of imperial reality caught up with the overlaying discourse of enlightened English beneficence. The discourses that contributed to the social signifi-cance of cricket were normally hidden behind the technical language of cricket reporting, obscured by the idyllic words of celebratory cricketing books, or drown in after match toasts of imperial good fellowship. However, because of the empire-wide coverage of these unprecedented events, these underlying discourses were brought to the forefront of public consciousness.

Repeatedly those trying to diffuse the controversy called upon Australia and England to remember their common history, especially their alleged common racial makeup and their common experience on various fields of battle. An English commentator defended the Australians by stating "Some are sneering at Australian courage. Well, 1914–1918 is not far distant. They took their whippings with as much whine as Tommy Atkins."[112] This was not simply in response to the devisive controversy. Before the English bowling attack had even been unveiled, Jardine spoke of the common Anglo-Australian racial tie as a great bulwark of the Empire. In reference to the uncertain economic situation in which the world then found itself, he stated: "Both countries have been passing through bad times, but both seem to be coming through them in a manner worthy of our race."[113]

The cricketing establishments of England and Australia had vested interests in retaining the status quo of Test cricket and imperial relations. On the most practical level, the revenue generated by the tours was the lifeblood of the counties' and states' cricket boards. More importantly, Test cricket bolstered England's and Australia's standing within the Empire. When the Australians instituted a new law for Australian cricket and forwarded their suggestions to the Imperial Cricket Conference, they ignored the MCC's dictatorial power to legislate the rules of cricket and by extension imperial relations. An article in the *Australian Cricketer* which was picked up and reprinted in the *Barbados Advocates* makes this argument explicitly by stating "Australia, by practically claiming the right to make laws, automatically ranked herself as equal first in cricketing nations."[114] The debacle that was Bodyline and the English tacit admission of wrongdoing allowed Australia to promote itself as an equal (or even superior) in every way to the "Mother Country." Although Australians were more egalitarian on the field than the English were, the game was still administered generally by men drawn from the elites of society, who were more likely than the average Australian to desire the retention of the social benefits attached to Test cricket. Bruce Harris, for example, commented on the fact that tour social life continued unabated at the elite level despite the animosity at large.[115]

Although the Australian reaction to Bodyline was undoubtedly an act of resistance, it was resistance only within a relationship in which Australia was seeking to be an equal partner at the top of the imperial power hierarchy. By protesting as they did and calling for a committee made up of English, Australian, and South African representatives to rule on the dispute, they did not reject the total English imperial project, just their subservient position within it despite three decades of political independence. Furthermore, they reinforced the wider imperial subjugation of the colonies of India and the West Indies, by denying them a vote in the matter.

The Bodyline controversy is important for historians of Britain, Australia, and the Empire because it was a key moment when popular culture was a reflection and engine of social consciousness, and when imperial values were contested and propagated. People in Britain did not think about Australia on a daily basis; nor did they regularly consciously articulate prevailing notions of masculinity, race, or class. These things were just part of their existence, part of the background to their lives. However, through a reading of Bodyline we are able to glimpse a snapshot of a moment in imperial history when those different threads of imperial existence came together and became visible.

CHAPTER SIX

Black Skin in White Flannel: The West Indies Join the Bodyline Fray

> I knew we were man for man as good as anybody. I had known that since my schooldays. But if that were the truth it was not the whole truth.[1]
>
> —C.L.R. James, *Beyond a Boundary*

A cricket tour to England for Australians and South Africans resembled pilgrimages to a holy site, complete with rituals (such as dinners, toasts, luncheons, tea breaks, gentleman/player divisions) and relics (such as tour blazers, team photographs, and above all, the mythical Ashes). An outward-bound English tour to the white settler colonies could be compared to a papal legate touring distant dioceses. In contrast, before World War II, an English MCC tour to the West Indies resembled a benevolent missionary effort beyond the bounds of civilization where natives needed enlightenment and instruction. Like most missionaries, the English cricketers believed they had nothing to learn from the West Indies, and treated their hosts with at best paternalism and at worst with outright disdain. While cricket encounters with white settler colonies and dominions normally called forth odes to imperial unity and common racial heritage and culture, cricket with multiracial West Indies teams brought condescending platitudes and references to grown men as "boys" and "niggers."

Relations between the British West Indies and Great Britain were strained and tense throughout the 1930s. The decade was one of political and labor turmoil throughout the Caribbean. The West Indian economies depended largely on agriculture, with over 50 percent of the population directly employed in agricultural production. When, following worldwide trends, agricultural prices fell by one half between 1928 and 1933, the West Indies experienced crippling unemployment, increased taxes, and wage cuts. When Lord Moyne conducted an investigation of the state of the West Indies in 1938–39, the findings were so damning that the British suppressed the report for the duration of the war to avoid any disruptions of imperial unity. The report detailed that in many parts of the West Indies, wages had not risen from the one shilling a day rate that was established a century earlier upon the emacipation of the slaves.[2]

Neither the soldiers of Britain nor the West Indian regiments contributed significantly to warm ties of mutual admiration, as they did in the Anglo-Australian case. At the end of World War I, West Indian soldiers in Italy briefly mutinied in the face of British racism in the army and at home.[3] A decade and a half later, on the second day of January 1933, less than two weeks before the Third Test at Adelaide, the military again figured prominently in an Anglo-West Indian dispute. Roughly 250 Northumberland Fusiliers stationed in Kingston rioted after one soldier died in a fight with a local. Despite widespread violence, injuries to Jamaican citizens and subjects of the crown, and great damage to property caused by the British soldiers, army quickly dismissed the incident as unimportant, a resolution indicative of the arrogant British treatment of West Indians in the Caribbean.[4] Unlike the independent dominion of Australia, the West Indies were colonies—a fact not unrelated to the racial compositions of each of the societies—and accordingly their relationships with the British were much more unequal and less important than Anglo-Australian relations.

Collective memories of World War I, along with race, constitute the significant areas of difference between the Anglo-Australian and the Anglo-West Indian imperial relationships. For the West Indians, there was no mass shared experience of World War I to tie them to the British as near-equals in the same manner as the Australians. Conversely, of course, there was also no Gallipoli in their recent collective memory to feed the fires of resentment against the British either. A local politician in Western Australia welcomed the MCC touring side, by saying, "We look upon these visits as a powerful influence in cementing the bonds of Empire. In that respect they are, I think, second only to the influence of Australian soldiers in the Great War. Australia is part of the British Empire, and its people are the same stock as those of England."[5] A West Indian politician would have been unable to make the same speech.

The standing of the British in West Indian eyes was not what it had once been. By the 1930s there were independence movements around the Empire, which garnered much attention in the West Indies. Furthermore, the prime advantage to being in the British Empire for many in the West Indies was that the British provided a market for West Indian sugar. After a high point in World War I, sugar prices had fallen steadily since 1923 and precipitously since 1929. By 1933, three years after the British Parliament ignored Lord Oliver's report recommending a British subsidy to the West Indian sugar industry, the price of sugar was still in a catastrophic decline. Moreover, as more West Indians immigrated to New York and Montreal, the United States and Canada began to rival Britain as potential metropoles. Hopelessness and resentment toward the British characterized West Indian public opinion in the 1920s and early 1930s.[6]

When the West Indian cricket team came to England in the summer of 1933, there were no anxious English commentators fretting about the Mother Country's chances against the tourists; the English expected victory. West Indians at home and in Britain followed the progress of the tour intensely. Trips to England were much rarer for West Indian teams than they were for the Australians and West Indians had never beaten the English in a test match, much less a series, in England.[7] Although the prospects for success on the field might have been slim, the West Indians went seeking the respect of the English and the acknowledgment that they were worthy opponents. The politics of race which permeated all things West Indian accompanied the West Indian cricket team to England in 1933 and this accounted for the tension that was expected to be lacking on the playing field.

One distinguishing feature of the West Indies team was that the players were not representing a nation or even a single colony, but rather a collection of small island colonies spread over a 1,000 miles of sea. Moreover, the 1933 team was composed of cricketers of European, African, and Chinese descent.[8] According to scholar Hilary Beckles, the white cricketing establishment in the West Indies before World War II saw a cricket match with England "as essentially a non-political event in which 'cousins' exchanged mutual admiration; black West Indians however did not share the outlook of their white teammates."[9] Rather, nonwhite West Indians tended to invest the success of the team with great significance and eventually "took the plough share of Empire and turned it into a sword which they later placed at the throats of the imperial order."[10] The 1933 season marked a key turning point in both the cricketing and, by extension, the general relations between the colonies of the British West Indies, and England. Although the West Indies did not win a single test match in their series against the English team, their level of play and their willingness and ability to employ Bodyline tactics marked them as a real presence in the cricketing world.

Learie Constantine, the star West Indian all-rounder, had recently become the first black man to play cricket professionally in the Lancashire League in the north of England. His West Indies teammate, George Headley, who was also black, would follow him the next year. From this point forward, West Indian cricketers would be a dominant force in English domestic cricket. In the 1934 season, Headley led the batting averages, with Constantine third, while Constantine led the bowling averages. Moreover, Constantine's Nelson club would win the championship in seven out of nine years that Constantine played and his electric performances helped swell the attendance of Lancashire League crowds.[11] The northern leagues provided opportunities for black cricketers to improve their cricket, eventually rendering white domination of West Indies cricket unsustainable.[12] More generally, by displaying an elevated quality of play while in England and against the England team, these cricketers challenged the stereotypical images of blacks as being indolent, weak, unskilled, uncivilized, and generally inferior to the English. Finally, by simultaneously embodying a "modern" sensibility in their cricket, which meant that they played with skill and a highly developed sense of the technicalities of the game, while being literally embodied with physiques which were deemed "primitive" by the English because of the darkness of their skin, the black West Indian cricketers confused and challenged English dichotomies between black and white, civilized and uncivilized, primitive and modern.

Stuart Hall has argued that "identity" is an ongoing "production" which is "always constituted within, not outside, representation."[13] Caribbean identity was perhaps less well formed than other areas of the British Empire because of the nature of West Indian colonization. In essence, everyone and everything was imported either by Europeans or for Europeans, whether it be the population or the cash crops they cultivated. Furthermore, the multiethnic composition of the West Indies encouraged a multitude of Caribbean identities. Ben Bousquet has written that "As a cultural and political melting pot, Britain was able to leave its mark on the Caribbean in a way it could not have achieved in any of its other colonies."[14] Cricket for black West Indians is one of the key performative arenas, along with the Garvey movement and labor organizations, where a dominant modern black West Indian identity has been represented, propagated, and consequently created. Success at cricket was for many black West Indians their proudest example of resistance to racist British imperialism and local planter-elite oligarchy and this success began in 1933 with the emergence of Headley, Constantine, and the West Indian fast bowling attack, including Bodyline. Despite the central role played by the West Indies in the affair, the literature on Bodyline has essentially ignored them.

The historiographic literature concerning West Indian cricket generally has overwhelmingly concentrated on issues of nationalism, race, color, and class, while, nationalism and cricket technicalities have dominated Bodyline historiography.[15] Both historiographies are fundamentally incomplete because of the general neglect of the issue of gender. The study of male West Indian cricketers *as men* has lagged far behind the study of them as West Indians or as people of the African diaspora. However, the issue of the comparative masculinity of the three nations involved was at the heart of the furor over the Bodyline scandal.

West Indian cricket was and is as profoundly gendered as the rest of imperial sport. The strong identification of cricket with masculinity is emblematic of the manner in which popular cultural institutions were instrumental in the marginalization of women from the national culture. Beckles argued that "since the nineteenth century, West Indian male have seen cricket as an exclusive manifestation of their activated world view. The social consumption and reproduction of its practice is guarded by gendered ideological boundaries that indicate the limits and nature of female involvement."[16] Michael Manley, former Jamaican Prime Minister as well as pioneering cricket historian, stated that "all cricket lovers share a regret that so few of the world's nations have a chance to experience this . . . subtle, exciting, and often dangerous game. Consequently, it is not surprising that nothing infuriates the true cricket fan more than the suggestion that it is a sissy's game."[17] What reason could there be for a "true cricket fan" to be incensed that the game was thought to be effeminate, unless things relating to women were inferior and unimportant? The ire with which cricket fans treat charges of effeminacy against cricket indicates that the game was an important site for the construction and public display of masculinity.

Bodyline allowed West Indians to participate in an Empire-wide discourse of manhood and civilization in a manner, which would have been impossible in purely economic or political arenas. More importantly, their refusal to abandon their tactics despite English pressure to do so allowed them to publicly turn the tables on the English and reject English perceptions of them as lazy, cowardly, childish, or effeminate. Furthermore, the West Indians were able to seize the moral high ground of sportsmanship and manhood by pointing out the English hypocrisy in the affair. Even though they lost the series to the English, they won a moral victory, in part because they played by the English rules. Moreover, unlike the Australians, they had done so without compromising their own standards of physical courage and masculine behavior. Furthermore, they disturbed the easy English binaries of black/white, civilized/uncivilized, and modern/primitive by excelling at a technique that the English had so recently claimed represented the modern face of cricket and athletic endeavor.

West Indian Cricket after World War I

Sport offers a somewhat unique site to explore the ideological contradictions that comprise a colonial situation because it freely mixes (seemingly without difficulty) official claims of individual meritocracy and equality with oppression and subjugation. This is especially true when it comes to West Indies cricket in the interwar period. Cricket, in part because of the participation of both colonial elites and the lower classes of colonial society, provides an excellent vantage point from which one can explore issues of identity formation with regard to race, class, and gender, especially in periods of turmoil like the 1930s when the sporting, economic, and imperial status quo were all coming under fire. Cricket had been one of the few topics about which the West Indies and the British could agree and then the British opened the floodgates of criticism with their transgressions against their own codes of ethical behavior.

Although the West Indies had been fielding representative cricket teams (colloquially called "elevens" and normally denoted as "XI's") since the turn of the century, it was not until 1928 that these matches were deemed first class by the arbiters of international cricket, the MCC. For the gentlemen at the MCC, the racial makeup of opposing sides had as much to do with the granting of official test status as did caliber of play.

For example, the MCC ranked New Zealand "first class" much more quickly than India or the West Indies despite a general parity of skill.

Maurice Tate played for England from 1924–35, although he saw no Test action on the Bodyline tour. He was a professional bowler and from a working-class background, yet he still saw himself as vastly superior to all the black West Indian cricketers he encountered, some of whom at least were undoubtedly far better educated than Tate. Education notwithstanding, black West Indians were all "darkies" to Tate, who was not aberrantly disdainful of black West Indians vis-à-vis his English contemporaries.[18]

A self-congratulatory air of tutelage hung over the tours from the English perspective, illustrated most dramatically by a cartoon published in the *Star* when a team of West Indian cricketers visited England in 1900. The cartoon depicted the father of English cricket, W.G. Grace standing tall and imposing and holding a bat surrounded by six small black men crying and pleading, "We have come to learn, sah."[19] Pelham Warner, Trinidadian-born English cricketer and manager of the 1932–33 Ashes tour to Australia, once wrote of an early non-test status tour of the West Indies that "[Lord] Martin Hawke . . . .was an object of much interests as a real live Lord. I believe they regarded him as a sort of god who descended from some glorified kind of palace or Government House to play cricket, and he was therefore considered a being highly to be commended for condescension and good-fellowship."[20] Even years later, for most English writers, the only possible explanation for the use of Bodyline by the West Indies was mimicry of their alleged English superiors. After the second test in Manchester when the West Indies unveiled their full-blown Bodyline attack for part of the match, the leading cricket commentator of the day, Neville Cardus, asked in the *Manchester Guardian*, "And if they did use body-line tactics, could they be blamed? What is sanctioned by Lord's and thought good enough to beat Australia, is legal and, presumably, desirable in this country."[21] Another writer stated unequivocally that "No one is more prone to imitation than they are."[22] The belief among Englishmen that West Indian men were in awe of them as icons of masculinity was recurrent and commonplace.

In an article about Bodyline by Warner which was originally published in the *Daily Telegraph* and then reprinted in *The Port of Spain Gazette* in Trinidad, the manager stated: "Now we are engaged in a dispute which savours of a civil war, for the Australian is bone of our bone, flesh of our flesh—he springs from the same stock."[23] Warner almost certainly would not have made the statement about his Trinidadian countrymen. Though the racial tie was preeminent for the Australians and the English, this was obviously less so for the majority of West Indians. The lack of a common racial heritage and close relations often made the social and cultural bond all the more important. For although there were certainly some white West Indians with close relations and ties to England, for the most part the West Indies had been settled much earlier than the Antipodes and the vast majority of the population were of African and East Indian, not

European, descent. Of course, the "English" side was drawn from all over the Empire and they were all not of English descent either, but for many Englishmen, it was easy to ignore the fact that Indians, Scots, Trinidadians, and Maltese men were not English while they played for and brought home victory to England and were for the most part white skinned.[24]

When the West Indies cricket team traveled to England in 1933 the black members of the team were for the most part viewed as child-like performers, although the better black players were at times considered something akin to idiot savants, whose great skills came not from hard-work and intelligence but from some indefinable and innate trait. A small group of white men who might be mediocre cricketers, but more often than not still "jolly good fellows" and who usually came from fabulously wealthy plantation families nominally "controlled" these dark-skinned "children of the sun." That several different ethnic groups were actually represented on the West Indies team went largely unnoticed in the discussion of the team, which was generally viewed, in black and white terms.

Despite the fact that throughout the twentieth century there have had been periods when they lacked impressively fast bowlers and when spin bowlers like Sonny Ramadhin, Alfred Valentine, and Lance Gibbs contributed greatly to West Indian success, from the 1930s, a distinct style of play came to be considered quintessentially West Indian. Exuberant fielding, flashy and dramatic batting, the predominance of very fast bowling, and the near absence of spin bowling were characteristic of this stereotype. Richard Burton has argued that a recognizably "West Indian" style of play developed and it relied heavily on fast bowling. Furthermore, it was more than simple adaptation of the game to local wickets and playing conditions. Rather it is, Burtons contends, a manifestation of West Indian masculine street culture.

> West Indian fast bowling confronts batsman and spectators alike with an all-out exteriorization of the methods and signs of attack: a run-up of (usually) exaggerated length and speed, a momentous heave of arms, legs and torso at the instant of delivery, with the ball unleashed at colossal speed straight at batsman and/or stumps, either bouncing half-way or two-thirds down the pitch and rearing up to around the batsman's chest and face. . . . a mode of attack apparently commonplace in black West Indian cricket in the 1920s and 1930s . . . and now banned . . . No concealment or mystery here: just aggression projected in a pure and naked state, a total spectacle complete in itself and instantly understood.[25]

In his autobiography-cum-cultural history of Trinidadian cricket, *Beyond a Boundary*, C.L.R. James stated that Trinidadian George John, who played in 1920s and 1930s, was in his opinion the ultimate fast bowler. James wrote, "John incarnated the plebs of his time, their complete independence from the values and aspirations that competed in the spheres above . . . Other bowlers can be qualified as hostile. John was not hostile, he was hostility itself...John was a formidable fast bowler. He was more than that. He was a formidable man."[26] This hostility expressed on the cricket pitch, albeit within limits, was part and parcel of black West Indian masculinity in this period. This is perhaps one reason why the furor over Larwood's and Voce's tactics in Australia bewildered many in the West Indies who saw it as a regular and indeed necessary facet of fast bowling and consequently of cricket.

The West Indian focus on fast bowling as the essence of cricket (and their only intermittent interest in spin bowling) was for many years responsible for their lack of success in competition with Australia and England because while they could conquer their fast bowlers, they were repeatedly done in by English and Australian spin.[27] West Indians who shied away from batting against hostile fast bowling could only be seen as afraid and hence "effeminate," which was, of course, pejorative. Even later, as we saw in the quote from Manley, the derogatory nature of cricket being compared to womanly activities was assumed to be self-evident and incontestable. This association of men with cricket in the West Indies was almost automatic due to the effective and nearly complete marginalization of women from playing the game in an organized setting.

Even women who played cricket well or who were as well versed in the theory of the game as any man, were kept off the formal playing field. Constantine wrote that he learned his cricket at home from his father and his uncle, Victor Pascall, both of whom played for Trinidad. The entire Constantine family would regularly practice together in the yard behind their house; uncle, father, mother, brothers, and sisters all competed equally and no distinction was made for age and gender. Although, as Constantine recalled, his "sister Leonara was able to hit a ball so that many a first-class cricketer, seeing her, would have felt like giving up the game," he never saw any injustice in the fact that she could not represent the West Indies or Trinidad or play organized cricket at all.[28] Her only role, so it seems, was to play in the yard and shame men into being better or giving up the game because they could not be better than a woman. In one tale recounting a tour to the West Indies, Warner told of his pleasure that there were so many women at the games because as one of his English teammates on the tour stated at a reception: "It has been said by some famous philosopher in the North of England, that cricket without the presence of ladies is like lamb without the mint sauce."[29]

While Warner's teammate was no doubt being glib, there is an element of truth in the observation of the centrality of the presence of women at cricket matches. This was true throughout the Empire, but was magnified in places like the West Indies and Australia where active and loud crowd participation was such a large element to the overall cricketing experience. Women become important because they are the target audience for much of the performance being enacted on the field and in the crowd. Men, either by playing or displaying their knowledge of the sport, perform explicitly male rituals and this is highlighted and reinforced by the presence of the gender "Other."

The main injustice of West Indian cricket as seen at the time was not one of the exclusion of women, but rather the unequal opportunities open to black men. C.L.R. James, the founding father of West Indian cricket writing, wrote about cricket on a daily basis as a reporter and was also able to appreciate the game's larger cultural meanings from a distance. James was able to put into eloquent words the common West Indian belief that cricket in the Caribbean was just as much "real cricket" as that played in England or Australia.[30] He summed up the basic tension between English sporting ideology and conceptions of race when he wrote: "The British tradition soaked deep into me was that when you entered the sporting arena you left behind you the sordid compromises of everyday existence. Yet for us to do that we would have had to divest ourselves of our skins."[31]

The political and racial hierarchies, which prescribed subservient behavior for non-whites and members of the working class, belied the meritocratic pretensions of cricket. Furthermore, middle-class black West Indians widely accepted the liberal ideology upon which English sporting philosophy was founded, and yet were confronted with the conflicting racialized practices of cricket in the West Indies.[32] Black West Indians thus found themselves in a matrix of multiple identities: British imperial subject, product of the African diaspora, resident of a particular colony, and finally, "West Indian." The meaning of this last identity—West Indian—grew tremendously via the only institution in which the colonies (and later nations) of the British Caribbean accomplished sustained cooperation: the West Indies cricket team.

Social relationships in colonial contexts were negotiated through shared-symbolism jointly adhered to by the colonizers and colonized alike. Nonetheless, even within a functioning hegemony as such, it is still necessary for the dominant parts of society to construct and maintain boundaries between themselves and those being subordinated. In the British Empire, one of the many ways that boundaries between and within the "races" and the colonizers were established and maintained was through the regulations and traditions of organized games. For example, careful gradations of class, race, and color determined an individual's access to club membership, team selection, the captaincy, and jobs.

Cricket historian Brian Stoddart has argued that of all the colonial cultural institutions, such as the church or the education system, cricket was the most effective at instilling the elite values, since it was so instrumental in creating "*virtually without protest* a consensual Barbadian society [Stoddart's emphasis]."[33] Unlike the church or educational systems, the racist and discriminatory nature of Barbadian cricket and the failure of the sport to live up to its ideals hardly ever raised a public protest because of the illusion of social mobility and meritocracy. However, in the end, the meeting of two or more cultures in social unity and equality was in fact, just that, an illusion. West Indian cricket's organizational and social practices helped to, in Stoddart's words, preserve "the exclusiveness of those cultures more effectively and for longer than other institutions, and also maintained traditional hierarchies within the cultures. The consensual as opposed to coercive manner in which this was achieved must be underlined."[34]

Deference to the white elite started to decline in the 1920s and 1930s as black teams began increasingly to dominate the domestic West Indian competitions and black players grew in stature on the West Indies team. In Trinidad, the main example of tenacious black cricket was the Shannon Club, which was made up of lower middle class and dark-skinned middle-class blacks and which dominated Trinidadian cricket in this period. For example, all the bowlers on the 1929 Trinidad team, which won the inter-colonial cup, were from Shannon. This was not a matter of simply superior skill. "They played as if they knew that their club represented the great mass of black people on the island . . . As clearly is if it were written across the sky, their play said: Here, on the cricket field if nowhere else, all men in the island are equal, and we are the best men in the island."[35]

James argued that the mastery of the art and science of cricket by West Indians was evidence of their ability and right to govern themselves. Moreover, he specifically aimed to show that the West Indians played the game as well as the English, as judged by the English standards. British analysts, in contrast, often attributed West Indian success to whimsical exuberance and "natural" athletic prowess rather than hard, disciplined work, intellectual, and tactical fluency in the game's "finer points." Around the world, presumed technological superiority significantly informed the civilizing mission ideology of colonizers aimed at uplifting the so-called "backward" colonials.[36] Similarly, the strategies, tactics, techniques, and equipment of cricket in which the British practices and material were deemed both normative and superior by many in the colonies. The ability to comprehend and implement the technical arguments surrounding the game of cricket was a badge not only of masculinity, but of civilized manliness as well.

In English cricket commentary, there often was a delineation between those who were technically brilliant batsmen, like the white Australian Donald Bradman, and so-called "natural" or "instinctive" batsmen, like the black West Indian George Headley. While the British and Australian press often referred to Headley as the "Black Bradman," the West Indian press rejected this construction of normative whiteness by knowingly referring to Bradman as the "White Headley." Manley argued that Healey's other nickname "Atlas" referred to more than just his on-field role of often carrying the rest of the West Indian team. Rather, the name was meant in a deeper sense. Manley wrote that Headley "carried at all times, wherever he went, the hopes of the black, English-speaking Caribbean man." Manley continued that Headley was "black excellence personified in a white world and in a white sport."[37]

In some sense, black West Indians were in the unenviable position of always being characterized according to English standards of language, ideology, and behavior. The end result was the marginalization of the colonized subject as a copy, often substandard, of an English original.[38] Even when colonial cricketers succeeded periodically, their success only bolstered the status of the English, in English eyes, as originators and propagators of cricketing tradition. However, sustained colonial success eventually began to erode this English national pride as the teachers and instructors to the world; rather colonial success quickly mutated from a point of pride to a threat to English superiority and required drastic measures to reassert English dominance. Bodyline was one of these drastic measures. However, once the English abandoned the traditions, which controlled proper behavior in cricket, or at least were seen to have abandoned them as they had with Bodyline, their ability to dictate to the colonies and dominions was weakened.

When Cricket is "Not Cricket"

Cricket did not always achieve the game's ideal of fair play and equal opportunity for all under uniformly enforced rules. Consequently, even cricket was sometimes "not cricket." However, for all the inequality, underhandedness, and discrimination, which had always been a part of imperial cricket, James argued that Bodyline was "the blow from which 'It isn't cricket' has never recovered."[39] Sport in general often directly acted to circumvent advancement merited by skill but in the end denied by color, class, and gender. Clifford Geertz wrote that a sporting event "is not a depiction of how things literally are among men, but, what is almost worse, of how from a particular angle, they imaginatively are."[40] This certainly can be seen in the world of interwar cricket. For example, Lord Hawke, without the least bit of irony, argued that "high and low, rich and poor, greet one another practically on an equality, and sad will be the day for England if socialism ever succeeds in putting class v. class and thus ending sports which have made England."[41] This was coming from a man who lived his whole adult life immersed in a first class cricket culture where teammates were addressed, ate, dressed, played, practiced, and were paid differently according to their class affiliations.

The English were not alone in equating cricket with anticommunism or antisocialism. The *Barbados Advocate* wrote, in response to the original flare-up of Bodyline between Australia and England: "Sport is the great bulwark against Bolshevism—the Empire's main safety valve in these troubled times" by keeping nations "cheerful" and encouraging "individual freedom of spirit and independence." However, this author then went on to criticize the amateur/professional divide in English cricket, which he argued was really just snobbery and attempted control by the upper-class legislators, thereby belying the chummy classlessness Lord Hawke envisioned.[42] Many Marxist critics of sport have decried the bread-and-circuses aspects of games, which channeled proletarian energies away from revolution and into activities, which were tangential to real power relations. James, an avowed Marxist himself, rejected Trotsky's belief that sports simply deflected the workers' attention from the class struggle. He noted that the nineteenth century, which created sports as we know it also produced great strides toward popular democracy for workers and those who were disenfranchised because of their race. Nonetheless, it should be noted that despite his later regret at his actions, when as a young man James had to choose a cricket club with which to affiliate, his choice was largely conditioned by class and color considerations which helped to maintain the divided nature of subordinate classes, thus belying his own position to a degree.[43]

The New Statesman and Nation, which reported on the 1933 West Indies tour with an article headlined, "Equality at Cricket," illustrated the English belief that the nominal egalitarianism of the cricket field somehow carried to off-field activities and attitudes. After noting the (of course) inferior quality of the West Indian play, the anonymous author commented that "no team could be more popular with the public. Their spontaneity alike in triumph and adversity wins all hearts, while the spectacle of a team half white and half black, living together in such perfect equality, is a delight to the philosopher. The Jamaican plantations, so long a disgrace to the British Empire, can now claim to be one of the major successes of imperialism."[44] Of course, there was not equality in cricket itself, much less in wider society, for black and working-class subjects of the crown; however the belief that the game was a great leveler was a strong one because cricket permitted players of different backgrounds to play on the same field, which was not possible elsewhere in English society. This "leveling" was consequently of a very upper-crust English sort at best and which in comparison to the racially segregated nature of American sport, appears to have been a very effective form of co-optation for many years. However, by the 1930s the period co-optation and uncritical acceptance of British ideals and superiority had come to an end.

English commentators maintained a much rosier perception of the egalitarianism of West Indies and indeed English cricket than the actual state of power dynamics warranted. Moreover, attempts by colonial athletes to conquer the British on the playing field are illustrative of the hegemonic nature of sport with, in this case, the West Indians attempting to defeat the British within the confines of British rules and institutions, and simultaneously alter the terms of engagement. The ideals of cricket were for the British and many white West Indians a depiction of "how things were." Yet for the black West Indians, the inequalities of cricket may have been a depiction of how things were, while the ethos of cricket provided an image of how things might be.

To black West Indians, this was not a radical position; in fact, it was largely a conservative movement which aimed not to replace English culture but rather to see English culture live up to its own ideals. Stoddart argued across the racial and class spectrum, West Indian society held up black cricketing heroes as examples of men who had "improved" or "bettered" themselves. "That is, they not so much symbolised a challenge to the dominant cultural elite as constituted a justification for that elite's ideology—many of the new stars were seen, significantly, not just as 'good' players but as 'good' blacks who had learned their social lessons. Many potential black stars failed to make the grade because of social rather than playing misdemeanors."[45] Likewise, in their work on the comparative ethnographies of masculinity, Andrea Cornwall and Nancy Lindisfarne argued that cultural conservatism amongst subordinate peoples is as much directed at their community as it is directed at the dominant group. In other words, subordinate black men might adopt the "idioms of white masculinity to gain prestige and control" vis-à-vis other black men.[46]

Images of Black Men

In England in the 1930s, a so-called color bar was firmly in place in British society. As a result, "respectable hotels" routinely and customarily refused service to people of color.[47] Blacks in Britain were not only treated unequally but they were viewed as objects of fun; characters which produced instantaneous mirth by their very existence. The explanation given for this was that Britons were unfamiliar with blacks, although since the 1890s there was a sizable black population in every port in Britain. Furthermore, despite claims of unfamiliarity with blacks, the popular media deemed blacks to be morally, socially, and intellectually inferior to whites.[48] English discussion and media coverage of the cricketers from the West Indies were rife with the then standard representations of black colonial men. These included perceptions of black men often as gifted athletes and physical specimens with natural strength and boundless enthusiasm for the superficial aspects of sport coupled with a childlike inability to concentrate, to master subtleties of the game, and to work hard for extended periods of time. The editor of the *Cricketer Annual 1933* wrote of the West Indies players: "their fielding was exuberant—often brilliant—sometimes too keen, I remember one of them stopping a ball quite beautifully; but then throwing unnecessarily hard at the wicket, scattering the stumps, and giving away an extra single. The action was characteristic of these light-hearted children of the sun."[49] Infantalization of course was a key recurring theme of British characterizations of colonial subjects, as was seen with regard to the Australians as well as the West Indians.

Even when the English complimented black West Indians, the racialization of their talent is ever present. For example, in an English *History of Cricket* published in the later 1930s, the authors write: "By any standards he [Headley] was an outstanding batsman, with a superb wrist and eye of the finest coloured athletes, and what is rather less common, a calm, almost phlegmatic temperament capable of stemming misfortune."[50] Cardus, in his capacity as cricketer editor for the *Manchester Guardian*, wrote that the West Indies star Learie Constantine was quintessentially and unmistakably West Indian. According to Cardus, no other culture could have produced a player like Constantine because "his cuts and drives, his whirling fast balls, his leapings and clutchings and dartings in the slips, are racial; we know they are the consequence of impulses born in the blood, heated by sun, and influenced by an environment and a way of life much more natural than ours—impulses not common to the psychology of the over-civilised quarter if the world."[51]

While the English of the 1930s did not use the term "noble savage" to describe the West Indies players, the sentiment permeated English reporting of the tour. The issue of "civilization" is key to the English perception of the West Indies cricketers vis-à-vis the Bodyline scandal. By dint of their black skin, regardless of their education or upbringing, the black cricketers were deemed more "natural" and "primitive" and therefore less "civilised" than their English counterparts. Whereas black athletic success was often attributed to this so-called primitivism, the case of Bodyline presented English commentators with a conundrum since it was this willingness to use brute force (i.e., Bodyline), which had given the English in Australia and the West Indies in England their greatest success. With the adoption of Bodyline, the English positioned themselves as closer to their black West Indian counterparts than to their normally closest dominion, Australia. Their reliance on brute force conflicted with the English self-perception as civilized.

As the newspapers of the West Indies often relied on wire service reports and reprints from British newspapers, the populations of the West Indies were keenly aware of English attitudes toward them. During the initial controversy between Australia and England, one Barbadian newspaper wrote: "In fact, the greatest part of the Empire exists on the fallacy that the incidental question of the colour of a person's epidermis is sufficient to proclaim his fitness to impose his will over people who are not similarly bleached."[52] This construction of the racial makeup of the empire is an inversion of the more commonly expressed notion that whiteness was normative and blackness was derivative as opposed to *The Advocate*'s contention that white skin was nothing more than bleached black skin.[53]

James and Constantine often spoke about West Indies and cricket to audiences around Nelson, England where the latter was a popular professional cricketer. James wrote, "One evening, Mr. Mayor, overflowing with good will, told my audience that when he saw Mr. Constantine and Mr. James with the children he knew . . . I cannot remember the phrase but it was to the effect that we were as human as the rest of them."[54] Nelsonians took pride in Constantine's presence, appreciating both the success he brought as well as the air of cosmopolitanism, which accompanied their exotic star. In effect, Constantine was given the status of "honorary white man." Furthermore, white Nelsonians derived a certain amount of pride from the fact that the Lancashire League clubs gave players like Constantine an opportunity, which they otherwise would not have. "His success reflected glory on the racial tolerance, as well as the sporting acumen, of Lancashire folk." Be that as it may, these northern communities were hardly devoid of racism or the belief in "white superiority," which "was as strongly entrenched as anywhere else and reproduced through a multiplicity of everyday ideologies, notably those associated with Empire, a community of which this part of the world was acutely conscious for economic reasons."[55]

The English belief that their culture was foundational and that colonials were doomed to be weak-hearted imitations at best, applied as much to conceptions of manhood as it did to conceptions of sport, literature, music, and manners. The English tradition viewed children not only as smaller versions of adults but as inferior versions of adults, and that the same applied to colonials. Within a colonial framework, the infantalization and effeminization of colonial men in comparison with English (or Australian vis-à-vis West Indian) men were a manner of reiterating a hierarchy where the former were inferior copies of the latter. For example, in a pamphlet encouraging British men to go to the West Indies and take up a career in estate management, one author writes that "the ordinary, native labourer has the mentality of a child, and must in consequence be treated as a child . . . and just as a child responds to firm, kindly, treatment, so in many instances will the native labourer." Later the same author writes: "Although the native labourer is simple-minded, he is able to discriminate, and will quickly take advantage of any weakness shewn [sic]."[56]

The Australians were often no better than the English. In fact, the Australians considered themselves quite liberal and open-minded for inviting a mixed-race team to come and play against their first class competition.[57] Don Bradman's first impression of the West Indies team "was what delightful schoolboyish enthusiasm they had for the game." He continued that the West Indies were "rather like a team of big children; they became vastly excited when they were being successful, utterly despairing when the were not."[58] In opposition to British attempts to portray them as children, black West Indian cricketers endeavored to play with intelligence, fearlessness, and skill as a means to publicly reject this hierarchy. This was accomplished without appearing overly threatening or revolutionary because their claims were couched within an accepted sporting dialogue.

A pamphlet entitled "Memorandum on Book Publication in Jamaica" published in 1937 for those British publishing companies interested in entering the West Indian market provides a common depiction of West Indians. The author, Robert Randall, in discussing the continuing prevalence of "black magic" writes that "It is true that the negro often goes about looking happy, but some of his more secret activities reveal a nature that is far from contented, and perhaps purposeless and restless . . . Gatherings take place . . . to the accompaniment of extravagant singing and shouting and the wild beating of drums, undisciplined minds and bodies seek a sense of ecstasy in romantic primitive fancy . . . What takes place . . . is an indulgence in extreme lack of self-control." Elsewhere he notes, "It is only by the help of European bastardy or by superb personal effort of mind and will that a few among the black population acquire a forceful and relevant sense of Western tradition."[59]

Depictions of black West Indians as physically powerful and active were often inconsistent with other strains of imperial discourse, which held that people of the tropics were naturally enervated by the heat and diseases in warm climates. In a 1925 pamphlet entitled "Practical Information of an Occupation for Young British Manhood—That of an Overseer on a Plantation in the Tropics" British readers are told: "Lowered vitality . . . in the northerly latitudes . . . is the exception rather than the rule, while in the tropics it is an experience common to all."[60] Articles about cricket tours abroad often acted as travelogues and ethnographies as well. One such article, which appeared in the *Cricketer Annual 1933*, stated that "Strong efforts are being made to induce the negroes to adopt more cleanly habits, and so prevent the spread of this fell disease [hookworm], which can be entirely stopped by wearing boots or shoes. British Boot Manufacturers kindly note."[61]

Although the West Indies cricket team displayed muscular athletic male bodies competing successfully, there was still the wider British perception of colonial men as effeminate in that they lacked the ability for concentration, rational thought, moral uprightness, and physically weak. However, race, like gender, can best be viewed as variable and shifting in form and meaning rather than as a coherently unified ideology or entity. Traits ascribed to any given race can be quite contradictory as seen earlier or in the manner in which the way black men were deemed to be simultaneously childlike yet sexually predatory, or physically underdeveloped and lacking endurance yet possessing bestial strength. Masculinity and race are relational categories of analysis; they affect and are affected by each other as well as by divergent femininities and alternate masculinities.

Many blacks agreed with whites that there were indeed racially determined differences. However, by choosing to argue whether West Indians possessed "natural" advantages or disadvantages, they reinforced the dominant discourse of biological difference. This entire debate is intimately tied to gender in two ways: the traits that were being discussed, namely, industry, strength, self-control, were coded "white" and "male" in the symbolic universe of imperial sport which automatically excluded women. Second, the belief in any biological determinism among men strengthens perceptions of the primacy of biology and therefore reinforces the biological difference between men and women.

In an article regarding the West Indies chances in the first Test match published in the *Port of Spain Gazette*, James wrote: "I have no hesitation in saying that in cricket, as in many other things, West Indians are among the most highly gifted people one can find anywhere. The English have, say, thirty times our population, vast organization, every conceivable advantage. Yet with all that, we could hold our own. Our trouble is that we have not yet learned to subordinate everything to winning."[62] In other words, James is arguing that the West Indies need to stop being gentleman-like and holding back in deference to their "social superiors" and simply concentrate on winning regardless of the social cost of winning, as the English had in Australia in 1932–33. It is doubtful that James really believed that this was a desirable choice for the West Indians, but it certainly would have led to more victories if that was the ultimate goal. However, since James roundly criticized Bodyline it would seem that for James, "playing the game" was more important than winning it.

Reactions to Bodyline

In the West Indies, reactions to the events of the 1932–33 English cricket tour of Australia were not uniform. The West Indian cricketing community was by no means an undivided fraternity happily engaged in frolicsome sport. Economic, political, racial, and religious divisions strongly characterized the organization of cricket on these islands, and these considerations were undoubtedly reflected in attitudes toward Britain and this assault on the spirit of the most tradition-bound of British games. However, the West Indian cricketing establishment, as well as the general public, had a vested interest in any dispute between a former colony and Great Britain due to its relevance to issues of imperial power and threats to the status quo. Any change or challenge to the current imperial power dynamic whether it be a call for self-governance for a dominion or a radical shift in the power relations in sporting administration, had repercussions in the rest of society. Australia's challenge to England was the greatest threat to the cricketing status quo since the legalization of overarm bowling in 1864. The *Barbados Advocate* called Australia's decision to draft laws for cricket without MCC permission "heresy" and continued "Australia, by practically claiming the right to make laws, automatically ranked herself as equal first in cricketing nations."[63]

The West Indian reactions to the initial controversy in Australia were largely supportive of the English, who until Bodyline were the practically unquestioned arbiters of fairness and legality within the context of cricket. However, some commentators expressed reservations about the political implications of the use of these tactics in a test match. The *Barbados Advocate* reported that "the English shock tactics again proved remarkably successful, Larwood, Allen, and Voce rendering the opposing batsmen almost impotent. The leg-theory bowling adopted by these men seems bound to occasion bitter controversy and to arouse much ill feeling before the tour is over."[64] Echoing common sentiments in the West Indian press, the *Barbados Advocate* continued, "It will be interesting to hear the views of the M.C.C. on the question. We need not now commit ourselves to any definite position as regards the ethics of leg-theory bowling . . . It is equally obvious that the leg-theory type of bowling introduces a new element of antagonism between batsman and bowler which is not in the true interests of the game."[65] Although this point appeared obvious to analysts in the West Indies, it seemed less so to the English. Furthermore, few West Indian sources questioned the ethics of the tactics, although many questioned their desirability for practical and tactical reasons. The practice of bowling short bumpers on the batsmen's body, albeit without a leg-side field placement, was standard practice on the domestic West Indian cricket scene. However, in an effort not to create ill will, West Indians normally suspended this practice out of social deference when playing English teams.

Owing to the widespread interest aroused by the dispute, West Indian papers presented the views of well-known authorities on the subject. The *Daily Gleaner* of Jamaica carried an interview with Karl Nunes, a white Jamaican and West Indies captain on the inaugural tour to England in 1928. Nunes argued that he never encouraged the *continuous* [emphasis added] bowling of short balls to a batsman when the intention was to hit the batsman. However, he said "it is unwise to express an opinion about the tactics of a particular bowler in a particular match unless one is present at the match."[66] Like many English commentators, Nunes expressed disbelief that Warner or Jardine would allow Larwood to bowl like this if his intention was to hit the batsman; his faith in English sportsmanship was too strong. Rather, he chalked the whole thing up to the incredible pace of Larwood which he believed must make the bowl bounce up even when pitched at a proper length.

The *Jamaica Times*, which reported the Woodfull–Warner encounter immediately, referred to the "shock troops" of England, which can be taken as a clear reference to the western front of the Great War. The *Jamaica Times* correspondent argued that Voce had attempted similar methods against the West Indies recently but that the West Indies men had batted well against these tactics. Importantly, much of the debate as described in the papers was not whether this was sportsmanlike or not, but whether it was an effective tactic for getting men out or whether the animosity it engendered from the Australians was worth the trouble. The sportsmanship of the action being taken for granted. Jamaican fast bowler Leslie Hylton, a black man, argued that as far as he could tell from the newspaper accounts, Larwood was perfectly entitled to pursue those tactics. George Headley was well sided with the English, blaming the hit batsmen for the problems and stating that their mis-timing and deficiencies in batting were responsible for the injuries.

Opinion in the West Indies was not completely on the English side, however. The *Jamaica Times* correspondent "Olympus" argued that from all accounts Woodfull is a "thorough sportsman and a right down jolly good fellow and that there must have been a good deal of provocation on somebody's part to have caused him to treat the Manager of the M.C.C.

team . . . as he did [by calling the English unsportsmanlike]." Yet, while he deferred his opinion to the English in the matter before coming to a conclusion, Olympus criticized the English for threatening to cancel the tour, believing that "as the mother of cricket, the M.C.C. should have used a little diplomacy."[67] The same paper also quoted English cricketing great, A.C. MacLaren who called the tactics "deplorable." MacLaren wrote that during the 1920s, "No Australian fast bowler . . . has ever bowled at or outside the body with five leg fieldsmen, which is the crux of the matter, from Australia's point of view."[68] The *Barbados Advocate* criticized *The Times* of London's argument that since Australia has produced the world's greatest fast bowlers in the persons of Arnst Jones, Albert Cotter, J.M. Gregory, and E.A. McDonald, they of all people should not complain. According to the *Barbados Advocate, The Times* had "missed the point of the controversy: which is not the pace but the direction of the ball which threatens injury to the batsman (something which the above four bowlers were not accused of)."[69] These comments, while illustrating a readiness of the part on some in the West Indies to follow the lead of the English in cricketing matters, also indicate their willingness to criticize the English and contest the English vision of civilization and sportsmanship. It would have been perhaps unthinkable three decades earlier for middle-class West Indian commentators to offer public criticism of British imperial diplomacy and etiquette.

The West Indies Go to Britain

When the West Indies cricket team to tour England in 1933 was selected, it was, as usual, placed under the captaincy of a white man. G.C. (Jack) Grant, was a relatively inexperienced recent graduate of Cambridge, who possessed exceptional, social, and racial qualifications to compensate for his middling cricketing ones. Warner noted that for any West Indies cricket touring team "the great difficulty [was] the selection of a captain, for the post is rendered even harder than usual by the inclusion of black men, some of whom will probably want a great deal of looking after."[70] This was actually belied by stories about the behavior of the black West Indies cricketers on tour. The English sportswriter William Pollack mockingly wrote that the off-field activity most enjoyed by the black West Indians was going to the movies. He reluctantly concluded his piece by stating: "Well, I suppose that it's better than sitting round the hotel lounges smoking and drinking and talking all the evening and well into the night, although to be sure, that is the time of the day when the stories begin to come out and you really get to know cricketers as they are."[71] Therefore, in many ways the black West Indians were in a no-win situation. Before they arrived they were held up as needing supervision to keep them out of trouble; after they arrived and behaved themselves, they were criticized for acting more like polite school boys than real men, who it seems have some (innocuous) vices at least. They could not escape criticism and they would not have had entree into the various social events their white teammates attended. However, the black West Indian players at least demonstrated that they did not need supervision.

Although there normally was a vice-captain appointed for a touring side to take the helm in minor matches and in case of sickness or injury to the captain, the West Indies Board of Control was faced with a dilemma in that the obvious, but racially unacceptable, choice was the black Jamaican, Headley. Rather than run the risk of having a black man lead whites, the Board chose to appoint no vice captain at all. The only other possible candidate was Learie Constantine, who as a black Trinidadian, was equally unacceptable to the white selectors. Moreover, Constantine was playing professional cricket in the English Lancashire League and was consequently unavailable for most of the tour matches because of conflicting league matches.

Maurice St. Pierre has argued that white West Indians were generally selected as batsmen, not bowlers and yet in the period 1928–59 they did demonstrably more poorly than black batsmen. He concluded that "since whites were not usually picked as bowlers and they did not perform as batsmen, then they must have been picked for some other reason. In view of the forgoing, one can only conclude that they were picked as administrators and as leaders."[72] This was not an issue only for West Indies cricketing community, although they had to confront it most often since they were the only nation, which regularly fielded a multiracial side. In an England v. Dominions match in August 1945, Warner encountered a problem in that the only man for the captaincy was Constantine; this would necessarily mean that a black man would be leading white men, which by definition was an issue. The fact that he would also be leading Indians was not commented upon. Warner recounts,

> Before this match started a difficulty arose when Hassett, who was to have captained the Dominions side, was taken ill and unable to play. His place as captain was filled by Constantine, the great West Indian player, who was the senior international cricketer on the sides. In this country, certainly on the cricket field, colour does not excite the feeling and prejudice that exists in some other parts for the Empire. It was however necessary to secure both the consent and co-operation of the rest of the Dominions side, and I went to their dressing-room. I chose my words with care, referring to his seniority and position in the cricket world.[73]

Therefore, although Constantine was the senior international cricketer with a worldwide reputation of more than 20 years at the international level, Warner still had to secure through diplomatic pressure the acquiescence of white men who were athletically junior although clearly socially superior.[74]

The issue of the captaincy was of special concern on the 1933 tour because it is the captain's job to select bowlers and oversee field placements during the match. Inevitably, the question arose of whether Grant would employ his fast bowlers in a Bodyline attack. The *Sydney Morning Herald* reported in April 1933 before the tests had started that the possibility of Bodyline from the West Indians was a central topic of press coverage in London. When asked, Grant pleaded ignorance of the finer points of the practice, but added that "Constantine formerly placed two or three men close in on the leg side and bowled short outside the leg stump, but I always stopped him or instructed him to bowl on the off side. In any event, if obliged to use body-line bowling, we have Griffith and Martindale, the latter very strong and fast."[75] The *Sydney Morning Herald* then noted that the more veteran West Indians recalled the vigorous protests by the English in 1930 over the West Indian practice of bowling short on the leg side.

In several of the county games and then in the second test at Old Trafford Oval in Manchester, Grant instructed his fast bowlers, Martindale and Constantine, to employ high, fast bumpers on or inside the leg stump with the appropriate Bodyline field placed. This was the first time that the English public witnessed a truly fast bowler employ these tactics in a test match.[76] Larwood, who had injured his foot in Australia, had not returned to form for the English season and had consequently missed most of his county games. The West Indies' employment of Bodyline tactics was a significant turning point for the tide of public opinion in England, which only a few months before had celebrated the tactics for bringing home the Ashes. This shift in popular opinion and the growing disgust of the English county captains would eventually ring the death knell for Bodyline as a legitimate tactic in organized cricket.

On June 15, 1933 C.L.R. James argued in an article in the *Port of Spain Gazette* that the vital issue was whether the West Indian captain Grant would permit his bowlers to bowl Bodyline. James wrote that if Grant "breaks the morale of his fast bowlers by expressing doubts as to whether the tactics of Constantine and Martindale are fair, the West Indies should flay him alive." James was disgusted by the fact that the English freely used the tactic in order to win the Ashes, but subsequently most English writers and cricketers "with the most barefaced effrontery condemns body line bowling" despite the fact that they had "shrieked to high heaven that there was nothing in it and the Australians were merely squealing." He concluded his article by arguing that this tour was the West Indies' chance to capitalize on the strength of their fast bowlers and "if weakness and lack of a sense of realism in the high command makes us lose it, then our blood be upon our own head."[77]

In his report of the second West Indies versus England test in Manchester, the correspondent from the Kingston, Jamaica *Daily Gleaner*, wrote: "I see there was quite a lot of genuine 'body-line' bowling, as opposed to genuine 'leg-theory' bowling by both sides—i.e., short pitched rising balls. But in spite of the fact that batsmen on both sides were hit several times, there was no 'squealing.'"[78] *The Times* triumphantly reported that although it was a slow wicket the day that the West Indies used leg theory, the tactic was not entirely successful. And yet, the fact that a slow pitch drastically limits the effectiveness of the tactic was left unmentioned. *The Times* wrote that "it has been suggested that a fast bowler banging the ball on the leg stump to a queerly disposed field will take wickets. Martindale bowls fast; so, too, does Constantine, but D.G. Jardine, railing himself to his full height, can defeat any manner of leg-theory bowling... This suggests that none of the batsmen who have had to deal with the ball which pitches on the leg stump can play it quite so well as Jardine."[79]

This was meant as a sleight to both the Australians, who had squealed in the face of unpleasant bowling rather than conquering it with their bats, and the West Indians, who in the opinion of *The Times* were unable to implement effectively Jardine's tactics. However, *The Times'* partisan coverage of cricket failed to stand up to the facts. The paper's correspondent chose to ignore that although the lanky skipper did do well against the West Indies, most of his runs came not against Bodyline but against an orthodox attack. Second, the atmosphere in Manchester was heavier and the pitch was slower than in Australia and chances are that his defense would have been unsuccessful on the Australian wickets on which Larwood took his victims. Finally, the rest of the England side did not fare well at all against Bodyline, including Hammond who was injured by a ball to his face.

Pelham Warner wrote the game report for *The Daily Telegraph* and noted that, although the West Indies had used Bodyline, the England players were not intimidated in the least and the crowd behaved itself, unlike the Australian spectators. While reiterating his opposition to the tactic, he still maintained that it was legal and that the English were able to face it with dignity and fearlessness.[80]

As late as June of 1933, the MCC was declaring the acceptability of Bodyline tactics. The *Sports Special* (popularly known as the "Green 'un") from Sheffield reported that a survey of the "flood of literature on Leg-theory" revealed an increasing division among the English over the propriety of Bodyline's continuing legality, although no one was apparently siding with the Australians who were still largely considered loud, ill-mannered, squealers with little sportsmanship themselves. The *Sports Special* wrote that the matter was nonetheless settled since "The M.C.C. have declared the 'leg theory' to be legitimate and have rightly refused to countenance the suggestion that any of our men did anything that was not sporting or contrary to the best interests of the game. They brook no argument on that score."[81] It continued to praise the MCC for being gracious enough to even consider reviewing Australian suggestions for rule changes, a fact that the English generally viewed as the height of generosity.

Despite the earlier rulings, the MCC eventually decided at the end of the summer to limit direct and intimidatory attacks on the batsman, a decision that was in part instigated by the widespread criticism in the English press of the West Indian bowlers for using these tactics in the

second test. Ironically, much of this criticism was infused with patroniz-
ing platitudes excusing the West Indian behavior as simple mimicry of the
English, but that this mimicry had revealed what an unpleasant, but
perfectly legal, tactic Bodyline was. In contrast, the English use of these
tactics in Australia had been hailed as a bold vision of the future. Consistently, the English admitted only that the tactics were aesthetically
unsightly, not unethical. The West Indies bowlers, especially Constantine,
took understandable offense at the *volte face* of the English.

Regarding the criticism that Martindale and he received from the
British press, Constantine wrote:

> Imagine our surprise when not only did a reporter interview
> Martindale about unfair tactics, but Mr. S. J. Southerton the editor of
> *Wisden's Almanack* published a statement that our bowling was
> "unpleasant, not to say dangerous." It was all the more surprising
> because *Wisden's Almanack* for 1933 had stated that intimidation was
> the charge against the English bowlers in Australia but that "it was
> inconceivable that English bowlers would descend to such means of
> getting a batsmen out."[82]

Constantine retorted that "in Test Match cricket there are no methods bar-
ring those which the umpire can detect which English bowlers will not
adopt to get their opponents out...I was not very satisfied at being treated
in this way, especially when paper after paper was protesting that the tactics
of Jardine and Larwood in Australia were spotless and without reproach."[83]
The charge that the English bowlers would employ underhanded and
therefore unsportsmanlike tactics raised a furor a year previously, but
by the end of 1933 when Constantine's *Cricket and I* was published, any
unfaltering belief in English sportsmanship was badly shaken.

Criticisms of the West Indies tactics as not being in the best interest of
the game were particularly galling to the men involved since they
regarded their own behavior as impeccable. The *Sports Special* reported
that in the second test, an English fielder threw the ball into the wickets,
which accidentally deflected off Constantine's bat to a remote part of
the field. Rather than running the two or three runs they could
have, Constantine and Headley stayed where they were and did not take
advantage of the accident. The correspondent wrote:

> Strictly speaking there is nothing in the rules of the game which
> would have prevented Constantine and Headley making as many
> more runs as they could in the circumstance (we must accept it that
> the ball, when thrown in, was turned aside accidentally.) At the same
> time I think the West Indies players did the correct thing in not taking
> advantage of the accident. I have often seen similar cases in first-class
> cricket. When the batsmen have run I have had the instinctive feeling
> that they were not quite living up to the highest traditions of the

game, and I think most people will agree when I say that Constantine did the sporting thing.[84]

Repeatedly, the West Indies cricket team in England established that they often lived up to English ideals much better than the English did themselves.

For their part, the West Indians attacked the English behavior on the grounds that they could not stand up to fast bowled bumpers, that they could not honorably take the type of intimidating bowling that they sent at the Australians, and that they were willing to use underhanded and unethical means to get opposing batsmen out. Furthermore, both Constantine and James alluded to the fact that the meritocratic pretensions of cricket were undermined and exposed as fraudulent by the political and racial hierarchies, which dictated subservient behavior for members of the working class and racial minorities.

Fear of Bodily Harm

As it was with the Australians, one of the key issues for the English when facing Bodyline was, at the heart of the matter, whether or not they were afraid of bodily harm, which they all steadfastly denied. Opponents of Bodyline argued that it was "not cricket" because it left the batsman no option but to be hit by the ball on his body and risk serious injury or get out and thereby let down his team. Its defenders argued that these were exactly the batsman's options and the traditions of the game required the batsman to choose to either possibly sustain injury while trying to help his team or go out because of fear of injury. There was no doubt for the tactic's defenders that a "real man" would not shirk from his duty and would accumulate runs as best he could regardless of the danger to him physically.

After the second test, a common line of reporting was represented by John Armitage in the English weekly, *The Cricketer*, which contrasted English behavior with Australian behavior when facing Bodyline. Armitage wrote that when the day began there had been "no sign that for much of the day we should be fated to watch in pained silence the full horror of 'bodyline.' " Of course, English spectators unlike Australian ones could be expected to suffer in silence. Armitage continued: "None of the England batsmen appeared intimidated, none complained, but they were all liable to be out in the leg direction . . . [English bowler] Clark indulged in a little leg-theory on his own account, which was singularly unsuccessful, unless scaring the batsmen be considered the criterion of accomplishment."[85] Therefore, despite all logic, Armitage argued that although the West Indies were successful against Bodyline and the English were largely not successful, the former were frightened by it and the latter were not.

The English press roundly criticized English professional cricketer Patsy Hendren and labeled him "hysterical" when he fashioned a

prototypical batting helmet after being struck in the head by the West
Indian bowling during a county match before the second Test.[86] Hendren
stated in July 1933: "People who have never been hit on the head by a
fast bowler have no right to enter the body-line controversy . . . If you
come across a batsman who tells you he doesn't mind body-line bowling,
you can reply with my compliments that he is a—prevaricator."[87]

Hendren wore a protective headgear/batting helmet that his wife made
for him when playing against Constantine in the West Indies versus MCC
at Lord's, an act that created quite a stir amongst commentators who saw
Hendren's "departure from tradition" as having "serious implications. It is
symbolic of the hysteria which appears to be prevalent at the moment
about fast bowling."[88] The paper considered his helmet to be a "lamentable confession of weakness," especially for a batsman of Hendren's caliber.
Hendren saw the headgear as a sensible precaution and felt that those
who were too afraid to look unmanly were the ones showing weakness.
He told the *Sydney Morning Herald*:

> The West Indies match was a good test for the cap. One of
> Constantine's deliveries was like a bullet. If it had hit me on the head
> I would have gone to Kingdom Come. My wife made the cap. It is of
> cloth lined with rubber, and it is a very fine job, but it is a little heavy
> on hot day. Nevertheless, it protects my temples. I don't mind having
> my face altered and my teeth knocked out if my head is protected. I
> don't think other players will get similar caps. They wear pads and
> abdominal and chest protectors, but they have not the courage to wear
> a head protector.[89]

In the official history of *Wisden*, editor Benny Green argued that it was
the effect of the West Indies' bowling on the English batsmen that finally
changed English minds on the issue of Bodyline's legality, or at least its
desirability. Green concluded, that the West Indian Bodyline was a "somewhat pale—but no less disturbing—imitation of Larwood in Australia."[90]
Between the time of the English side's homecoming from Australia and the
employment of Bodyline tactics by the West Indies, there were numerous
county, league, school, and university matches played in England. The
papers reported increasingly common use of Larwood's style including a
display of Bodyline by Cambridge in the University Match against Oxford.
However, not a single English bowler (other than Larwood and Voce) possessed the skill and athleticism necessary to render Bodyline dangerous or
even particularly effective. It took two West Indians—Martindale and
Constantine—to convince the English public of the barbarity of the practice. This in itself speaks volumes about the level of play in the West Indies
despite British criticism of the team as sub-par. The Australians had criticized without being able to retaliate, which led many English commentators to conclude that the Australian lack of a sufficiently fast bowler was at
the root of the so-called squealing. The English had supported the tactic but

were left with no one who could implement it after Larwood and Voce fell out of form. Only the West Indies supported the tactic and could back it up. For making good on their word, they were heavily criticized.

In his autobiography of this period, Constantine discussed his feelings about Bodyline. First, he argued that he refrained from using it against Lancashire League cricketers, because they were not up to the standard and it "would be taking advantage and absolutely spoiling the fun to terrorise them, as it would be very easy to do."[91] Although boastful, this is undoubtedly accurate and points to a long-held tradition in cricket that an honorable fast bowler bowls to batsman only as fast as they can safely handle. For example, a bowler who is batting was unlikely to face the same speed and hostility as a recognized batsman would. However, this "rule" by tradition was more or less likely to be invoked in direct relation to the status of the batsman or bowler concerned.

An episode that James recounts in *Beyond a Boundary* during the 1926 MCC tour to the West Indies illustrates this well. The West Indians thought the English were bowling at the head of H.G.B. Austin, captain of the West Indies. According to James, Constantine determined that if they were going to bowl at his captain as such, he would return it in kind and duly bowled at the head of F.S.G. Calthorpe the captain of the MCC touring team. When James told him to stop, Constantine is reported to have said: "What's wrong with you? It is cricket." James writes that he "told him bluntly: 'Do not bump the ball at that man. He is the M.C.C. captain, captain of an English county and an English aristocrat. The bowling is obviously too fast for him, and if you hit him and knock him down there'll be a hell of a row and we don't want to see you in any such mess. Stop it.'" Constantine acquiesced eventually so as not to make waves.[92]

Conclusion

The Bodyline affair created the opportunity for a yearlong imperial conversation between Australia, England, and the West Indies in which the long-held English assumptions of their superiority were questioned and contested by Australians and West Indians. At the heart of the debate was the question of which nation's men were the strongest, the most civilized, and the most sportsmanlike. Coming as it did, in a moment of supreme crisis of confidence for England due to the precarious position of the world economy and with the English still reeling after the calamity of World War I, the Bodyline affair allowed the facade of unquestioned English superiority to be broken down and revealed to be hypocritical and hollow.

The West Indian and Australian reactions to Bodyline can be viewed both primarily as counterhegemonic movements within the larger frameworks of imperial masculinity and imperial sporting relations. Neither the Australians nor the West Indies sought to fundamentally alter the nature of sporting relations and the ideology of the games revolution.

The Australians did not begin to advocate that losers should be encouraged to complain or throw tantrums and threaten not to play again when they lose. Likewise, West Indians did not argue that by sheer speed of fast bowling one cricket team should be able to batter and bruise another team into submission. Rather, both teams wanted not to change the rules of engagement between themselves and the English, but rather they sought to have the rules as they saw them fairly and evenly applied and followed. Neither side ever threatened to abandon cricket, although the Australians did threaten to abandon cricket with the English.

In the realm of imperial masculinity, the Australians sought to assert their equality with (and even superiority to) English men by being more English than the English while maintaining what were viewed as uniquely Australian traits. That is to say, they endeavored to be the ultimate sportsmen, sacrificing their bodies for the game, maintaining their dignity and silence as long as possible in the face of unprecedented antagonisms, while enjoying a more egalitarian society than that found in England. The Australians were the source of the most obvious and blatant challenge to English privilege, but in the end, they only sought to join the English at the pinnacle of the imperial hierarchy, not displace them. Furthermore, by stressing their common racial background, they did not seek to upset the racial status quo; rather they wanted to strengthen it and benefit from it.

For their part, the nonwhite West Indian cricketers presented a less ostentatious challenge on the surface while representing the much more radical and revolutionary challenge to the empire at a structural level. While not rejecting the basic tenets of normative British masculinity, they sought only to remove the color bar. Most of the black West Indian cricketers on the national team in 1933 were educated and were uninterested in denouncing British culture in general, just the racism which was at that point inherent in the system. J.A. Mangan has argued that education in the British Empire was concerned largely with "establishing the presence and absence of *confidence* in those controlling and those controlled."[93] The socialization and normalization of hierarchy worked very well until subject peoples gained the confidence to challenge the system. Success at cricket was one way in which black middle class West Indians gained confidence, and through them the entire black population. By coming to England and performing well and in a disciplined manner against the English while using tactics which the English deemed to be English in a manner which the mother country could no longer employ them themselves, the West Indian cricket team made a bid for the competence and worth of West Indians generally. Specifically, they demonstrated that West Indians could be a productive, self-disciplining entity within the British Empire. In that sense, they were able to use cricket to push a revolutionary agenda without arousing the fear and disapproval of the English because the aims of that agenda were well within an English-defined worldview and culture.

CHAPTER SEVEN

Conclusions: Sport, Masculinity, and Nationalism

In 1897 a company called London Exhibitions Ltd., held an exposition in honor of the Diamond Jubilee of the reign of Queen Victoria, which celebrated the Empire at the end of the nineteenth century, including a large section on imperial sport. One director told *The Sporting News* that the sport display was "the most popular attraction of the exhibition." In the opinion of the director, this was entirely just. He argued:

> The most spontaneous expression of individual and national character is found in the great democratic sports of a country, and if history is philosophy teaching by example, the inference is inevitable that the patriotic citizen cannot set too great store on the development of the natural force—the physical energy—of his race. And sport promotes not merely bodily health and vigour, but all the higher forms of manliness, alertness in observation, promptitude in judgment and action, the determination never to deserve to lose and always deserve to win, and the disciplined temper to accept defeat without degradation, and victory without vaunting. Sport promotes, in a word, that magnanimity of soul which is the noblest characteristic of British statesmanship, and the redeeming grace and glory of our ubiquitous Empire.[1]

While there is of course an element of a huckster in the exhibition promoter's pronouncements, it is unlikely that this proclamation would have sounded outlandish to the average reader in Britain or the Empire. Claims such as this had been commonplace for decades by the time of Victoria's Diamond Jubilee and were largely taken for granted as a truism.

It was the widespread acceptance of this creed by middle- and upper-class Britons and imperial subjects which enabled the British to export their pastimes to the rest of the world and allowed British subjects all over the globe to connect to Britain through those games. However, as this study has shown, sport was also a more complicated arena than the exhibition promoter admitted. The fact that different races and nationalities participated in these sports made simplistic correlations between the games and British ideal problematic. Furthermore, the exclusion of women from most of the playing fields and gymnasiums, complicated automatic associations between games and any ungendered conception of nationalism. Finally, the values and ideals promulgated by English sporting traditions changed over time.

If in 1897 the purpose of sport was to inculcate in British men "the disciplined temper to accept defeat without degradation," by the 1910s, British sport seemed to be more about maintaining the status quo of British power. This shift is seen most prominently in the British reluctance in the 1910s and 1920s to allow high-profile fights, which included boxers of color to be staged and in the Bodyline scandal of the 1930s when victory at whatever cost became a viable goal. These instances were indicative of a strategic British reaction to wider global issues being played out in sport. By the eve of World War I, it was no longer enough to let the best man win, whomever that may have been. Rather, athletically elite sports for the British were supposed to confirm that the British were the best men and therefore should remain in control.

One of the questions raised by this study is how and to what degree did sport support or undermine British imperial hegemony from the 1880s through the 1930s. On balance, for the men of the British Empire, it was a progressive institution, although not always in the manner in which British advocates of the games revolution would have thought. On the one hand, there was a widespread diffusion around the Empire of middle-class games and the middle-class values, which informed them. These to a greater or lesser extent depending on the specific circumstance were adopted in one form or another. For example, Australian Rules footballers held to largely the same code of sportsmanship (in the abstract) as English rugby players or West Indian cricketers did at any given time. There was a general acceptance of the role of referees and umpire, although the deference due to these figures varied greatly with context. However, subordinate groups did not blindly accept these codes; they resisted and altered them, including for example, the common practice of bending rules while not breaking them, cheating strategically up to the point of detectability, and adding innovative tactics which took advantage of loopholes in the rules of a given game.

Despite general acceptance of the sports, the widespread adoption of English games (or, in the case of the Irish and Australians, indigenous games inspired by the English games revolution) did not always serve the interests of the colonizers or help to maintain the Empire. The British elites sought to win the hearts, minds, and bodies of their imperial subjects through the hegemonic propagation of imperial sport and the associated middle-class white values to the peoples of the Empire and the working classes. It was thought that these values then would be absorbed and applied to all aspects of life by these social subordinates. However, sportsmanship was more than just an evangelical creed, it was also a marker of social difference when only middle- and upper-class athletes adhered to its tenets. The very success of the games revolution in spreading middle-class values also limited the exclusivity previously found in the games. Moreover, the games often in the end came to be used as tools of resistance by subordinate groups of men in the empire, including the Irish, the Australians, West Indians, men of color, and working-class men.

The freedom these groups found in sport to resist middle-class British dominance and values came at a cost to the women of Britain and the Empire, whose exclusion from yet another realm of public contestation and nation building could only have had detrimental effects on women's drive for equality in society. The very shared masculinity upon which subordinate men seized to stake their claims to nationalized conceptions of manliness was based on the banishment of women from the public sphere. While sports presented an avenue for counterhegemonic forces to be publicly produced and trumpeted, they rarely, at the athletically elite level at least, were beneficial to women regardless of their national, class, or racial background.

These challenges to British practices and mores were not simply accepted by the British either. When the All Blacks and the Springboks beat the British rugby teams through superior fitness and tactics, British rugby responded to the challenge by altering their own ways of playing. Likewise, the working-class innovation in soccer of shin pads allowed working-class footballers to play much more aggressively than their middle-class opponents who had to either adapt or be uncompetitive. The creation of the Bodyline tactics in an attempt to stop the young Bradman is another, albeit extreme, example.

Pressures outside the actual games also influenced the manner in which they were played and organized. Colonial subjects acted as class surrogates for the British. Colonial resistance to British supremacy was seen to have domestic ramifications. When the ABC threatened the unwritten conventions of imperial sport, in that case the practice of losing silently no matter what perceived wrong had been done, they challenged by extension the unwritten code of class and racial behavior which supported British society.

Underlying all of these changes in social behavior, class relations, and conceptions of nationalism related to sports was the issue of what it meant to be a man. From the creation of Australian Rules football in 1859 to the founding of Football Association, the parent body of soccer, in 1863 to the formation of the GAA in 1884, the prime consideration of the founders was what type of men would be produced by these various sports. Once sport had been marked as a site for the production of men, the sports could not help but to be points of contestation, propagation, and resistance. The result of this was a varied assortment of different conceptions of true manhood which were produced by different geographical, political, racial, and class contexts.

Sport in the New Millennium

As the millennium begins, the institutions and practices, which were formerly known as "British imperial sport," occupy an ambiguous place in the cultural life of the erstwhile Empire and the wider world. The games have not only outlived the Empire, but their practice has far outgrown the boundaries of lands ever controlled by the British. The largest single sporting event in the world, certainly among the most universally watched and followed world events, is the quadrennial World Cup of soccer. The 2002 World Cup final between Brazil and Germany was watched by an estimated 1.7 billion people, or almost 30 percent of the world's population watched the game. Likewise, rugby and cricket tours between and amongst Britain and her former colonies still attract massive public attention and remain lightning rods for political activism. Demonstrations against competition with South Africa and Rhodesia in the apartheid era fomented great controversy in the West Indies, Africa, and New Zealand in the last three decades. In 2003, protests over the Zimbabwean government affected the outcome of the cricket World Cup by causing teams to forfeit much needed games. In short, organized sport has become a global phenomenon perhaps second only to industrial capitalism in its scope.

This globalization undoubtedly has had an effect on the relationships between masculinity, nationalism, and sport. The British hegemony that once existed has been replaced by a more diffuse Western, industrial capitalist, often but not always American, hegemony. Like the British dominance before it, the contemporary sporting culture is not a unified, monolithic entity, which produces a single masculinity. The so-called major sports are still dominated by men with a substantially coherent conception of sport, based on the ideal of a heterosexual, muscular (to a greater or lesser extent dictated by the individual sport), hardplaying, male (or at least masculinized) athlete who eschews and ridicules the feminine and homosexual. International rugby, soccer, American, Australian, and Gaelic football, hurling, baseball, cricket, sumo wrestling, ice hockey, basketball, and auto racing all largely subscribe to this view of masculinity. All traces of so-called womanliness or effeminacy are banned from public view.

This holds true as much for elite female athletes as for men. In baseball or softball, the epithet that one "throws like a girl" can be equally applied to males or females. However, the meaning remains clear: to throw like a boy means to throw well and to throw like a girl means to throw poorly. Likewise, although there is more room in sport of emotion to be shown, witness teary retirement speeches, the moments when this is acceptable behavior is clearly defined. If a boxer breaks down and starts crying in the middle of the ring, as Oliver McCall did in his February

1997 match with Lennox Lewis, his reputation and/or sanity are called into immediate question.

Finally, in contrast to these more traditional sports, there has been in the last two decades a proliferation of new sports and events that have produced the possibility of a myriad different athletic masculinities and femininities. Some, like the Gay Games, self-consciously oppose normative athletic masculinity, which situate heterosexualized violent male strength and competition at the apex of the hierarchy of desired values.[2] Others, like the National Basketball Association's sister (or is it daughter?) league, the WNBA, or international women's world cup soccer, seem to have positioned themselves not in opposition to normative masculine ideals, but rather in a manner which is meant to suggest that women can be exactly like men (violent, hypercompetitive, merciless) if only given the chance. Furthermore, the so-called "extreme sports" of snowboarding, skateboarding, street luge, and the like, seem to have developed the rhetoric and style at least of a more communal and less hypercompetitive, albeit still hypermasculine, manly ideal in opposition to traditional sports. Finally, sports like figure skating and female gymnastics have come to be associated largely, if not exclusively, with female participants and spectators and have expanded enormously due to the desire of advertisers to reach an important consumer demographic, namely adult women who have in the past watched less televised sport than their male counterparts.

As a result of these innovations and evolutions in the world of sport, the construction of athletic masculinities can no longer be located so easily in any one place. However, since masculinism still pervades the sporting world either as a normative ideal or as a presence against which new sports and sporting practices can react, it remains a matter of vital interest. Sport continues to be a major way in which the sexes learn to relate to one another and by which competing countries measure their national worth. The ethos and self-perception of the British as a sporting nation remained strong despite encroachments on the sporting ideal and the visible cracks in the exterior of the sporting ideal. For example in a 1927 book credited the sporting nature of the British with enabling them to defeat the Germans in the Great War. Theodore Cook in his book *Character and Sportsmanship* argued that "the most deep-seated instinct of the English race—the instincts of sportsmanship and fair-play" gave the British "sufficient endurance, sufficient good humour and good sense, to over come not only the perils that are past"—such as onslaught of "Prussian Imperialism" in 1914, attacks by "socialists and communist's of the Trade Unions" in the General Strike—"but the dangers of the future."[3]

J. Nelson Fraser, a professor of English Literature at Deccan College in Poona, India, wrote a book entitled *England: An Account of English Life for Indian Readers* to introduce the home country to the Indian subjects of the crowd. In a chapter devoted to English leisure, attempted to define the role of "sport" in British society. He wrote: "The word and the idea are alike peculiarly English... The essential idea of sport is that of context on fair terms, and a sportsman is one who delights in such a contest . . . The truest form of sport is that which involved difficulty and danger, where there is room for courage, skill, and endurance. The end in view is to exercise these qualities, and to win, if possible, but not to triumph loudly over your foe, or to resent his victory, if you are fairly beaten. What marks a sportsman more than almost anything else is the power of taking a defeat well, without denying it, or explaining it away, or grudging it. This ideal, which all forms of sport encourage, is very influential in English, and is one of he most notable forms of the national love of justice."[4]

Notes

Chapter One   Gender and Imperial Sport

1. John Nauright, "Colonial Manhood and Imperial Race Virility: British Responses to Post-Boer War Colonial Rugby Tours," in John Nauright and Timothy J.L. Chandler, eds., *Making Men: Rugby and Masculine Identity* (London: Frank Cass, 1996), 121–39.
2. For a discussion of the Games Revolution, see Richard Holt, *Sport and the British: A Modern History* (Oxford: Clarendon Press, 1989); J.A. Mangan, *Athleticism in the Victorian and Edwardian Public School: The Emergence and Consolidation of an Educational Ideology* (Cambridge: Cambridge University Press, 1981).
3. Edward Said discusses the process of interplay between the culture of colonial metropoles and subject peoples in *Culture and Imperialism* (New York: Vintage Books, 1993).
4. Allen Guttmann, *Women's Sports: A History* (New York: Columbia University Press, 1991), 71–78.
5. Kathleen E. McCrone, *Playing the Game: Sport and the Physical Emancipation of English Women, 1870–1914* (Lexington: University Press of Kentucky, 1988), 7–18, 192–95. For an American comparison, see Susan K. Cahn, *Coming on Strong: Gender and Sexuality in Twentieth-Century Women's Sport* (New York: The Free Press, 1994), 7–30.
6. Alan R. Haig-Brown, "Women and Sport," *Baily's Magazine*, lxxxiii: 539 (January 1905), 25.
7. Clifford Geertz, *Myth, Symbol, and Culture* (New York: W.W. Norton, 1971), 23–29.
8. J.A. Mangan, *The Games Ethic and Imperialism: Aspects of the Diffusion of an Ideal* (Cambridge: Cambridge University Press, 1981); idem, *Pleasure, Profit, Proselytism: British Culture and Sport at Home and Abroad 1700–1914* (London: Frank Cass, 1988); idem, ed., *"Benefits bestowed?" Education and British Imperialism* (Manchester: Manchester University Press, 1988).
9. Paul Dimeo and James Mills, eds., *Soccer in South Asia: Empire, Nation, Diaspora* (London: Frank Cass, 2001), 1–15.
10. Jean-Marie Brohm, *Sport: A Prison of Measured Time* (London: Ink Lins, 1978).
11. Cheryl L. Cole, "Resisting the Canon: Feminist Cultural Studies, Sport and Technologies of the Body, " in Susan Birrell and Cheryl L. Cole, *Women, Sport, and Culture* (Champaign, IL: Human Kinetics, 1994), 5–29. Although Foucault does not address modern sport per se, for his theories of panopticism, see Michel Foucault, *Discipline and Punish: The Birth of the Prison* (New York: Vintage Books, 1979), 195–228.
12. John Hargreaves, "Sport and Hegemony: Some Theoretical Problems" in Cantelon, Hart, and Richard Grueau, eds., *Sport, Culture and the Modern State* (Toronto: University of Toronto Press 1982), 104–05. I use the term "dialectical" here in the Marxian connotation as described by Raymond Williams; he writes that the Marxian sense of "dialectic" was used to indicate: "a progressive unification through the contradiction of opposites." Raymond Williams, *Keywords: A Vocabulary of Culture and Society* (New York: Oxford University Press, 1983), 107.
13. Jim Bullock, O.B.E., *Bowers Row: Recollections of a Mining Village* (London: EP Publishing, 1976), 74–77.
14. For some detailed regional studies which illustrate this general process, see Martin Johnes, *Soccer and Society: South Wales, 1900–1939* (Cardiff: University of Wales Press, 2002); Tony Collins, *Rugby's Great Split: Class, Culture and the Origins of Rugby League Football* (London: Frank Cass, 1998); Grant Jarvie and John Burnett, eds., *Sport, Scotland and the Scots* (East Lothian: Tuckwell Press, 2000).

15. Antoinette Burton, *Burdens of History: British Feminists, Indian Women, and Imperial Culture, 1865–1915* (London: University of North Carolina Press, 1994); Nupur Chaudhuri and Margaret Strobel, eds., *Western Women and Imperialism: Complicity and Resistance* (Bloomington: Indiana University Press, 1992); Mrinalini Sinha, "Gender in the Critique of Colonialism and Nationalism: Locating the 'Indian Woman,'" in Ann-Louise Shapiro, ed., *Feminists Revision History* (New Brunswick: Rutgers University Press, 1994); Leila Ahmed, *Women and Gender in Islam: Historical Roots of a Modern Debate* (New Haven: Yale University Press, 1992); Anna Davin, "Imperial Motherhood," in Raphael Samuel, ed., *Patriotism: The Making and Unmaking of British National Identity* (New York: Routledge, 1989); Clare Midgley, ed., *Gender and Imperialism* (New York: Manchester University Press, 1998).

16. Edward Said, *Orientalism* (New York: Vintage Books, 1979); Mrinalini Sinha, *Colonial Masculinity: The "Manly Englishman" and the "Effeminate Bengali" in the Late Nineteenth Century* (Manchester: Manchester University Press, 1995).

17. Catherine Hall, "Gender Politics and Imperial Politics: Rethinking the Histories of Empire," in Verene Shepherd, Bridget Brereton, and Barbara Bailey, eds., *Engendering History: Caribbean Women in Historical Perspective* (Kingston, Jamaica: I. Randle, 1995), 48–52.

18. David Andrews, "Sport and the Masculine Hegemony of the Modern Nation: Welsh Rugby, Culture and Society, 1890–1914," in Nauright and Chandler, eds., *Making Men*, 50.

19. Jock Phillips, *A Man's Country? The Image of the Pakeha Male—A History* (Auckland: Penguin Books, 1987), 108–22, 163–65.

20. Mary Poovey, *Uneven Developments: The Ideological Work of Gender in Mid-Victorian England* (Chicago: Chicago University Press, 1988), 10.

21. This follows the logic of Mary Douglas, *Purity and Danger: Analysis of the Concepts of Pollution and Taboo* (London: Routledge & Kegan Paul, 1966).

22. For a parallel examination of the American context, see Gail Bederman, *Manliness and Civilization: A Cultural History of Gender and Race in the United States 1880–1917* (Chicago: University of Chicago Press, 1995), 1–44.

23. David D. Gilmore, *Manhood in the Making: Cultural Concepts of Masculinity* (London: Yale university Press, 1990), 1–12. See also Judith A. Allen, "Men Interminably in Crisis? Historians on Masculinity, Sexual Boundaries, and Manhood," *Radical History Review* 82 (2002): 199–202.

24. Joan Wallach Scott, *Gender and the Politics of History* (New York: Columbia University Press, 1988), 41–61; also, Andrea Cornwall and Nancy Lindisfarne, eds., *Dislocating Masculinities: Comparative Ethnographies* (London: Routledge, 1994), 20.

25. Ann Laura Stoler, *Race and the Education of Desire: Foucault's History of Sexuality and the Colonial Order of Things* (Durham: Duke University Press, 1995), 8.

26. Homi Bhabha discusses this ambivalence in other, non-sporting colonial contexts in "Of Mimicry and Man: The Ambivalence of Colonial Discourse" in Frederick Cooper and Ann Laura Stoler, eds., *Tensions of Empire: Colonial Cultures in a Bourgeois World* (Berkeley: University of California Press, 1997), 152–60.

27. E.P. Thompson, *The Making of the English Working Class* (New York: Vintage Books, 1966), 9–10. While Thompson's inattention to gender has been well criticized, most notably by Scott in *Gender and the Politics of History*, 68–90, the virtual invisibility of Empire in his work has received less analysis. Robert Gregg and Madhavi Kale provide an insightful critique of the necessary role of Empire in the construction of an adequate history of the development of the working classes in England in "The Empire and Mr. Thompson: The Making of Indian Princes and the English Working Class," in Gregg, *Inside Out, Outside In: Essays in Comparative History* (New York: St. Martin's Press, 2000), 39–80.

28. C.L.R. James, *Beyond a Boundary* (Durham: Duke University Press, 1993), 49–56. See also R. Gregg "Beyond Silly Mid-Off: C.L.R. James, Ranjitsinhhi, and the Boundaries of Englishness," in *Inside Out, Outside In*, 96–123; Grant Farred, "The Maple Man: How Cricket Made a Postcolonial Intellectual," in Farred, ed., *Rethinking C.L.R. James* (Cambridge, Massachusetts: Blackwell, 1996), 165–86.

29. Paul Gilroy, *The Black Atlantic: Modernity and Double Consciousness* (Cambridge: Harvard University Press, 1993).

30. Mangan, *The Games Ethic and Imperialism*, 24–25.

31. Asa Briggs, *Victorian People: Some Reassessments of People, Institutions, Ideas and Events 1851–1867* (London: Odhams Press, 1954), 152–53; David Newsome, *Godliness and Good Learning* (London: Cassell Publishers, 1961), 37; J.A. Mangan, *Athleticism in the Victorian and Edwardian Public*

School: The Emergence and Consolidation of an Educational Ideology (London: The Falmer Press, 1981), 13–21.

32. Henry Newbolt, *Selected Poems of Henry Newbolt*, ed., Patrick Dickinson (London: Hodder & Stoughton, 1981).

33. Mangan, *The Games Ethic and Imperialism*, 48. This connection between public school sporting ideology and volunteerism is examined in Colin Veitch, " 'Play Up! Play Up! and Win the War!' Football, The Nation and the First World War," *Journal of Contemporary History* 20 (1985): 363–78.

34. Mangan, *The Games Ethic and Imperialism*, 42.

35. Leonie Sandercock and Ian Turner, *Up Where Cazaly? The Great Australian Game* (London: Granada, 1981), 33.

36. Sandercock and Turner, *The Great Australian Game*, 70.

37. Allen J. Greenberger, *The British Image of India: A Study in the Literature of Imperialism* (Delhi: Oxford University Press, 1969), 47.

38. Mangan, *The Games Ethic and Imperialism*, 37.

39. Mangan, *The Games Ethic and Imperialism*, 22.

40. W.F. Mandle, "Games People Played: Cricket and Football in England and Victoria in the Late Nineteenth Century," *Historical Studies* 15: 60 (1973), 526.

41. Martin Barker, *Cosmics: Ideology, Power and the Critics* (Manchester: Manchester University Press, 1989), 292.

42. John Tomlinson, *Cultural Imperialism: A Critical Introduction* (Baltimore: Johns Hopkins University Press, 1991), 7–12.

43. It has been argued, most prominently by Ranajit Guha in his *Dominance Without Hegemony: History and Power in Colonial India* (Cambridge: Harvard University Press, 1997) that "hegemony" is an inaccurate way to describe the colonial relationship because it neglects certain class dynamics which were central to Gramsci's use of the term. Here however, "hegemony" is meant simply to imply an area in which there was a substantial level of agreement between colonizers and colonized, but that also simultaneously exhibited points of disagreement. In other words, sport in this case acted both as a point of mutuality and of self-assertion. See T.J. Jackson Lears, "The Concept of Cultural Hegemony: Problems and Possibilities," *American Historical Review* 90 (1985).

Chapter Two   Strong Men, Free Men: Gaelic Team Sports and Irish Masculinity

1. P.J. Devlin, *Our Native Games* (Dublin: M.H. Gill and Son, 1935), 35–36.

2. The dates mark the creation of the GAA, which sparked the revival and organization of hurling and Gaelic football, and the 1916 Easter Rebellion, which inaugurated the more violent and revolutionary phase of Irish republican struggles.

3. Although the "games" of hurling and football would fall under the heading of "sports" in today's terminology, this was less so at the time of the founding of the GAA. In general, "sports" then referred to hunting and horse racing and "games" referred to organized, physical team competitions. However, this began to change later in the period, as evidenced by one Irish commentator which distinguished between Irish games and British sports, making the payment of athletes the key distinction. Gaelic games were originally, and remain to this day, technically amateur endeavors. As this represented a period of transition for the terms, both will be used interchangeably. *The Gaelic Athletic Annual and County Directory 1908–1909*, no. 2 (Dundalk: Dundalgon Press, 1909), 20. The authorship is unknown except for the statement that the collection was "Compiled and Edited by Gaels for Gaels."

4. Mark Tierney, *Croke of Cashel: The Life of Archbishop Thomas William Croke, 1823–1902* (Dublin: Gill and Macmillan, 1976), 191.

5. Marcus de Búrca, *The G.A.A.: A History* (Dublin: Cumann Lúthchleas Gael, 1980), 1–6; W.F. Mandle, *The Gaelic Athletic Association and Irish Nationalist Politics 1884–1924* (London: Christopher and Helm, 1987), 10–17.

6. *Freeman's Journal*, April 30, 1888.

7. H.V. Brasted, "Irish Nationalism and the British Empire in the Late Nineteenth Century," in Oliver MacDonagh, W.F. Mandle, and Pauric Travers, eds., *Irish Culture and Nationalism 1750–1950* (London: Macmillan Press, 1983), 84–85.

8. Nicholas Mansergh, *The Irish Question 1840–1921* (London: George Allen and Unwin, 1975), 243–46. For an alternate view of 1891–1916, see R.F. Foster, *Paddy and Mr. Punch: Connections in Irish and English History* (London: Alen Lane, 1993), 262.

9. Donal McCartney, "Gaelic Ideological Origins of 1916," in O. Edwards, Dudley, and Fergus Pyle, eds., *1916: The Easter Rising* (London: Macgibbon and Kee, 1968), 48.

10. Sir Derek Birley, *Sport and the Making of Britain* (Manchester: Manchester University Press, 1993), 157.

11. Richard Holt, *Sport and the British: A Modern History* (Oxford: Clarendon Press, 1989), 203.

12. The main historiographical debate to date has concerned the extent of Cusack's relationship to the revolutionary Irish Republican Brotherhood. See Marcus de Búrca, *G.A.A.: A History and Michael Cusack and the G.A.A.* (Dublin: Anvil Books, 1989); Padraig Puirseal, *The G.A.A. in its Time* (Dublin: privately published, 1982); W.F. Mandle, *The Gaelic Athletic Association*; see also Padraig Griffin, *The Politics of Irish Athletics* (Ballinamore, Co. Leitrim: Marathon Publications, 1990) for a discussion of track and field in Ireland in this period.

13. Eric Hobsbawm, "Inventing Traditions," in Eric Hobsbawm and Terence Ranger, eds., *The Invention of Tradition* (New York: Cambridge University Press, 1983), 1–14.

14. W.F. Mandle, "The Gaelic Athletic Association and Popular Culture, 1884–1924," in MacDonagh et al., eds., *Irish Culture and Nationalism 1750–1950*, 115.

15. The argument that Australian Rules football represented a similar type of rebellion is belied by chronology. The initial rules for the Australian code were framed in 1859, four years before the English Football Association (e.g., soccer) was formed and 12 before the Rugby Union. Also, Australian Rules is played only in a portion of the country as opposed to cricket, which is the truly national sport of Australia during this period.

16. Ashis Nandy examined similar issues with regard to Indian cricket. See Nandy, *The Tao of Cricket: On Games of Destiny and the Destiny of Games* (New Delhi: Penguin Books, 1988), xi, 1–4.

17. For a discussion of the clerical–I.R.B. split, see James O'Shea, *Priest, Politics and Society in Post-Famine Ireland: A Study of County Tipperary 1850–1891* (Dublin: Wolfhound Press, 1983), 150, 171–76.

18. Nandy, *The Tao of Cricket*, 1–4.

19. Henry Glassie, *Passing the Time in Ballymenone: Culture and History of an Ulster Community* (Philadelphia: University of Pennsylvania Press, 1982), 165, 284–89.

20. L. Perry Curtis, Jr., *Apes and Angels: The Irishman in Victorian Caricature* (Washington: Smithsonian Institution Press, 1971); R.F. Foster, *Paddy and Mr Punch*; Ashis Nandy, *The Intimate Enemy: Loss and Recovery of Self Under Colonialism* (New York: Oxford University Press, 1983), 14–15; Ronald Hyam, *Britain's Imperial Century 1815–1914: A Study of Empire and Expansion* (London: B.T. Batsford, 1976), 88; Richard Ned Lebwow, *White Britain and Black Ireland: The Influence of Stereotypes on Colonial Policy* (Philadelphia: Institute for the Study of Human Issues, 1976), 20.

21. Benedict Anderson, *Imagined Communities: Reflections on the Origin and Spread of Nationalism* (New York: Verso, 1983).

22. For a wide-ranging and excellent discussion of the movement of Irish women from paid employment to unpaid domestic labor, see Joanna Bourke, *Husbandry to Housewifery: Women, Economic Change, and Housework in Ireland 1890–1914* (Oxford: Clarendon Press, 1993).

23. *The Gaelic Athletic Annual and County Directory 1910–1911, no. 3* (Dublin: Cahill, 1911) "Compiled and Edited by Gaels for Gaels," 58.

24. *Celtic Times*, February 26, 1887.

25. *Celtic Times*, February 26, 1887.

26. Devlin, *Our Native Games*, 14.

27. Clifford Geertz, "Centers, Kings and Charisma: Reflections on the Symbolics of Power," in Joseph Ben-David and Terry Nichols Clark, eds., *Culture and Its Creators: Essays in Honor of Edward Shils* (Chicago: Chicago University Press, 1977), 168–71.

28. Devlin, *Our Native Games*, 48.

29. Emmit Larken, "The Devotional Revolution in Ireland, 1850–1875," *The American Historical Review* 77 (1972), 625–52.

30. Donal McCartney, *The Dawning of Democracy: Ireland 1800–1870* (Dublin: Helicon, 1987), 207–08.

31. Two notable exceptions are Oscar Wilde and James Joyce, neither of whom were fond of games, but both of whom were Irish nationalists and represented alternate conceptions of Irish masculinity.

32. For an interesting reaction by this community to a divergent presentation of Irish gender roles, see James Kilroy, *The "Playboy" Riots* (Dublin: The Doleman Press, 1971); Stephen Tifft, "The

Parricidal Phantasm: Irish Nationalism and the 'Playboy' Riots," in Andrew Parker et al., eds., *Nationalisms and Sexualities* (New York: Routledge, 1992). Both works examine the week-long disruptions of Synge's opening run of the play "Playboy of the Western World" in 1907.

33. Griffin, *The Politics of Irish Athletics*, 26. The Ban was eventually lifted in November 2001 after the GAA's member counties voted to eliminate Rule 21; however, five of the six counties in Northern Ireland voted against the lifting of the Ban.

34. Cited in *The United Irishman*, September 24, 1904.

35. Devlin, *Our Native Games*, 20.

36. John Sugden and Alan Bairner, *Sport, Sectarianism and Society in a Divided Ireland* (Leicester: Leicester University Press, 1993), 29.

37. For examples of this process at work around the Empire, see Mangan, *"Benefits bestowed"?* idem, *The Games Ethic and Imperialism*; Nauright and Chandler, eds., *Making Men*.

38. Mandle, *The Gaelic Athletic Association*, 221.

39. *The Gaelic Athletic Annual* (1910–11), 18.

40. de Búrca, *Michael Cusack*, 120, and *G.A.A.: A History*, 26.

41. As cited in Fr. Michael Gilsenan, S.S., C.C., *Hills of Magheracloone 1884–1984* (Monaghan: Magheracloone Mitchells, 1985), 19.

42. *The Gaelic Athletic Annual* (1910–11), 19.

43. *The Gaelic Athletic Annual* (1910–11), 19.

44. Brasted, "Irish Nationalism and the British Empire in the Late Nineteenth Century," 93–94.

45. Kerby Miller, *Emigrants and Exiles: Ireland and the Irish Exodus to North America* (New York: Oxford University Press, 1985), 448–50.

46. Devlin, *Our Native Games*, 62–63.

47. C.L. Innes, *Woman and Nation in Irish Literature and Society, 1880–1935* (London: Harvester Wheatsheaf, 1993), 46–47; Seán Farrell Moran, *Patrick Pearse and the Politics of Redemption: The Mind of the Easter Rising, 1916* (Washington: The Catholic University of America Press, 1994), 146–54.

48. Oliver MacDonagh, *States of Mind: A Study of Anglo-Irish Conflict 1780–1980* (London: George Allen and Unwin, 1983), 87.

49. *Celtic Times*, April 16, 1887.

50. *United Ireland* and the *Irishman*, October 11, 1884, as cited in de Búrca, *Michael Cusack*, 96.

51. Ronald Hyam, *Britain's Imperial Century 1815–1914: A Study of Empire and Expansion* (London: B.T. Batsford Ltd., 1976), 88; L. Perry, Curtis, Jr., *Anglo-Saxons and Celts: A Study of Anti-Irish Prejudice in Victorian England* (Bridgeport: Conference on British Studies, 1968), 61–62.

52. Wolfgang Mock, "The Function of 'Race' in Imperialist Ideologies: The Example of Joseph Chamberlain," in Paul Kennedy and Anthony Nicholls, eds., *Nationalist and Racialist Movements in Britain and Germany Before 1914* (London: Macmillan Press, 1981), 193.

53. George Mosse, *Nationalism and Sexuality: Respectability and Abnormal Sexuality in Modern Europe* (New York: Howard Fertig, 1985), 98.

54. Innes, *Woman and Nation in Irish Literature*, 1–4, 177–79.

55. *Irish Daily Independent and Nation*, November 7, 1904.

56. Michael A. Messner and Donald F. Sabo, *Sex, Violence and Power in Sports* (The Freedom, California: Crossing Press, 1994), 96.

57. *The Gaelic Athletic Annual* (1910–11), 14.

58. *The Gaelic Athletic Annual* (1908–09), 45.

59. Tierney, *Croke of Cashel*, 195.

60. *Celtic Times*, February 26, 1887.

61. Carol Coulter, *The Hidden Tradition: Feminism, Women and Nationalism in Ireland* (Cork: Cork University Press, 1993), 9–18.

62. Bourke, *Husbandry to Housewifery*, 157.

63. de Búrca, *The G.A.A.: A History*, 93.

64. *The United Irishman*, July 29, 1905.

65. Tierney, *Croke of Cashel*, 195.

66. Coulter, *The Hidden Tradition*, 11.

67. Coulter, *The Hidden Tradition*, 5.

68. Janet A. Nolan, *Ourselves Alone: Women's Emigration from Ireland 1885–1920* (Lexington: University Press of Kentucky, 1989).

69. *The Shamrock*, January 24, 1884, as cited in de Búrca, *Michael Cusack*, 83.

70. Griffin, *The Politics of Irish Athletics*, 16.

71. In the mid-eighteenth century, gentry-supported hurling flourished in the southern half of Ireland. It was the withdrawal of this support along with the Famine which hastened the decline of the game. Kevin Whelan, "The Geography of Hurling," *History Ireland* 1 (1993), 28–31.

72. *The United Irishman*, March 18, 1899, as cited in Tom Graven, *Nationalist Revolutionaries in Ireland 1858–1928* (Oxford: Clarendon Press, 1987), 67.

73. Griffin, *The Politics of Irish Athletics*, 6.

74. *The United Irishman*, August 19, 1905.

75. Mosse, *Nationalism and Sexuality*, 90.

76. *The Irish Independent*, October 19, 1914.

77. Norbert Elias and Eric Dunning, *Quest for Excitement: Sport and Leisure in the Civilizing Process* (New York: Basil Blackwood, 1986), 227–31.

78. Jock Phillips, *A Man's Country? The Image of the Pakeha Male—A History* (Auckland: Penguin Books, 1987), 103–05.

79. *Clare Journal*, October 14, 1889, cited in Tim Moloney, ed., *The Claret and Gold: A History of the Tulla Hurling Club 1887–1987* (Ennis: Clare Champion Printers, 1987), 62.

80. T.O. hAongusa, ed., *An Gaeoeal Óg* (Louth: Drogheda Independent, Drogheda, Co., 1923), 19–21.

81. *The Gaelic Athletic Annual* (1910–11), 19.

82. *Freeman's Journal*, November 30, 1914; *G.A.A. 1915: Yearbook* (Dublin: The Gaelic Press, 1915), 29–30. A key promoter of the Kerry teams was P.D. Mehigan, who was perhaps the most widely read sports commentator of his era and was better known to Irish readers by his pen name, "Carbery." *Vintage Carbery* (Dublin: Beaver Row Press, 1984).

83. Devlin, *Our Native Games*, 12.

84. *G.A.A. 1915: Yearbook*, 39.

85. Gilsenan, *Hills of Magheracloone 1884–1984*, 127.

86. *Clare Journal*, October 14, 1889, cited in Moloney, ed., *The Claret and Gold*, 58.

87. Devlin, *Our Native Games*, 21.

88. *Freeman's Journal*, April 3, 1888.

89. de Búrca, *The G.A.A.: A History*, 62; Griffin, *The Politics of Irish Athletics*, 25.

90. de Búrca, *The G.A.A.: A History*, 124–27.

91. Devlin, *Our Native Games*, 56.

92. *Wicklow People*, January 21, 1911, cited in W. Alison Phillips, *The Revolution in Ireland: 1906–1923* (London: Longmans, Green and Co., 1923).

93. Séamus King, *A History of Hurling* (Gill and Macmillan, Dublin, 1998), 25–31.

94. Foster, *Modern Ireland,* 448–49; Moran, *Patrick Pearse and the Politics of Redemption*, 53.

95. Messner/Sabo, *Sex, Violence and Power in Sports*, 3.

Chapter Three   The King of Sports: Polo in
Late Victorian and Edwardian India

1. Pigsticking was a noble activity in India whereby hunters on horseback would hunt wild boar with long spears. Unlike big game hunting which took on airs of modernizing rational scientific efficiency, the rudimentary and atavistic use of spears in pigsticking were seen as central to the sport's value as a school of manhood. See John M. MacKenzie, *The Empire of Nature: Hunting Conservation and British Imperialism* (Manchester: Manchester University Press, 1988).

2. Lawrence James, *Raj: The Making and Unmaking of British India* (New York: St. Martin's Press, 1997), 323–24.

3. See Mrinalini Sinha *Colonial Masculinity: The "Manly Englishman" and the "Effeminate Bengali" in the Late nineteenth Century* (Manchester: Manchester University Press, 1995).

4. *The Indian Sportsman* (Calcutta), December 3, 1898.

5. J. Moray Brown and T.F. Dale, *The Badminton Library of Sports and Pastimes: Polo* (London: Longmans, Green, and Co., 1901), 266, 272–73 and Captain G.J. Younghusband, *Polo in India* (London: W.H. Allen & Co., 1890), 1.

6. Marquess of Kedleston Curzon, *A Viceroy's India: Leaves from Lord Curzon's Note-Book* (London: Sidgwick & Jackson, 1984), 190.

7. Brown and Dale, *The Badminton Library of Sports and Pastimes*, 254–55.

8. Younghusband, *Polo in India*, 3–9, 23–27.
9. Brown and Dale, *The Badminton Library of Sports and Pastimes*, 254–255.
10. "Tactics: Development" by Brigadier-General Robert Lumsden Ricketts in John Wodehouse, Earl of Kimberly, ed., *Polo* (London: Seeley, Service, 1936), 68–75.
11. Ricketts in Wodehouse, 68–75.
12. Ricketts in Wodehouse, 71.
13. Inden, Ronald, "Orientalist Constructions of India," *Modern Asian Studies* 20: 3 (1986), 403.
14. E.D. Miller, *Modern Polo* (London: Hurst & Blackett, 1922), 356.
15. "A Lover of the Game," *Letters on Polo in India: Written to a Beginner* (Calcutta: Thacker, Spink & Co., 1918). Letters originally written in 1910–11 and were "addressed to one about to dedicate his life to service in India" after graduating from Sandhurst, 12–14.
16. Miller, *Modern Polo*, 311.
17. Robert Baden-Powell, *Indian Memories: Recollections of Soldiering, Sport, etc.* (London: Herbert Jenkins, 1915) chapter entitled "The Sport of Kings and the King of Sports," 30–51.
18. Baden-Powell, *Indian Memories*, 30–51.
19. *Letters on Polo in India: Written to a Beginner*, v; also, *Pioneer Mail and India Weekly News* (Allahabad), October 6, 1911.
20. Letter quoted in Younghusband, *Polo in India*, 7.
21. *Letters on Polo in India: Written to a Beginner*, 9–10.
22. Richard Holt, *Sport and the British: A Modern History* (Oxford: Clarendon Press, 1989), 210.
23. Sir George Arthur, *Lord Haig* (London: William Heinemann, 1928), 8–9.
24. Gerard J. De Groot, *Douglas Haig, 1861–1928* (London: Unwin Hyman, 1988), 22.
25. "Marco," Preface by Earl Mountbatten of Burma. *An Introduction to Polo (6th ed)* (London: J.A. Allen, 1976). Anthony Kirk-Greene, "Badge of Office: Sport and His Excellency in the British Empire," in J.A. Mangan, ed., *The Cultural Bond: Sport, Empire, Society* (London: Frank Cass, 1992), 181.
26. A "practice bowl" was a circular depression at the bottom of which a saddled, wooden saw-horse was placed. Novice polo players could then practice their swings by themselves as the curved sides of the "bowl" would naturally return the ball to them after it was struck.
27. J. Nelson Fraser, *England: An Account of English Life for Indian Readers* (London: The Christian Literature Society for India, 1903), 96–97.
28. Benita Parry, *Delusions and Discoveries: Studies on India in the British Imagination, 1880–1930* (London: Allen Lane, 1972), 34.
29. William Manchester, *The Last Lion: Visions of Glory 1874–1932* (New York: Bantam Doubleday Dell, 1983), 238.
30. Oriental and India Office Collection at the British Library (OIOC), MSS.Eur.B235/1, Col. Harry Ross, British Army in India 1890–92, Indian Army 1892–1924.
31. Baden-Powell, *Indian Memories*, 34–35.
32. Manchester, *The Last Lion*, 241, 286–87.
33. Parry, *Delusions and Discoveries*, 34.
34. P.E. Razzell, "Social Origins of Officers in the Indian and British Home Army," *The British Journal of Sociology* 14: 3 (1963), 248–60.
35. Lt.-Col H. deB. deLisle, *Polo in India* (Bombay: Thacker, 1907), 225.
36. Ann Laura Stoler examines a similar dynamic in "Rethinking Colonial Categories: European Communities and the Boundaries of Rule," *Comparative Studies in Society and History* 31: 1 (1989), 134–61.
37. OIOC, MSS.Eur.C597, Two letters from Mrs. Edith Glascock, wife of L.C.B. Glascock of the Indian Police.
38. deLisle, *Polo in India*, ii–iii.
39. *Pioneer Mail and India Weekly News* (Allahabad) October 6, 1911.
40. *Pioneer Mail and India Weekly News* (Allahabad) October 27, 1911.
41. OIOC: MSS.Eur.D1235/5. Lt.-Col Arthur John Maitland-Hudson of the 1st Hyderabad (Nizam's Own) Imperial Service Lancers 1934.
42. *Letters on Polo in India: Written to a Beginner*, 73–74.
43. *Letters on Polo in India: Written to a Beginner*, 60.
44. T. Wilfred Sheppard, *A Guide to Training and Stable Management of Polo Ponies for Beginners in India* (Calcutta: Caledonian Printing, 1927), 25.

45. OIOC, MSS.Eur.C823, Scrap book kept by J.H.E. Reid.

46. deLisle, *Polo in India*, 166.

47. Miller, *Modern Polo*, 349.

48. *Pioneer Mail and India Weekly News* (Allahabad) October 27, 1911.

49. George MacMunn, *The Living India: Its Romance and Realities* (London: G. Bell and Sons, 1934), 18–20.

50. Ian Copland, *The Princes of Indian in the Endgame of Empire, 1917–1947* (Cambridge: Cambridge University Press, 1997), 1–14.

51. Thomas R. Metcalf, *The Aftermath of Revolt: India 1857–1870* (New Delhi: Manohar Publications, 1990), 222.

52. Metcalf, *The Aftermath of Revolt*, 236.

53. Parry, *Delusions and Discoveries*, 20. See also David Cannadine, *Ornamentalism: How the British Saw Their Empire* (New York: Oxford University Press, 2001), 41.

54. Metcalf, *The Aftermath of Revolt*, 236. See also Bernard S. Cohn "Representing Authority in Victorian India," in Eric Hobsbawm and Terence Ranger, eds., *The Invention of Tradition* (Cambridge: Cambridge University Press, 1983), 179–85.

55. Henry Cotton, *New India or India in Transition* (London: Kegan Paul, Trench, Trubner, 1907), 35–36.

56. Rev. W. Bonnar, "The English in India," *The Contemporary Review* 68 (October 1895), 572.

57. Cannadine, *Ornamentalism*, 41, 51.

58. M.B. Belsare, *The System of Government in India* (Ahmedabad: Guzerat Gazette Press, 1888), 10–11.

59. Curzon, *Lord Curzon in India: Being a Selection from his Speeches as Viceroy and Governor-General of India 1898–1905*, ed., Thomas Raleigh (London: Macmillan Press, 1906), 251.

60. Similarly, Lawrence James also views the 1903 Durbar as a stunningly successful demonstration of imperial unity and princely devotion to the monarchy. See James, *Raj: The Making and Unmaking of British India*, 316–19.

61. *Voice of India, Indian Spectator and Champion*, January 10, 1903.

62. Bonnar, "The English in India," 573.

63. *The Indian Daily News (Overland Summary)* (Calcutta) January 3, 1894.

64. John Campbell Oman, *The Brahmans, Theists and Muslims of India* (London: T. Fisher Unwin, 1907), 236–37.

65. Oman, *The Brahmans, Theists and Muslims of India*, 228–29.

66. Bonnar, "The English in India," 567.

67. Mihir Bose, *The Aga Khans* (Kingswood: World's Work, 1984), 93.

68. Parry, *Delusions and Discoveries*, 51.

69. OIOC: MSS.Eur.D1235/5 Maitland-Hudson, 1934.

70. deLisle, *Polo in India*, 200.

71. Brown and Dale, *The Badminton Library of Sports and Pastimes*, 276–77.

72. deLisle, *Polo in India*, 200.

73. deLisle, *Polo in India*, 198–99.

74. *Coronation Durbar, 1911: Being a Reprint of Articles and Telegrams Previously Published in the Pioneer* (Allahabad: Pioneer Press, 1912), 219–38.

75. Deslandes, Paul R, " 'The Foreign Element': Newcomers and the Rhetoric of Race, Nation, and Empire in 'Oxbridge' Undergraduate Culture, 1850–1920," *Journal of British Studies* 37 (January 1998), 71.

76. *Coronation Durbar, 1911: Being a Reprint of Articles and Telegrams Previously Published in the Pioneer* (Allahabad: Pioneer Press, 1912), 238.

77. Brown and Dale, *The Badminton Library of Sports and Pastimes*, 276–77.

78. A. Vadivelu, *The Ruling Chiefs, Nobles and Zamindars of India* (Madras: G.C. Loganadham Bros., 1915), 170.

79. Vadivelu, *The Ruling Chiefs, Nobles and Zamindars of India*, 1–14.

80. *The Indian Mirror* (Calcutta) February 20, 1889.

81. Vadivelu, *The Ruling Chiefs, Nobles and Zamindars of India*, 27–32.

82. Pandit Shri Dhar Lal, *The Glories of Rajasthan* (Jodhpur: 1922), 88.

83. Vadivelu, *The Ruling Chiefs, Nobles and Zamindars of India*, 167.

84. Vadivelu, *The Ruling Chiefs, Nobles and Zamindars of India*, 167.

85. Dhananajaya Singh, *The House of Marwar* (New Delhi: Roli Books, 1994), 130.
86. R.B. Van Wart, *The Life of Lieut.-General H.H. Sir Pratap Singh* (London: Oxford University Press, 1926), 79–80.
87. Van Wart, *The Life of Lieut.-General H.H. Sir Pratap Singh*, 1–4, 36–37, 174.
88. Barbara N. Ramusack, "The Indian Princes as Fantasy: Palace Hotels, Palace Museums and Palace on Wheels," in Carol A. Breckenridge, ed., *Consuming Modernity: Public Culture in a South Asian World* (Minneapolis: University of Minnesota Press, 1995), 67.
89. Van Wart, *The Life of Lieut.-General H.H. Sir Pratap Singh*, 196.
90. Henry Newbolt, *Poems: New and Old* (London: John Murray, 1919), 123–24.
91. Van Wart, *The Life of Lieut.-General H.H. Sir Pratap Singh*, 196.
92. Van Wart, *The Life of Lieut.-General H.H. Sir Pratap Singh*, 200.
93. Singh, *The House of Marwar*, 154.
94. Pandit Shri Dhar Lal, *The Glories of Rajasthan* (Jodhpur: 1922), 95.
95. Singh, *The House of Marwar*, 154.
96. Mihir Bose, *A History of Indian Cricket* (London: Andre Deutsch, 1990), 40.
97. Richard Cashman, *Patrons, Players and the Crowd: The Phenomenon of Indian Cricket* (New Delhi: Orient Longman, 1980), 27–28.
98. Cashman, *Patrons, Players and the Crowd*, 47.
99. Bose, *A History of Indian Cricket*, 47 and Cashman, *Patrons, Players and the Crowd*, 27–28.
100. Cashman, *Patrons, Players and the Crowd*, 33.
101. United Provinces of Agra and Oudh Misc. Government Publications, *Manual on Indian Etiquette For the use of European Officers Coming to India* (Allahabad: Government Press, 1910), 5–6.
102. John M. MacKenzie, ed., *Popular Imperialism and the Military 1850–1950.* (Manchester: Manchester University Press, 1986), 10.
103. OIOC, MSS.Eur.F206/223–37, Macnabb Collection: Lt.-Col. Rawdon Macnabb, Indian Political Service 1906–35, Program from the Bengal Polo Tournment 1905–06.
104. Oman, *The Brahmans, Theists and Muslims of India*, 230.
105. MacMunn, *The Living India*, 205.
106. W. Hogarth Todd, *Work, Sport and Play: An Englishman's Life in India Before the War* (London: Heath Cranton, 1928), 149–50.
107. Todd, *Work, Sport and Play*, 153.
108. OIOC, MSS.Eur.D1004, Sir Philip Crawford Vickery, Indian Police 1909–47.
109. Francis Younghusband, *The Light of Experience: A Review of Some Men and Events of My Time* (London: Constable, 1927), 184.
110. United Provinces of Agra and Oudh Misc. Government Publications, *Manual on Indian Etiquette For the use of European Officers Coming to India* (Allahabad: Government Press, 1910), 3. See also, Oman, *The Brahmans, Theists and Muslims of India*, 230.
111. Antoinette M. Burton "The White Woman's Burden: British Feminists and 'The Indian Woman,' 1865–1915," 137–57 and Barbara N. Ramusack "Cultural Missionaries, Maternal Imperialists, Feminist Allies: British Women Activists in India, 1865–1945," 199–36, in Nupur Chaudhuri and Margaret Strobel eds., *Western Women and Imperialism: Complicity and Resistance* (Bloomington: Indiana University Press, 1992).
112. Baden-Powell, *Indian Memories*, 263.
113. Charles Allen and Shararda Dwivedi, *Lives of the Indian Princes* (London: Century Publishing, 1984), 129.
114. Pamphlet Title: "More opportunity for Sport (Economically), for officers of the Indian Infantry, and how to get it, Some suggestions by an Indian Infantry Officer in 1908," Poona. Scottish Mission Industries Co. [1908?] OIOC- T50870, 19–20.
115. *Letters on Polo in India: Written to a Beginner*, 12–14.
116. *Quarterly Review* 196 (1902), 50–51, as cited in Parry, *Delusions and Discoveries*, 53.
117. *Letters on Polo in India: Written to a Beginner*, 3–4.
118. William Barton, *The Princes of India* (London: Nisbet, 1934), 47.
119. *Pioneer Mail and India Weekly News* (Allahabad) December 6, 1894.
120. For example, see Curzon's address to the students of Rajkumar College Rajkot in 1900, Curzon, *Lord Curzon in India*, 245.
121. H. Caldwell Lipsett, *Lord Curzon in India, 1898–1903* (London: R.A. Everett, 1903), 112.
122. Vincent Smith, rewritten and edited by Percival Spear, *The Oxford History of India, fourth edition* (Delhi: Oxford University Press, 1981), 744.

123. J.A. Mangan, ed., *The Cultural Bond: Sport, Empire, Society* (London: Frank Cass, 1992), 6.

124. Lionel Caplan, " 'Bravest of the Brave': Representations of 'The Gurkha' in British Military Writings," *Modern Asian Studies* 25: 3 (1991), 590–91.

125. Philip Mason, *A Matter of Honour: An Account of the Indian Army Its Officers and Men* (London: Jonathan Cape, 1974), 314.

126. George MacMunn, *The Martial Races of India* (London: Sampson, Low, Marston, 1933), 233, 354–55 and Lionel Caplan, " 'Bravest of the Brave': Representations of 'The Gurkha' in British Military Writings," *Modern Asian Studies* 25: 3 (1991), 587.

127. Mihir Bose, *The Lost Hero: A Biography of Subhas Bose* (London: Quartet Books, 1982), xi–xii.

128. Mihir Bose, *The Lost Hero: A Biography of Subhas Bose*, 1; Subhas Bose, Prison Notebook III, 1925–27 quoted in Bose, *The Lost Hero*, 1.

Chapter Four   May the Best White Man Win:
Boxing, Race, and Masculinity

1. W.J. Doherty, *In the Days of Giants: Memories of a Champion of the Prize-Ring* (London: George G. Harrap, 1931), 80–81.

2. *Baily's Magazine of Sports and Pastimes* xci (April 1909), 274.

3. Norbert Elias, *The Civilizing Process* (New York: Urizen Books, 1978).

4. Bonnie G. Smith, *Changing Lives: Women in European History Since 1700* (Lexington, MA: D.C. Heath, 1989), 317–34.

5. Eugene Corri, *Gloves and the Man: The Romance of the Ring* (London: Hutchinson, 1927), 53.

6. Licensed Victualler's Mirror, July 12, 1897.

7. Walter J. Ong, *Fighting for Life: Contest, Sexuality and Consciousness* (Ithaca: Cornell University Press, 1981), 94.

8. *The Mirror of Life*, March 24, 1897.

9. J.G.B. Bohun Lynch, *The Complete Amateur Boxer* (London: Methuen, 1913), 170.

10. John Bagriel, *The Professional Gentleman* (London: G.H. Robertson and J. Birch, 1921).

11. Lynch, *The Complete Amateur Boxes*, 158.

12. *The Referee* (London), July 10, 1910.

13. Introduction by J.G.B. Bohun Lynch in Joe Palmer, *Recollections of a Boxing Referee* (London: John Lane The Bodley Head, 1927), x.

14. Ong, *Fighting for Life*, 94.

15. J. Nelson Fraser, *England: An Account of English Life for Indian Readers* (London: The Christian Literature Society for India, 1903), 55–56.

16. Peter Fryer, *Black People in the British Empire: An Introduction* (London: Pluto Press, 1988), 66–67.

17. *Boxing*, October 2, 1909.

18. *Boxing*, October 2, 1909.

19. *The Referee* (London) July 10, 1910.

20. J.A. Mangan, "Images for Confident Control: Stereotypes in Imperial Discourse," in Mangan, *The Imperial Curriculum: Racial Images and Education in the British Colonial Experience* (London: Routledge, 1993), 12–13.

21. Anne McClintock, *Imperial Leather: Race Gender and Sexuality in the Colonial Contest* (New York: Routledge, 1995), 5.

22. *Boxing*, September 25, 1909.

23. *Mirror of Life*, May 18, 1895.

24. Corri, *Gloves and the Man*, 51–52.

25. *Boxing New Year Annual 1913*, 27–28.

26. Doherty, *In the Days of Giants*, 83–84.

27. Doherty, *In the Days of Giants*, 213, 221–32.

28. Edward Scobie, *Black Britannia: A History of Blacks in Britain* (Chicago: Johnson Publishing Company, 1972), 128.

29. Doherty, *In the Days of Giants*, 224.

30. *Sporting Life*, December 26, 1908.

31. Lynch, *The Complete Amateur Boxer*, 170.

32. Lynch, *The Complete Amateur Boxer*, 170.

33. *Sydney Morning Herald*, December 28, 1908.

34. *The Age*, December 28, 1908.
35. *The Observer*, January 2, 1909.36. *Tasmanian Mail*, January 2, 1909.
37. *Sydney Morning Herald*, December 28, 1908.
38. *The Observer*, January 2, 1909.
39. *Punch* (Melbourne) July 14, 1910.
40. *Sydney Morning Herald*, December 29, 1908.
41. *Sydney Morning Herald*, December 30, 1908.
42. *Sydney Morning Herald*, December 30, 1908.
43. *Sydney Morning Herald*, December 30, 1908.
44. *Sydney Morning Herald*, December 30, 1908.
45. *Punch* (Melbourne) December 31, 1908.
46. *The Argus*, December 28, 1908.
47. *The Argus*, December 28, 1908.
48. *Sporting Life*, December 28, 1908.
49. *Sporting Life*, December 28, 1908.
50. *The Referee* (London) July 10, 1910.
51. *Boxing*, July 9, 1910.
52. *The Parliamentary Debates (Official Report)* (London: HM Stationary Office, 1910, v. 19), 19.
53. *Sports Times*, July 9, 1910.
54. *The Referee* (London) July 10, 1910.
55. *The Referee* (London) July 10, 1910.
56. *Sports Times*, July 2, 1910.
57. *Boxing*, July 9, 1910.
58. *Boxing World and Athletic Chronicle*, July 14, 1910.
59. *Boxing World and Athletic Chronicle*, July 14, 1910.
60. Scobie, *Black Britannia*, 124.
61. Scobie, *Black Britannia*, 128.
62. Gail Bederman, *Manliness and Civilization: A Cultural History of Gender and Race in the United States 1880–1917* (Chicago: University of Chicago Press, 1995), 8.
63. Letter dated September 21, 1922 in PRO MEPO 2/1474.
64. Letter dated August 30, 1911 in PRO MEPO 2/1474.
65. September 10, 1911, Report summation in PRO MEPO 2/1474.
66. September 20, 1911, Letter/memo from Under Secretary of State PRO MEPO 2/1474.
67. Memo dated September 22, 1911 PRO HO 45/11880.
68. PRO HO 45/11880.
69. Letter dated January 29, 1923 PRO HO 45/11880.
70. Letter dated November 1, 1922 PRO HO 45/11880.
71. Letter dated January 1, 1923 PRO HO 45/11880.
72. For example, the *Licensed Victualler's Gazette and Hotel Courier* of London May 24, 1901 carried a report on a fight that had occurred in 1790.

Chapter Five   Defending White Manhood: The Bodyline Affair in England and Australia

1. "Gryllus," *Homage to Cricket* (London: Desmond Harmsworth, 1933), 2.
2. Horace, Epistle 19.
3. "Bowling" is the action by which the team in the field delivers the ball to the batsman standing at "wicket," which is comprised of three stakes stuck in the ground. In essence the bowler is analogous to the pitcher in baseball and the wicket or "stumps" are roughly analogous to home plate. Since the bowler usually delivers the ball so that it bounces once before it gets to the batsman, bowling "short" makes the ball bounce high on the batsman's body. The three stumps are called leg, middle, and off stumps as they move away from the batsman.
4. Richard Holt, *Sport and the British* (Oxford: Clarendon Press, 1989), 233. See Ric Sissons and Brian Stoddart, *Cricket and Empire: The 1932–33 Bodyline Tour of Australia* (London: George Allen & Unwin, 1984); Laurence Le Quesne, *The Bodyline Controversy* (London: Secker & Warburg, 1983);

R. Mason, *Ashes in the Mouth: The Story of the Bodyline Tour 1932–1933* (London: Hambledon, 1982); Gilbert Mant, *A Cuckoo in the Bodyline Nest* (Kenthurst, New South Wales: Kangaroo Press, 1992); Brian Stoddart, "Cricket's Imperial Crisis: The 1932–33 MCC Tour of Australia," in Richard Cashman and Michael McKernan, eds., *Sport in History: The Making of Modern Sporting History* (St. Lucia: University of Queensland Press, 1979); Phillip Derriman, *Bodyline* (London: Grafton, 1986); Edward Wyburgh Docker, *Bradman and the Bodyline* (London: Angus & Robertson, 1983); Jack Fingleton, *Cricketing Crisis: Bodyline and Other Lines* (London: Pavilion, 1984, originally 1947); J.B. Hobbs, *The Fight for the Ashes 1932–33: A Critical Account of the English Tour in Australia* (London: George G. Harrap, 1933); Harold Larwood, *Body-Line?* (London: Elkin Matthews & Marrot, 1933); Arthur Mailey—*And Then Came Larwood: An Account of the Test Matches 1932–33* (London: John Lane The Bodley Head, 1933); D.R. Jardine *Ashes—And Dust* (London: Hutchinson, 1934); Bruce Harris, *Jardine Justified: The Truth about the Ashes* (London: Chapman & Hall, 1933), and Richard S. Whitington, *Bodyline Umpire* (Adelaide: Rigby, 1974).

5. Sissons and Stoddart, *Cricket and Empire*, 21.

6. County cricket was the premier cricket competition in the same way that major league baseball was the premier baseball competition in this period. Similar to the Negro League in America, the Lancashire League of professional cricketers offered play at a level often equal to that of county teams, but was deemed inferior because of the prominence of professionalism and the lower class status of the players, organizers, and fans in the northern league. See Jeffrey Hill, "Reading the Stars: A Post-Modernist Approach to Sports History," *The Sport Historian: The Journal of the British Society of Sports History* 14 (1994), 50–52.

7. *Nottingham Evening Post*, January 19, 1933.

8. C.L.R. James, *Beyond a Boundary* (Durham: Duke University Press, 1993), 187.

9. James, *Beyond a Boundary*, 188.

10. League of Nations, *Statistical Year-Book of the League of Nations* (Geneva, 1934).

11. Robert Wohl, *The Generation of 1914* (Cambridge: Harvard University Press, 1979), 84–121; Fussell, Paul, *The Great War and Modern Memory* (New York: Oxford University Press, 1975), 75–113.

12. Wohl, *The Generation of 1914*, 105.

13. Joanna Bourke, *Dismembering the Male: Men's Bodies, Britain and the Great War* (Chicago: University of Chicago Press, 1996), 14.

14. For a wide-ranging discussion of the conflicts and debates surrounding interwar gender and sexuality, see Susan Kingsley Kent, *Making Peace: The Reconstruction of Gender in Interwar Britain* (Princeton: Princeton University Press, 1993).

15. League of Nations, *International Statistics Yearbook*, 1926; *Statistical Year-Book of the League of Nations*, (Geneva, 1934).

16. Roland Perry, *The Don* (London: Sidgwik & Jackson, 1996), 286–87.

17. Patricia Grimshaw, et al., *Creating a Nation* (New York: Viking Penguin, 1994), 241.

18. For a European-wide perspective on this, see Michael Adas, "'High' Imperialism and 'New History,'" in Adas, Michael, ed., *Islamic and European Expansion: The Forging of a Global Order* (Philadelphia: Temple University Press, 1993), 326.

19. Robert Graves and Alan Hodge, *The Long Week-End: A Social History of Great Britain, 1918–1939* (New York: W.W. Norton, 1940), 295.

20. Larwood, *Body-line?*, 44–45.

21. H.S. Altham and E.W. Swanton, *A History of Cricket* (London: George Allen & Unwin, 1938), 436.

22. Teams representing the MCC and England often were comprised of players who were English on the cricketing field only. Some prominent examples of this include the Indians K.S. Ranjitsinhji, K.S. Duleepsinhji, and the Nawab of Patudi, the Trinidadian Pelham Warner, the Australian G.O. Allen, and the Scotsman Jardine, to name just a few.

23. Sissons/Stoddart, *Cricket and Empire*, 35.

24. Altham/Swanton, *A History of Cricket*, 360–61.

25. The name comes from a *faux* obituary published in the *Sporting Times* on September 2, 1882 which announced "In Affectionate Remembrance of ENGLISH CRICKET, which died at the Oval on 29 August, 1882. Deeply lamented by a large circle of Sorrowing Friends and Acquaintances, R.I.P.—The body will be cremated, and the Ashes taken to Australia."

26. While the West Indies were not actually a "nation," they are generally referred to as such in cricketing matters since the cricketers from the colonies of Jamaica, Barbados, Trinidad and Tobago, British Guiana, the Leeward and Windward Islands play as one team.

27. Altham/Swanton, *A History of Cricket*, 337.

28. *The Times*, January 24, 1933.
29. *The Times*, January 24, 1933.
30. Curiously, Woodfull is nearly always described by Australian sources as being struck "over the heart" which is I believe meant to make it sound worse than just being struck in the chest.
31. *The Australian Worker*, February 8, 1933.
32. *Wisden* (1934) has all the cables' texts in their entirety. I 328–331.
33. The control of language is central to the success of any hegemonic system. T.J. Jackson Lears wrote: "The available vocabulary helps mark the boundaries of permissible discourse, discourages the clarification of social alternatives, and makes it difficult for the dispossessed to locate the source of their unease, let alone remedy it." T.J. Jackson Lears, "The Concept of Cultural Hegemony: Problems and Possibilities," *American Historical Review* 90 (1985), 569–70.
34. Larwood, *Body-line?*, 16.
35. Harris, *Jardine Justified*, 3.
36. F.J.C. Gustard, *England v. Australia: A Guide to the Tests 1934* (London: Herbert Joseph, 1934), 24–26.
37. James, *Beyond a Boundary*, 189.
38. Put in a baseball context, this might be the equivalent of maintaining a .425 batting average over a 20-year career.
39. Matthew Engel, ed., *Wisden Cricketer's Almanack*, 133rd edition (Guilford: John Wisden, 1996), 119.
40. A cricket captain is responsible for all on the field decisions regarding personal changes, tactics, and strategies. In essence, the captain acts as a player/coach in American parlance.
41. Le Quesne, *The Bodyline Controversy*, 34.
42. Stoddart, "Cricket's Imperial Crisis," 132.
43. Donald Bradman, *My Cricketing Life* (London: Stanley Paul, 1938), 96.
44. Mant, *A Cuckoo in the Bodyline Nest*, 81, 111.
45. Williams, Marcus, ed., *The Way to Lord's: Cricketing Letters to the Times* (London: Willow Books, 1983), 6.
46. Patsy Hendren, *Big Cricket* (London: Hodder & Stoughton, 1934), 104–05.
47. A.W. Carr, *Cricket with the Lid Off* (London: Hutchinson, 1938), 67.
48. "Barracking" is the practice of spectators actively participating in the game by usually loudly critiquing, cajoling, insulting the players, umpires, or games in general. While first class English cricket was played in virtual silence, not unlike a modern tennis match, Australian and West Indian cricket was played in a more carnival atmosphere.
49. Harris, *Jardine Justified*, 66.
50. Richard Cashman, "Cricket," in Wray Vamplew and Brian Stoddart, eds., *Sport in Australia: A Social History* (Cambridge: Cambridge University Press, 1994), 72.
51. *Sydney Morning Herald*, May 9, 1933.
52. Neville Cardus, *Good Days: A Book of Cricket* (London: Jonathan Cape, 1934), 26–27.
53. Herbert Sutcliffe, *For England and Yorkshire* (London: Edward Arnold, 1935), 117.
54. Carr, *Cricket with the Lid Off*, 42.
55. Carr, *Cricket with the Lid Off*, 47.
56. *Morning Post*, January 21, 1933.
57. *Morning Post*, January 24, 1933.
58. Hobbs, *Fight for the Ashes*, 238–39
59. Jardine, *In Quest of the Ashes*, 196–97.
60. *Manchester Guardian*, January 20, 1933.
61. *South Wales Football Echo and Express*, May 6, 1933.
62. *The Advertiser*, January 18, 1933.
63. *The Daily Telegraph*, July 29, 1933.
64. Jardine, *In Quest of the Ashes*, 198.
65. Larwood, *Body-line?*, 33.
66. Carr, *Cricket with the Lid Off*, 44.
67. "Is Cricket This?" *The Saturday Review*, January 21, 1933.
68. Grimshaw, *Creating a Nation*, 242–43.
69. Joanna Bourke, *Working Class Cultures in Britain 1890–1960: Gender, Class & Ethnicity* (London: Routledge, 1994), 44.

70. John Gillis, "Vanishing Youth: The Uncertain Place of the Young in a Global Age," *Young: Nordic Journal of Youth Research* 1 (1993), 5–7.
71. *The Referee* (Sydney), January 25, 1933.
72. Alistair Thomson, "The Anzac Legend: Exploring National Myth and Memory in Australia" in Raphael Samuel and Paul Thompson, ed., *The Myths We Live By* (London: Routledge, 1990), 74.
73. Thomson *The Myths We Live By*, 74–75.
74. Jardine, *Ashes and Dust*, 90–91.
75. Bill O'Reilly, "*Tiger*" (Sydney: William Collins Pty., 1985), 93.
76. *Liverpool Post & Mercury*, January 17, 1933.
77. *Morning Post*, January 24, 1933.
78. *Liverpool Post & Mercury*, January 21, 1933.
79. *The Referee*, February 1, 1933.
80. See Ann Laura Stoler, "Rethinking Colonial Categories: European Communities and the Boundaries of Rule," *Comparative Studies in Society and History,* 31 (1989).
81. See J.A. Mangan, *Athleticism in the Victorian and Edwardian Public School: The Emergence and Consolidation of an Educational Ideology* (Cambridge: Cambridge University Press, 1981), and idem. *The Imperial Curriculum: Racial Images and Education in the British Colonial Experience* (New York: Routledge, 1993).
82. *The Referee*, January 18, 1933.
83. Harris, *Jardine Justified*, 69.
84. *The Argus*, January 17, 1933.
85. Hobbs, *Fight for the Ashes*, 255.
86. *The New Statesman*, August 5, 1933, 170.
87. Harris, *Jardine Justified*, 19.
88. Jardine, *In Quest of the Ashes*, 209–10.
89. *The Argus*, November 11, 1932.
90. Jardine, *In Quest of the Ashes*, 212.
91. *Morning Post*, January 24, 1933.
92. Irving Rosenwater, *Sir Donald Bradman: A Biography* (London: B.T. Batsford, 1978), 257.
93. For some examples, see *The Argus*, January 5, 1933 and Derriman, Phillip, ed., *Our Don Bradman: Sixty Years of Writings About Sir Donald Bradman* (Melbourne: The Macmillan Company of Australia, 1987), 73–74.
94. *The Referee*, January 18, 1933.
95. Jim Bullock, O.B.E., *Bowers Row: Recollections of a Mining Village* (London: EP Publishing, 1976), 77.
96. William Pollock, *The Cream of Cricket* (London: Methuen, 1934), 70.
97. *The New Statesman*, July 1, 1933.
98. Perry, *The Don*, 287.
99. *The Times*, January 20, 1933.
100. R.S. Whitington, *Time of the Tiger: The Bill O'Reilly Story* (London: Stanley Paul, 1970), 187.
101. *Morning Post*, January 24, 1933.
102. *Daily Telegraph*, July 28, 1933.
103. Larwood, *Body-line?*, 20.
104. *Daily Telegraph*, January 19, 1933.
105. *The Advertiser*, December 30, 1932.
106. *The Referee*, January 25, 1933.
107. O'Reilly, *Tiger*, 195.
108. Alan Kippax, *Anti Body-Line* (London: Hurst & Blackett, 1933), 19–20.
109. Kippax, *Anti Body-Line*, 82–83, 86–87.
110. Carr, *Cricket with the Lid Off*, 45–46.
111. Nandy, *Tao of Cricket*, 5.
112. *Morning Post*, January 24, 1933.
113. *The Argus*, November 11, 1932.
114. *Barbados Advocate*, August 2, 1933.
115. Harris, *Jardine Justified*, 55.

Chapter Six   Black Skin in White Flannel:
The West Indies Join the Bodyline Fray

1. C.L.R. James, *Beyond a Boundary*, 112.
2. Ben Bousquet, *West Indian Women at War: British Racism in World War II* (London: Lawrence & Wishart, 1991), 29–32.
3. Peter Fryer, *Black People in the British Empire: An Introduction* (London: Pluto Press, 1988), 101.
4. Bousquet, *West Indian Women at War*, 31–33.
5. Sissons and Stoddart, *Cricket and Empire*, 38.
6. J.H. Parry et al., *A Short History of the West Indies* (New York: St. Martin's Press, 1987), 252–55.
7. The first Test victory for the West Indies in England would not come until 1950 when the English lost at Lord's by 326 runs.
8. Ellis "Puss" Achong, who earned six Test caps for the West Indies between 1930 and 1935, was of Chinese origin. Sonny Ramadhin would be the first cricketer of East Indian descent to represent the West Indies in 1950.
9. Hilary McD. Beckles, "The Political Ideology of West Indies Cricket Culture," in Hilary McD. Beckles and Brian Stoddart, eds., *Liberation Cricket: West Indies Cricket Culture* (Manchester: Manchester University Press, 1995), 152.
10. Ibid., 149.
11. Jeffrey Hill, "Reading the Stars: A Post-Modernist Approach to Sports History," *The Sport Historian: The Journal of the British Society of Sports History* 14 (1994), 49.
12. White West Indies cricketers came largely from the plantocratic elite and professional classes of West Indies and were not likely to pursue a career as a professional cricketer in either the more plebeian Lancaster League or the elite English county system. Garfield Sobers and J.S. Barker, *Cricket in the Sun: A History of West Indies Cricket* (London: Arthur Barker, 1967), 11.
13. Stuart Hall, "Cultural Identity and Diaspora," in Jonathan Rutherford, ed., *Identity, Community, Culture Difference* (London: Lawrence & Wiskart, 1990), 222.
14. Bousquet, *West Indian Women at War*, 45.
15. Some examples include: Hilary Beckles, ed., *An Area of Conquest: Popular Democracy and West Indies Cricket Supremacy* (Kingston: Ian Randle Publishers, 1994); Michael Manley, *A History of West Indies Cricket* (London: Andre Deutsch, 1995); Clyde Walcott, *Island Cricketers* (London: Hodder and Stoughton, 1958); C.L.R. James, *Cricket* ed., Anna Grimshaw (London: Allison & Busby, 1989); L. O'Brien Thompson, "How Cricket is West Indian Cricket?: Racial and Colour Conflict," *Caribbean Review* 12 (1983); F. Birbalsingh and C. Shiwcharan, eds., *Indo-Westindian Cricketers* (London: Hansib Publishing, 1988).
16. H.M. Beckles, "A Purely Natural Extension: Women's Cricket in West Indies Cricket Culture," in Beckles/Stoddart, *Liberation Cricket*, 223.
17. Manley, *A History of West Indies Cricket*, 13.
18. Maurice Tate, *My Cricketing Reminiscences* (London: Stanley Paul, 1934), 118.
19. Manley, *A History of West Indies Cricket*, 22.
20. Pelham Warner, *Cricket in Many Climes* (London: William Heinemann, 1900), 14.
21. *Manchester Guardian*, July 26, 1933.
22. "Second Slip," "A Review of 1933," *The Cricketer Annual* (1933), 8. See Homi Bhabha "Of Mimicry and Man: The Ambivalence of Colonial Discourse," in Cooper and Laura Stoler, eds., *Tensions of Empire: Colonial Cultures in a Bourgeois World* (Berkeley: University of California Press, 1997), 152–60.
23. *The Port of Spain Gazette*, July 18, 1933.
24. Ric Sissons and Brian Stoddart, *Cricket and Empire: The 1932–33 Bodyline Tour of Australia* (London: George Allen & Unwin), 38–46.
25. Richard D.E. Burton, "Cricket, Carnival and Street Culture in the Caribbean," in Beckles/Stoddart, *Liberation Cricket*, 89–106.
26. James, *Beyond a Boundary*, 79–85.
27. Clayton Goodwin, *Caribbean Cricketers : From the Pioneers to Packer* (London: Harrap, 1980), 24.
28. Gerald Howat, *Learie Constantine* (London: George Allen & Unwin, 1975), 28–29.
29. Warner, *Cricket in Many Climes*, 68–69.
30. Manthia Diawara, "Englishness and Blackness: Cricket as Discourse on Colonialism," *Callaloo: A Journal of African-American and African Arts and Letters* 13 (1990), 839.
31. James, *Beyond a Boundary*, 66.

32. For a discussion of "double consciousness" among people of the African diaspora as described by W.E.B. Du Bois and further examined by Paul Gilroy; see Gilroy, *The Black Atlantic: Modernity and Double Consciousness* (Cambridge: Harvard University Press, 1993).

33. Brian Stoddart, "Cricket, Social Formation and Cultural Continuity in Barbados: A Preliminary Ethnohistory," *Journal of Sport History* 14 (1987), 321–22.

34. Stoddart, "Cricket, Social Formation and Cultural Continuity in Barbados," 321–22.

35. James, *Beyond a Boundary*, 55.

36. Michael Adas, *Machines as the Measure of Men: Science, Technology, and Ideologies of Western Dominance* (Ithaca: Cornell University Press, 1989).

37. Manley, *A History of West Indies Cricket*, 37–38.

38. Diawara, *Callaloo*, 830.

39. James, *Beyond a Boundary*, 185.

40. Clifford Geertz, "Centers, Kings and Charisma: Reflections on the Symbolics of Power" in Joseph Ben-David and Terry Nichols Clark, eds., *Culture and Its Creators: Essays in Honor of Edward Shils* (Chicago: The University of Chicago Press, 1977), 25.

41. Sissons/Stoddart, *Cricket and Empire*, 64.

42. *Barbados Advocate*, January 28, 1933.

43. James, *Beyond a Boundary*, 49–56, 153. See also Grant Farred, "The Maple Man: How Cricket Made a Postcolonial Intellectual," in Farred, ed., *Rethinking C.L.R. James* (Cambridge, Massachusetts: Blackwell, 1996), 165–86.

44. *The New Statesman and Nation*, July 1, 1933.

45. Stoddart, "Cricket, Social Formation and Cultural Continuity in Barbados," 335.

46. Cornwall, Andrea, Nancy Lindisfarne, eds., *Dislocating Masculinities: Comparative Ethnographies* (London: Routledge, 1994), 19.

47. Dilip Hiro, *Black Britain, White Britain* (New York: Monthly Review Press, 1973), xx.

48. Edward Scobie, *Black Britannia: A History of Blacks in Britain* (Chicago: Johnson Publishing Company, 1972), 119–21.

49. *The Cricketer Spring Annual 1933*, 14 (1933), 74.

50. H.S. Altham and E.W. Swanton, *A History of Cricket* (London: George Allen & Unwin, 1938), 362.

51. Neville Cardus, *Good Days: A Book of Cricket* (London: Jonathan Cape, 1934), 38.

52. *Barbados Advocate*, February 4, 1933.

53. I thank Martin Summers for this observation.

54. James, *Beyond a Boundary*, 120–21.

55. Jeffrey Hill, "Reading the Stars: A Post-Modernist Approach to Sports History," *The Sport Historian: The Journal of the British Society of Sports History*, 14 (1994), 53.

56. "Busha," *Practical Information of an Occupation for Young British Manhood—That of an Overseer on a Plantation in the Tropics* (Westcliff-on-Sea: C.E. Dainton, 1925), 3.

57. Bridgette Lawrence, *Masterclass: The Biography of George Headley* (London: Polar Publishing, 1995), 28.

58. Donald Bradman, *My Sporting Life* (London: Stanley Paul, 1938), 62–65.

59. Robert Randall, *Memorandum on Book Readership in Jamaica* (London: Robert Randall, 1937).

60. "Busha," *Practical Information*, 5.

61. *Cricketer Annual*, (1933), 48.

62. C.L.R. James, "Chance of West Indies in First Test," *Port of Spain Gazette*, June 15, 1933.

63. *Barbados Advocate*, August 2, 1933.

64. *Barbados Advocate*, January 20, 1933.

65. *Barbados Advocate*, January 20, 1933.

66. *Barbados Advocate*, January 30, 1933.

67. *Jamaica Times*, January 28, 1933.

68. *Jamaica Times*, January 21, 1933.

69. *Barbados Advocate*, January 20, 1933.

70. Warner, *Cricket in Many Climes*, 9.

71. William Pollack, *The Cream of Cricket* (London: Methuen, 1934), 101.

72. Maurice St. Pierre, "West Indian Cricket—Part I: A Socio-Historical Appraisal," in Beckles/Stoddart *Liberation Cricket*, 110.

73. Pelham Warner, *Long Innings* (London: George G. Harrap, 1951), 162–63.

74. Constantine was eventually knighted and later made a peer. He was the first Black to enter the House of Lords as a member.

75. *Sydney Morning Herald*, April 18, 1933.
76. It was noted however that the bowlers were slower than Larwood and the wicket was slower than those in Australia. However, even this diminished version of Bodyline was highly unpleasant to watch.
77. *Port of Spain Gazette*, June 15, 1933.
78. *The Daily Gleaner*, July 27, 1933.
79. *The Times*, July 25, 1933.
80. *The Daily Telegraph*, July 25, 1933.
81. *Sports Special ("Green 'un")*, June 10, 1933.
82. Learie Constantine, *Cricket and I* (London: Philip Allen, 1933), 194–95.
83. Constantine, *Cricket and I*, 194–95.
84. *Sports Special ("Green 'un")*, July 29, 1933.
85. *The Cricketer* (weekly), July 29, 1933.
86. Hard-shelled batting helmets would not come into widespread use for decades and to this day, it is considered a sign of weakness in some circles to wear one in one-day internationals.
87. *The Star*, July 1, 1933; reprinted in *Barbados Advocate*, Bridgetown, August 8, 1933.
88. "Mark Over," "Sport with the Lid Off" originally in *The Bystander*; reprinted in the *Port of Spain Gazette*, June 15, 1933.
89. *Sydney Morning Herald*, May 25, 1933.
90. Benny Green, ed., *The Wisden Papers 1888–1946* (London: Stanley Paul, 1989), 159–60.
91. Constantine, *Cricket and I*, 189.
92. James, *Beyond a Boundary*, 111–12.
93. J.A. Mangan, "Images for Confident Control: Stereotypes in Imperial Discourse" in *The Imperial Curriculum: Racial Images and Education in the British Colonial Experience* (London: Routledge, 1993), 6.

Chapter Seven   Conclusions: Sport, Masculinity, and Nationalism

1. *Sporting Times*, March 20, 1897.
2. For an interesting discussion of gay athletes, see Michael Messner, Michael and Donald Sabo, *Sex, Violence, and Power in Sports: Rethinking Masculinity* (Freedom, CA: The Crossing Press, 1994).
3. Cooke, Theodore *Character and Sporstmanship* (London: Williams and Norgate, Ltd., 1927), vii–viii.
4. Fraser, J. Nelson *England: An Account of English Life for Indian Readers* (London: The Christian Literature Society for India, 1903), 55.

Bibliography

Periodicals and Newspapers

Advertiser, The (Adelaide)
Age, The (Melbourne)
Argus, The (Melbourne)
Australian Worker, The (Sydney)
Baily's Magazine of Sports and Pastimes (London)
Barbados Advocate (Bridgetown)
Boxing (London)
Boxing World and Athletic Chronicle (London)
Bystander, The (London)
Celtic Times (Ennis, Co. Clare)
Contemporary Review (London)
Cricketer, The (London)
Cricket Chronicle and Herald (Bath)
Daily Express (London)
Daily Gleaner, The (Kingston)
Daily Sport (London)
Daily Telegraph, The (London)
Evening News (London)
Football Post (Nottingham)
Freeman's Journal (Dublin)
Gaelic Athletic Annual, The (Dublin)
Illustrated Sporting and Dramatic News, The (London)
Indian Daily News, The (Overland Summary) (Calcutta)
Indian Mirror, The (Calcutta)
Indian Sportsman, The (Calcutta)
Irish Daily Independent and Nation (Dublin)
Irish Independent, The (Dublin)
Jamaica Times (Kingston)
Licensed Victualler's Mirror (London)
Liverpool Post and Mercury (Liverpool)
Manchester Guardian (Manchester)
Mirror of Life, The (London)
Morning Post (London)
Nassau Daily Tribune, The (Nassau)
New Society (London)
New Statesman and Nation, The (London)
Nottingham Evening Post (Nottingham)
Observer, The (Adelaide)

Pioneer Mail and India Weekly News (Allahabad)
Port of Spain Gazette, The (Port of Spain)
Punch (Melbourne)
Referee, The (London)
Referee, The (Sydney)
St. Kitts-Nevis Daily Bulletin (Basseterre, St. Kitts)
Saturday Review, The (London)
South Wales Football Echo and Express
Sporting Life (London)
Sporting Times (Bristol)
Sporting Times (London)
Sports Argus (Birmingham)
Sportsman, The (London)
Sports Special ("Green 'un") (Sheffield)
Sports Trades Journal: Yearbook and Diary for 1920 (London)
Star, The (London)
Sydney Morning Herald (Sydney)
Tasmanian Mail, The (Hobart)
Times, The (London)
United Irishman, The (Dublin)
Voice of India, Indian Spectator and Champion (Bombay)
Wisden Cricketer's Almanack (London)

Document Collections

Public Records Office of the United Kingdom, London
PRO CRIM   Central Criminal Court
PRO HO   Home Office
PRO MEPO   Metropolitan Police

British Library
OIOC   Oriental and India Office Collection

Books and Articles

Adas, Michael. *Machines as the Measure of Men: Science, Technology, and Ideologies of Western Dominance.* Ithaca: Cornell University Press, 1989.

Adas, Michael. " 'High' Imperialism and 'New History,' " in Michael, Adas ed., *Islamic and European Expansion: The Forging of a Global Order.* Philadelphia: Temple University Press, 1993.

Adelman, Melvin. *A Sporting Time: New York City and the Rise of Modern Athletics, 1820–1870.* Chicago: University of Illinois Press, 1990.

Ahmed, Leila. *Women and Gender in Islam: Historical Roots of a Modern Debate.* New Haven: Yale University Press, 1992.

Allen, Charles and Shararda Dwivedi. *Lives of the Indian Princes.* London: Century Publishing, 1984.

"A Lover of the Game," *Letters on Polo in India: Written to a Beginner.* Calcutta: Thacker, Spink, 1918.

Allen, Judith A. "Men Interminably in Crisis? Historians on Masculinity, Sexual Boundaries, and Manhood," *Radical History Review* 82 (2002), 199–202.

Altham, H.S. and E.W. Swanton. *A History of Cricket.* London: George Allen and Unwin, 1938.

Anderson, Benedict. *Imagined Communities: Reflections on the Origins and Spread of Nationalism.* New York: Verso, 1983.

Arthur, Sir George. *Lord Haig.* London: William Heinemann, 1928.

Baden-Powell, Sir George. *The Saving of Ireland: Industrial, Financial, Political.* London: William Blackwood and Sons, 1898.

Baden-Powell, Robert. *Indian Memories: Recollections of Soldiering, Sport, Etc.* London: Herbert Jenkins, 1915.

Barker, Martin. *Cosmics: Ideology, Power and the Critics*. Manchester: Manchester University Press, 1989.

Barton, William. *The Princes of India*. London: Nisbet, 1934.

Beckles, Hilary, ed. *An Area of Conquest: Popular Democracy and West Indies Cricket Supremacy*. Kingston: Ian Randle Publishers, 1994.

Beckles, Hilary McD. and Brian Stoddart, eds. *Liberation Cricket: West Indies Cricket Culture*. Manchester: Manchester University Press, 1995.

Bederman, Gail. *Manliness and Civilization: A Cultural History of Gender and Race in the United States 1880–1917*. Chicago: University of Chicago Press, 1995.

Belsare, M.B. *The System of Government in India*. Ahmedabad: Guzerat Gazette Press, 1888.

Bettinson A.F. and W. Outram Tristram, eds. *The National Sporting Club: Past and Present*. London: Sands and Co., 1901.

Bhabha, Homi. "Of Mimicry and Man: The Ambivalence of Colonial Discourse" in Cooper Frederick and Stoler Ann Laura, eds. *Tensions of Empire: Colonial Cultures in a Bourgeois World*. Berkeley: University of California Press, 1997.

Birbalsingh F. and C. Shiwcharan, eds. *Indo-Westindian Cricketers*. London: Hansib Publishing, 1988.

Birley, Sir Derek. *Sport and the Making of Britain*. Manchester: Manchester University Press, 1993.

Birley, Sir Derek. *Land of Sport and Glory: Sport and British Society 1887–1910*. Manchester: Manchester University Press, 1995.

Birley, Sir Derek. *Playing the Game: Sport and British Society 1910–45*. Manchester: Manchester University Press, 1995.

Birrell, Susan and Cheryl L. Cole, eds. *Women, Sport, and Culture*. Champaign, Illinois: Human Kinetics Press, 1994.

Booth, J.B. *Sporting Times: The "Pink 'Un" World*. London: T. Werner Laurie, 1938.

Bose, Mihir. *The Lost Hero: A Biography of Subhas Bose*. London: Quartet Books, 1982.

Bose, Mihir. *The Aga Khans*. Kingswood: World's Work, 1984.

Bose, Mihir. *A History of Indian Cricket*. London: Andre Deutsch, 1990.

Bourke, Joanna. *Husbandry to Housewifery: Women, Economic Change, and Housework in Ireland 1890–1914*. Oxford: Clarendon Press, 1993.

Bourke, Joanna. *Working Class Cultures in Britain 1890–1960: Gender, Class and Ethnicity*. London: Routledge, 1994.

Bourke, Joanna. *Dismembering the Male: Men's Bodies, Britain and the Great War*. Chicago: University of Chicago Press, 1996.

Bousquet, Ben. *West Indian Women at War: British Racism in World War II*. London: Lawrence and Wishart, 1991.

Bradman, Don. *How to Play Cricket*. London: Associated Newspapers, 1935.

Bradman, Don. *My Cricketing Life*. London: Stanley Paul, 1938.

Breckenridge, Carol A., ed. *Consuming Modernity: Public Culture in a South Asian World*. Minneapolis: University of Minnesota Press, 1995.

Briggs, Asa. *Victorian People: Some Reassessments of People, Institutions, Ideas and Events 1851–1867*. London: Odhams Press, 1954.

Brohm, Jean-Marie. *Sport: A Prison of Measured Time*. London: Ink Lins, 1978.

Broome, Richard. *Aboriginal Australians: Black Response to White Dominance, 1788–1980*. Sydney: George Allen and Unwin, 1982.

Brown, J. Moray and T.F. Dale. *The Badminton Library of Sports and Pastimes: Polo*. London: Longmans, Green and Co., 1901.

Buchan, John. *The African Colony: Studies in the Reconstruction*. Edinburgh: William Blackwood and Sons, 1903.

Bullock, Jim. *Bowers Row: Recollections of a Mining Village*. London: EP Publishing, 1976.

Burnett, John, David Vincent, and David Mayall, eds. *The Autobiography of the Working Class: An Annotated, Critical Bibliography*. Brighton: The Harvester Press, 1989.

Burton, Antoinette. *Burdens of History: British Feminists, Indian Women, and Imperial Culture, 1865–1915*. London: University of North Carolina Press, 1994.

"Busha." *Practical Information of an Occupation for Young British Manhood—That of an Overseer on a Plantation in the Tropics*. Westcliff-on-Sea: C.E. Dainton, 1925.

Butler, Frank. *A History of Boxing in Britain: A Survey of the Noble Art from it's Origins to the Present-Day*. London: Arthur Baker, 1972.

Butler, Judith and Joan W. Scott, eds. *Feminists Theorize the Political*. New York: Routledge, 1992.

Cahn, Susan K. *Coming on Strong: Gender and Sexuality in Twentieth-Century Women's Sport*. New York: The Free Press, 1994.

Cannadine, David. *Ornamentalism: How the British Saw Their Empire*. New York: Oxford University Press, 2001.

Cantelon, Hart and Richard Grueau. *Sport, Culture and the Modern State*. Toronto: University of Toronto Press, 1982.

Caplan, Lionel. " 'Bravest of the Brave': Representations of 'The Gurkha' in British Military Writings," *Modern Asian Studies* 25: 3 (1991), 590–91.

Cardus, Neville. *Good Days: A Book of Cricket*. London: Jonathan Cape, 1934.

Cardus, Neville. *The Wisden Papers of Neville Cardus*, ed. Benny Green. London: Stanley Paul, 1989.

Carr, A.W. *Cricket With the Lid Off*. London: Hutchinson and Co., 1935.

Cashman, Richard. *Patrons, Players and the Crowd: The Phenomenon of Indian Cricket*. New Delhi: Orient Longman, 1980.

Cashman, Richard and Amanda Weaver. *Wicket Women: Cricket and Women in Australia*. Kensington NSW: New South Wales University Press, 1991.

Cashman, Richard and Michael McKernan, eds. *Sport in History: The Making of Modern Sporting History*. St. Lucia: University of Queensland Press, 1979.

Cashman, Richard, David Headon, and Graeme Kinross-Smith. *The Oxford Book of Australian Sporting Anecdotes*. Melbourne: Oxford University Press, 1993.

Cashmore, Ernest. *Black Sportsmen*. London: Routledge and Kegan Paul, 1982.

Chaudhuri, Nupur and Margaret Strobel, eds. *Western Women and Imperialism: Complicity and Resistance*. Bloomington: Indiana University Press, 1992.

Collins, Tony. *Rugby's Great Split: Class, Culture and the Origins of Rugby League Football*. London: Frank Cass, 1998.

Comitas, Lambros and David Lowenthal, eds. *Work and Family Life: West Indian Perspectives*. Garden City, NY: Anchor Books, 1973.

Constantine, Learie. *Cricket and I*. London: Philip Allan, 1933.

Constantine, Learie. *Cricketers' Carnival*. London: Stanley Paul, 1948.

Cook, Theodore Andrea. *The Fourth Olympiad: The Official Report of the Olympic Games of 1908*. London: British Olympic Association, 1919.

Copland, Ian. *The Princes of Indian in the Endgame of Empire, 1917–1947*. Cambridge: Cambridge University Press, 1997.

Cornwall, Andrea and Nancy Lindisfarne, eds. *Dislocating Masculinities: Comparative Ethnographies*. London: Routledge, 1994.

Corri, Eugene. *Gloves and The Man: The Romance of the Ring*. London: Hutchinson, 1927.

Corri, Eugene. *Thirty Years a Boxing Referee*. New York: Longmans, Green, 1915 and 1919.

Cotter, Gerry. *England Versus West Indies: A History of the Tests and Other Matches*. Swindon, Wiltshire: Crowood Press, 1991.

Cotton, Henry. *New India or India in Transition*. London: Kegan Paul, Trench, Trubner, 1907.

Coulter, Carol. *The Hidden Tradition: Feminism, Women and Nationalism in Ireland*. Cork: Cork University Press, 1993.

Coxhead, Elizabeth. *Daughters of Erin: Five Women of the Irish Renascence* [sic]. Geerrards Cross: Colin Smythe, 1965.

Curtis, Jr., L. Perry. *Anglo-Saxons and Celts: A Study of Anti-Irish Prejudice in Victorian England*. Bridgeport: Conference on British Studies, 1968.

Curtis, Jr., L. Perry. *Apes and Angels: The Irishman in Victorian Caricature*. Washington: Smithsonian Institution Press, 1971.

Curzon, Marquess of Kedleston. *Lord Curzon in India: Being a Selection from his Speeches as Viceroy and Governor-General of India 1898–1905*, ed. Thomas Raleigh. London: Macmillan, 1906.

Curzon, Marquess of Kedleston. *A Viceroy's India: Leaves from Lord Curzon's Note-Book*. London: Sidgwick & Jackson, 1984.

Davin, Anna. "Imperial Motherhood," in Raphael Samuel, ed. *Patriotism: The Making and Unmaking of British National Identity*. New York: Routledge, 1989.

Davis, Captain F.J. *A Handbook on Refereeing and Judging Boxing under Imperial Services Boxing Association Rules*. Aldershot: Wm. May, 1935.

de Búrca, Marcus. *The G.A.A.: A History*. Dublin: Cumann Lúthchleas Gael, 1980.

de Búrca, Marcus. *Michael Cusack and the GAA*. Dublin: Anvil Books, 1989.

Deghy, Guy. *Noble and Manly: The History of the National Sporting Club*. London: Hutchinson, 1956.

De Groot, Gerard J. *Douglas Haig, 1861–1928*. London: Unwin Hyman, 1988.

deLisle, Lt.-Col H. deB. *Polo in India*. Bombay: Thacker, 1907.

Derriman, Phillip. *Bodyline*. London: Grafton, 1986.

Derriman, Philllip, ed. *Our Don Bradman Sixty Years of Writings about Sir Donald Bradman*. Melbourne: The Macmillan Company of Australia, 1987.

de Sélincourt, Hugh. *Moreover: Reflections on the Game of Cricket*. London: Gerald Howe, 1934.

Deslandes, Paul R. " 'The Foreign Element': Newcomers and the Rhetoric of Race, Nation, and Empire in 'Oxbridge' Undergraduate Culture, 1850–1920," *Journal of British Studies* 37 (January 1998), 71.

Devlin, P.J. *Our Native Games*. Dublin: M.H. Gill and Son, 1935.

Diawara, Manthia. "Englishness and Blackness: Cricket as Discourse on Colonialism," *Callaloo: A Journal of African-American and African Arts and Letters* 13: 4 (1990).

Dimeo, Paul and James Mills, eds. *Soccer in South Asia: Empire, Nation, Diaspora*. London: Frank Cass, 2001.

Dixon, David. *From Prohibition to Regulation: Bookmaking, Anti-Gambling, and the Law*. Oxford: Clarendon Press, 1991.

Docker, Edward Wyburgh. *Bradman and the Bodyline Series*. London: Angus & Robertson, 1983.

Doherty, W.J. *In the Days of Giants: Memories of a Champion of the Prize-Ring*. London: George G. Harrap, 1931.

Douglas, Mary. *Purity and Danger: Analysis of the Concepts of Pollution and Taboo*. London: Routledge and Kegan Paul, 1966.

Doyle, Tommy. *A Lifetime in Hurling*. London: Hutchinson, 1955.

Ducat, Andrew. *Cricket*. London: Hutchinson, 1933.

Dunning, Eric. "Sport as a Male Preserve: Notes on the Social Sources of Masculine Identity and Its Transformations," *Theory, Culture and Society* 3: 1 (1986).

Dunning, Eric, Patrick Murphy, and John Williams. *The Roots of Football Hooliganism: An Historical and Sociological Study*. New York: Routledge and Kegan Paul, 1988.

Dunning, Eric, Patrick Murphy, and John Williams. *Hooligans Abroad: The Behaviour and Control of English Fans in Continental Europe*. Boston: Routledge and Kegan Paul, 1984.

Edwards, Harry. *Sociology of Sport*. Homewood, IL: Dorsey Press, 1973.

Edwards, Wil Jo. *From the Valley I Came*. London: Angus and Robertson, 1956.

Elias, Norbert. *The Civilizing Process*. New York: Urizen Books, 1978.

Elias, Norbert and Eric Dunning. *Quest for Excitement: Sport and Leisure in the Civilizing Process*. New York: Basil Blackwood, 1986.

Faber, Richard. *The Vision and the Need: Late Victorian Imperialist Aims*. London: Faber and Faber, 1966.

Farred, Grant, ed. *Rethinking C.L.R. James*. Cambridge, MA: Blackwell, 1996.

Field, Dick. *Up and Down the Valley: Growing Up in the Cotswolds in the 1920s*. Cirencester, Gloucestershire: Gryffon Publications, 1985.

Fingleton, J.H. *Cricket Crisis*. London: Cassell, 1946.

Fingleton, Jack. *Batting from Memory*. London: Collins, 1981.

Fingleton, Jack. *Cricketing Crises: Bodyline and Other Lines*. London: Pavilion, 1984, originally 1947.

Fishwick, Nicholas. *English Football and Society 1910–1950*. Manchester: Manchester University Press, 1989.

Fiske, John, Bob Hodge, and Graeme Turner. *Myths of Oz: Reading Australian Popular Culture*. Boston: Allen and Unwin, 1987.

Fitzpatrick, David. "Women, Gender and the Writing of Irish History," *Irish Historical Studies* 27 (107): 267–273 (1991), 1991.

Fitzsimmons, Robert. *Physical Culture and Self-Defense*. London: Gale and Polden, 1906.

Forman, Charles. *Industrial Town: Self-Portrait of St. Helens in the 1920s*. London: Granada Publishing, 1978.

Foster, R.F. *Modern Ireland 1600–1972.* London: Penguin, 1989.

Foster, R.F. *Paddy and Mr. Punch: Connections in Irish and English History.* London: Allen Lane, 1993.

Foucault, Michel. *Discipline and Punish: The Birth of the Prison.* New York: Vintage Books, 1979.

Frankenberg, Ruth. *White Women, Race Matters: The Social Construction of Whiteness.* London: Routledge, 1993.

Fraser, J. Nelson. *England: An Account of English Life for Indian Readers.* London: The Christian Literature Society for India, 1903.

Frindall, Bill, ed. *The Wisden Book of Test Cricket: Volume I 1877–1977.* London: Headine Book Publishing, 1995.

Fryer, Peter. *Black People in the British Empire: An Introduction.* London: Pluto Press, 1988.

Fussell, Paul. *The Great War and Modern Memory.* New York: Oxford University Press, 1975.

G.A.A. 1915: Yearbook. Dublin: The Gaelic Press, 1915.

Gaelic Athletic Annual and County Directory 1908–1909, The. Dundalk: Dundalgon Press, 1909.

Geertz, Clifford. *Myth, Symbol, and Culture.* New York: W.W. Norton, 1971.

Geertz, Clifford. "Centers, Kings and Charisma: Reflections on the Symbolics of Power," in Joseph Ben-David and Terry Nichols Clark, eds. *Culture and Its Creators: Essays in Honor of Edward Shils.* Chicago: The University of Chicago Press, 1977.

Gerber, Ellen W. and William J. Morgan. *Sport and the Body: A Philosophical Symposium.* Philadelphia: Febiger, 1979.

Gibbons, J. Wynfred. *Barbados Cricketers' Annual.* Bridgetown: Globe Office, 1909–13.

Gibbons, Luke. "Identity Without a Centre: Allegory, History and Irish Nationalism," *Cultural Studies* 6: 3 (1992).

Gibbs, Harry and John Morric. *Box on: The Autobiography of Harry Gibbs.* London: Pelham Books, 1981.

Gillis, John R. "Vanishing Youth: The Uncertain Place of the Young in a Global Age," *Young: Nordic Journal of Youth Research* 1 (1993).

Gilmore, David D. *Manhood in the Making: Cultural Concepts of Masculinity.* London: Yale University Press, 1990.

Gilroy, Paul. *The Black Atlantic: Modernity and Double Consciousness.* Cambridge: Harvard University Press, 1993.

Gilsenan, Fr. Michael, S.S., C.C., *Hills of Magheracloone 1884–1984.* Monaghan: Magheracloone Mitchells, 1985.

Glassie, Henry. *Passing the Time in Ballymenone: Culture and History of an Ulster Community.* Philadelphia: University of Pennsylvania Press, 1982.

Goodwin, Clayton. *Caribbean Cricketers: From the Pioneers to Packer.* London: Harrap, 1980.

Gorn, Elliot J. *The Manly Art: The Lives and Times of the Great Bare-Knuckle Champions.* London: Robson Books, 1989.

Grant, David. *On a Roll: A History of Gambling and Lotteries in New Zealand.* Wellington: Victoria University Press, 1994.

Graven, Tom. *Nationalist Revolutionaries in Ireland 1858–1928.* Oxford: Clarendon Press, 1987.

Graves, Charles L. *Mr. Punch's History of Modern England.* London: Cassell, 1921.

Graves, Robert and Alan Hodge. *The Long Week-End: A Social History of Great Britain, 1918–1939.* New York: W.W. Norton, 1940.

Green, Benny, ed. *Wisden Anthology 1900–1940.* London: Macdonald Futura Publishers, 1980.

Greenberger, Allen J. *The British Image of India: A Study in the Literature of Imperialism.* Delhi: Oxford University Press, 1969.

Gregg, Robert. *Inside Out, Outside In: Essays in Comparative History.* New York: St. Martin's Press, 2000.

Gregory, Kenneth, ed. *The First Cuckoo: A Selection of the Most Witty Amusing and Memorable Letters to The Times 1900–1975.* London: Book Club Associates, 1977.

Griffin, Padraig. *The Politics of Irish Athletics.* Ballinamore, Co. Leitrim: Marathon Publications, 1990.

Grimshaw, Patricia et al. *Creating a Nation.* New York: Viking Penguin, 1994.

"Gryllus." *Homage to Cricket.* London: Desmond Harmsworth, 1933.

Guha, Ramachandra. *A Corner of a Foreign Field: The Indian History of a British Sport.* London: Picador, 2002.

Guha, Ranajit. *Dominance Without Hegemony: History and Power in Colonial India.* Cambridge: Harvard University Press, 1997.

Gustard, F.J.C. *England v. Australia: A Guide to the Tests 1934.* London: Herbert Joseph, 1934.

Guttmann, Allen. *From Ritual to Record: The Nature of Modern Sport.* New York: Columbia University Press, 1978.

Guttmann, Allen. *Women's Sports: A History.* New York: Columbia University Press, 1991.

Guttmann, Allen. *Games and Empires: Modern Sports and Cultural Imperialism.* New York: Columbia University Press, 1994.

Hain, Peter. *Don't Play with Apartheid: The Background to the Stop the Seventy Tour Campaign.* London: George Allen and Unwin, 1971.

Haley, Bruce. *The Healthy Body and Victorian Culture.* London: Harvard University Press, 1978.

Hall, Catherine. "Gender Politics and Imperial Politics: Rethinking the Histories of Empire," in Verene Shepherd, Bridget Brereton, Barbara Bailey, eds. *Engendering History: Caribbean Women in Historical Perspective.* 48–59. Kingston, Jamaica: I. Randle, 1995.

Hall, Stuart and Tony Jefferson. *Resistance Through Rituals: Youth Subcultures in Post War Britain.* London: Unwin Hyman, 1976.

Hall, Stuart. "Cultural Identity and Diaspora," in Jonathan Rutherford, ed. *Identity, Community, Culture Difference.* London: Lawrence & Wiskart, 1990.

hAongusa, T.O., ed. *An Gaeoeal Óg.* Drogheda: Drogheda Independent, 1923.

Harding, Arthur. *East End Underworld: Chapters in the Life of Arthur Harding.* History Workshop Series, general editor Raphael Samuel, London: Routledge and Kegan Paul, 1981.

Hargreaves, Jennifer. *Sport, Culture and Ideology.* London: Routledge and Kegan Paul, 1982.

Hargreaves, Jennifer. *Sporting Females: Critical Issues in the History and Sociology of Women's Sports.* London: Routledge, 1994.

Hargreaves, Jennifer. "Where's the Virtue? Where's the Grace? A Discussion of the Social Production of Gender Relations in and through Sport," *Theory, Culture and Society* 3: 1 (1986), 109–21.

Hargreaves, John. "Sport and Hegemony: Some Theoretical Problems," in Cantelon, Hart and Richard Grueau, eds. *Sport, Culture and the Modern State.* Toronto: University of Toronto Press, 1982.

Harkness, David and Mary O'Dowd, eds. *The Town in Ireland.* Belfast: Appletree Press, 1991.

Harris, Bruce. *Jardine Justified: The Truth about the Ashes.* London: Chapman and Hall, 1933.

Hartley, R.A. *History and Bibliography of Boxing Books: Collectors Guide to the History of Pugilism.* Alton, Hants: Nimrod Press, 1989.

"H.B.," *Letters From Ireland.* Dublin: Office of the *New Ireland Review*, 1902. (Reprinted from the *New Ireland Review*.)

Henderson, J.E. *A Visit to the West Indies.* London: The Cargate Press, 1939.

Hendren, Patsy. *Big Cricket.* London: Hodder and Stoughton, 1934.

Higginbotham, Evelyn Brooks. "African-American Women's History and the Metalanguage of Race," *Signs: Journal of Women in Culture and Society* 2: 2 (1992).

Hill, Jeffrey. "British Sports History: A Post-Modern Future?" *Journal of Sport History* 23: 1 (1996).

Hill, Jeffrey. "Reading the Stars: A Post-Modernist Approach to Sports History," *The Sport Historian: The Journal of the British Society of Sports History* 14 (1994).

Hiro, Dilip. *Black Britain, White Britain.* New York: Monthly Review Press, 1973.

Hitchin, George. *Pit-Yacker.* London: Jonathan Cape, 1962.

Hobbs, J.B. *The Fight for the Ashes 1932–33: A Critical Account of the English Tour in Australia.* London: George G. Harrap, 1933.

Hoberman, John. "Toward a Theory of Olympic Internationalism," *Journal of Sport History* 22: 1 (1995).

Hobsbawm, Eric. "Inventing Traditions," in Eric Hobsbawm and Terence Ranger, eds. *The Invention of Tradition.* New York: Cambridge University Press, 1983.

Hobsbawm, E.J. *Nations and Nationalism since 1870.* New York: Cambridge University Press, 1990.

Hogge, J.M. *The Facts of Gambling.* London: Andrew Moelrose, 1907.

Holmes, Colin. *John Bull's Island: Immigration and British Society.* London: Macmillan Education, 1988.

Holt, Richard. "Contrasting Nationalisms: Sport, Militarism, and the Unitary State in Britain and France Before 1914," *International Journal of the History of Sport* 12: 2 (1995).

Holt, Richard. *Sport and Society in Modern France.* London: Macmillan Press, 1981.

Holt, Richard. *Sport and the British: A Modern History.* Oxford: Clarendon Press, 1989.

Howat, Gerald. *Learie Constantine.* London: George Allen and Unwin, 1975.

Howell, Maxwell and Reet A. Howell, eds. *History of Sport in Canada*. Champaign, IL: Stipes Publishing, 1985.

Hugman, Barry, ed. *The George Wimpey Amateur Boxing Yearbook*. London: Wimpey Group Services, 1982.

Hyam, Ronald. *Britain's Imperial Century 1815–1914: A Study of Empire and Expansion*. London: B.T. Batsford, 1976.

Inden, Ronald, "Orientalist Constructions of India," *Modern Asian Studies* 20: 3 (1986), 403.

Innes, C.L. *Women and Nation in Irish Literature and Society, 1880–1935*. New York: Harvester Wheatsheaf, 1993.

James, C.L.R. *Cricket*. Edited by Anna Grimshaw. London: Allison & Busby, 1989.

James, C.L.R. *Beyond a Boundary*. Durham: Duke University Press, 1993 (1963 originally).

James, Lawrence. *Raj: The Making and Unmaking of British India*. New York: St. Martin's Press.

Jardine, D.R. *Ashes—And Dust*. London: Hutchinson, 1934.

Jardine, D.R. *In Quest of the Ashes*. London: Hutchinson, 1933.

Jarvie, Grant and John Burnett, eds. *Sport, Scotland and the Scots*. East Lothian: Tuckwell Press, 2000.

Johnes, Martin. *Soccer and Society: South Wales, 1900–1939*. Cardiff: University of Wales Press, 2002.

Joint Sports Council/Social Science Research Panel. *Report on Public Disorder and Sporting Events*. London, 1978.

Jones, Stephen G. "State Intervention in Sport and Leisure in Britain between the Wars," *Journal of Contemporary History* 22: 1 (1987).

Joyce, Patrick. *Visions of the People: Industrial England and the Question of Class 1848–1914*. Cambridge: Cambridge University Press, 1991.

Karl B. Raitz, ed. *The Theater of Sport*. Baltimore: Johns Hopkins University Press, 1995.

Kearney, Richard. *Dialogues with Contemporary Continental Thinkers: The Phenomenological Heritage*. Manchester: Manchester University Press, 1984.

Kennedy, Paul and Anthony Nicholls, ed. *Nationalist and Racialist Movements in Britain and Germany before 1914*. London: Macmillan Press, 1981.

Kent, Cecil. *The Story of the Tests in England (1880–1934)*. London: Hutchinson, 1934.

Kent, Susan Kingsley. *Making Peace: The Reconstruction of Gender in Interwar Britain*. Princeton: Princeton University Press, 1993.

Kilroy, James. *The "Playboy" Riots*. Dublin: The Doleman Press, 1971.

King, Seamus J. *A History of Hurling*. Dublin: Gill & Macmillan, 1996.

Kippax, Alan. *Anti Body-Line*. London: Hurst and Blackett, 1933.

Lal, Pandit Shri Dhar. *The Glories of Rajasthan*. Jodhpur: 1922.

Laqueur, Thomas. "Orgasm, Generation and the Politics of Reproductive Biology," in Catherine Gallagher and Thomas Laqueur, eds. *The Making of the Modern Body: Sexuality and Society in the Nineteenth Century*. Berkeley: University of California Press, 1987.

Laqueur, Thomas. *Making Sex: Body and Gender from the Greeks to Freud*. London: Harvard University Press, 1990.

Larken, Emmit. "The Devotional Revolution in Ireland, 1850–1875," *The American Historical Review* 77 (1972), 625–52.

Larwood Harold. *Body-Line?* London: Elkin Matthews and Marrot, 1933.

Laurence, John C. *Race, Propaganda and South Africa*. London: Victor Gollancz, 1979.

Lawrence, Bridgette. *Masterclass: The Biography of George Headley*. London: Polar Publishing, 1995.

Lawson, Jack. *A Man's Life*. London: Hodder and Stoughton, 1932.

League of Nations. *International Statistics Yearbook*, Geneva: 1926.

League of Nations. *Statistical Year-Book of the League of Nations*, Geneva: 1934.

Lears, T.J. Jackson. "The Concept of Cultural Hegemony: Problems and Possibilities," *American Historical Review* 90 (1985).

Lebow, Richard Ned. *White Britain and Black Ireland: The Influence of Stereotypes on Colonial Policy*. Philadelphia: Institute for the Study of Human Issues, 1976.

Lee, J.J. *Ireland 1912–1985*. Cambridge: Cambridge University Press, 1989.

Lenskyi, Helen. *Out of Bounds: Women, Sport, and Sexuality*. Toronto: The Women's Press, 1986.

Le Quesne, Laurence. *The Bodyline Controversy*. London: Secker & Warburg, 1983.

Levine, Lawrence W. *Black Culture and Black Consciousness: Afro-American Folk Thought from Slavery to Freedom*. New York: Oxford University Press, 1977.

Lewis, W.J. *The Language of Cricket*. London: Oxford University Press, 1934.

Linton, David. *The Twentieth-Century Newspaper Press in Britain: An Annotated Bibliography*. London: Mansell Publishing, 1994.

Lipsett, H. Caldwell. *Lord Curzon in India, 1898–1903*. London: R.A. Everett, 1903.

Little, K.L. *Negroes in Britain: A Study of Racial Relations in English Society*. London: Kegan Paul, Trench, Trubner, 1947.

Lovesey, Peter. *The Official Centenary History of the Amateur Athletic Association*. Enfield, Middlesex: Guinness Superlatives, 1979.

Lowerson, John. *Sport and the English Middle Classes 1870–1914*. New York: University of Manchester Press, 1993.

Luddy, Maria. "An Agenda for Women's History in Ireland, 1500–1900, Part II: 1800–1900," *Irish Historical Studies* 28: 109 (1992).

Luddy, Maria. *Women in Ireland, 1800–1918: A Documentary History*. Cork: Cork University Press, 1995.

Lynch, J.G.B. Bohun. *The Complete Amateur Boxer*. London: Methuen, 1913.

MacAloon, John J. *This Great Symbol: Pierre de Coubertin and the Origins of the Modern Olympic Games*. Chicago: University of Chicago Press, 1981.

MacCurtain, Margaret and Mary O'Dowd. "An Agenda For Women's History in Ireland, 1500–1900, Part I: 1500–1800," *Irish Historical Studies* 28: 109 (1992).

MacCurtain, Margaret and Donncha Ó Corráin. *Women in Irish Society: The Historical Dimension*. Dublin: Arlen House, 1978.

Macdonald, Herbert G. *History of the Kingston Cricket Club*. Kingston: The Gleaner Co., 1938.

MacDonagh, Oliver. *States of Mind: A Study of Anglo-Irish Conflict 1780–1980*. London: George Allen and Unwin, 1983.

MacDonagh, Oliver, W.F. Mandle, and Pauric Travers, eds. *Irish Culture and Nationalism 1750–1950*. London: Macmillan Press, 1983.

MacIntosh, Donald et al. *Sport and Politics in Canada: Federal Government Involvement Since 1961*. Montreal: McGill-Queen's University Press, 1987.

MacKenzie, John M., ed. *Popular Imperialism and the Military 1850–1950*. Manchester: Manchester University Press, 1986.

MacKenzie, John M. *The Empire of Nature: Hunting, Conservation and British Imperialism*. New York: St. Martin's Press, 1989.

MacMunn, George. *The Martial Races of India*. London: Sampson, Low, Marston, 1933.

MacMunn, George. *The Living India: Its Romance and Realities*. London: G. Bell and Sons, 1934.

Mailey, Arthur. *—And Then Came Larwood: An Account of the Test Matches 1932–33*. London: John Lane The Bodley Head, 1933.

Malcolmson, Robert W. *Popular Recreation in English Society 1700–1850*. Cambridge: Cambridge University Press, 1973.

Manchester, William. *The Last Lion: Visions of Glory 1874–1932*. New York: Bantam Doubleday Dell, 1983.

Mandle, W.F. "Games People Played: Cricket And Football in England and Victoria in the Late Nineteenth Century," *Historical Studies* 15: 60 (1973).

Mandle, W.F. *The Gaelic Athletic Association and Irish Nationalist Politics 1884–1924*. London: Christopher and Helm, 1987.

Mangan, J.A. *Athleticism in the Victorian and Edwardian Public School: The Emergence and Consolidation of an Educational Ideology*. Cambridge: Cambridge University Press, 1981.

Mangan, J.A. *The Games Ethic and Imperialism: Aspects of the Diffusion of an Ideal*. Cambridge: Cambridge University Press, 1981.

Mangan, J.A., ed. *"Benefits bestowed?" Education and British Imperialism*. Manchester: Manchester University Press, 1988.

Mangan, J.A. *Pleasure, Profit, Proselytism: British Culture and Sport at Home and Abroad 1700–1914*. London: Frank Cass, 1988.

Mangan, J.A., ed. *The Imperial Curriculum: Racial Images and Education in the British Colonial Experience*. New York: Routledge, 1993.

Mangan, J.A. "Duty Unto Death: English Masculinity and Militarism in the Age of the New Imperialism," *International Journal of the History of Sport* 12: 2 (1995).

Mangan, J.A. and James Walvin, eds. *Manliness and Morality: Middle-Class Masculinity in Britain and America 1800–1941*. Manchester: Manchester University Press, 1987.

Manley, Michael. *A History of West Indies Cricket*. London: Andre Deutsch, 1995.

Mansergh, Nicholas. *The Irish Question, 1840–1921, Third Edition*. London: George Allen and Unwin, 1975.

Mant, Gilbert. *A Cuckoo in the Bodyline Nest*. Kenthurst, NSW: Kangaroo Press, 1992.

Markus, Andrew. *Australian Race Relations 1788–1993*. Saint Leonards, NSW: Allen and Unwin, 1994.

Marqusee, Mike. *Anyone But England: Cricket and the National Malaise*. New York: Verso, 1994.

Mason, Philip. *A Matter of Honour: An Account of the Indian Army Its Officers and Men*. London: Jonathan Cape, 1974.

Mason, Ronald. *Ashes in the Mouth: The Story of the Bodyline Tour 1932–1933*. London: Harmondsworth Penguin, 1984.

Mason, Tony. *Sport in Britain: A Social History*. Cambridge: Cambridge University Press, 1989.

McCartney, Donal. "Gaelic Ideological Origins of 1916," in O. Edwards, Dudley and Fergus Pyle, eds. *1916: The Easter Rising*. London: Macgibbon and Kee, 1968.

McCartney, Donal. *The Dawning of Democracy: Ireland 1800–1870*. Dublin: Helicon, 1987.

McCrone, Kathleen E. *Playing the Game: Sport and the Physical Emancipation of English Women, 1870–1914*. Lexington: University Press of Kentucky, 1988.

McGhee, Frank. *England's Boxing Heroes*. London: Bloomsbury Publishing, 1989.

McIntyre, W. David. *The Commonwealth of Nations: Origins and Impact 1869–1971*. Minneapolis: University of Minnesota Press, 1977.

McKay, Jim. *No Pain, No Gail? Sport and Australian Culture*. New York: Prentice Hall, 1991.

McKay, Jim and Iain Middlemiss. "Mate Against Mate, State Against State: A Case Study of Media Constructions of Hegemonic Masculinity in Australian Sport," *Masculinities: Interdisciplinary Studies on Gender* 3: 3 (1995).

Mehigan, P.D. *Vintage Carbery*. Dublin: Beaver Row Press, 1984.

Messner, Michael and Donald Sabo. *Sex, Violence, and Power in Sports: Rethinking Masculinity*. Freedom, CA: The Crossing Press, 1994.

Metcalfe, Alan. *Canada Learns to Play: The Emergence of Organized Sport, 1807–1914*. Toronto: McClelland and Stewart, 1987.

Metcalfe, Alan. "Power: A Case Study of the Ontario Hockey Association, 1890–1936," *Journal of Sport History* 19: 1 (1992).

Metcalf, Thomas R. *The Aftermath of Revolt: India 1857–1870*. New Delhi: Manohar Publications, 1990.

Metcalf, Thomas R. *Ideologies of the Raj*. Cambridge: Cambridge University Press, 1998.

Midgley, Clare, ed. *Gender and Imperialism*. New York: Manchester University Press, 1998.

Miller, E.D. *Modern Polo*. London: Hurst & Blackett, 1922.

Miller, Kerby. *Emigrants and Exiles: Ireland and the Irish Exodus to North America*. New York: Oxford University Press, 1985.

Mock, Wolfgang. "The Function of 'Race' in Imperialist Ideologies: The Example of Joseph Chamberlain," in Paul Kennedy and Anthony Nicholls, eds. *Nationalist and Racialist Movements in Britain and Germany before 1914*. London: Macmillan Press, 1981.

Moloney, Tim, ed. *The Claret and Gold: A History of the Tulla Hurling Club 1887–1987*. Ennis: Clare Champion Printers, 1987.

Moran, Seán Farrell. *Patrick Pearse and the Politics of Redemption: The Mind of the Easter Rising, 1916*. Washington: The Catholic University of America Press, 1994.

Morris, Barry. *Bradman: What they Said About Him*. Harpenden, Herts: Queen Anne Press, 1994.

Mosse, George. *Nationalism and Sexuality: Respectability and Abnormal Sexuality in Modern Europe*. New York: Howard Fertig, 1985.

Mountbatten of Burma, Earl ("Marco"). *An Introduction to Polo 6th ed.* London: J.A. Allen, 1976.

Mullan, Harry. *Heroes and Hard Men*. London: Stanley Paul, 1989.

Mulvey, Laura. *Visual and Other Pleasures*. Bloomington: Indiana University Press, 1989.

Munting, Brian. *An Economic and Social History of Gambling in Britain and the U.S.A.* Manchester: Manchester University Press, 1996.

Nandy, Ashis. *The Intimate Enemy: Loss and Recovery of Self Under Colonialism*. Oxford: Oxford University Press, 1983.

Nandy, Ashis. *The Tao of Cricket: On Games of Destiny and the Destiny of Games*. New Delhi: Penguin Books, 1988.

Nauright, John and Timothy J.L. Chandler. *Making Men: Rugby and Masculine Identity*. London: Frank Cass, 1996.

Navy, Army and Air Force Institutes. *The Army Boxing Association and ISBA Rules 1928–1929*, 1929.

Newbolt, Henry. *Selected Poems of Henry Newbolt*, ed. Patrick Dickinson. London: Hodder & Stoughton, 1981.

Newbolt, Henry. *Poems: New and Old*. London: John Murray, 1919.

Newsome, David. *Godliness and Good Learning*. London: Cassell Publishers, 1961.

Nicole, Christopher. *West Indian Cricket*. London: Phoenix Sports Books, 1957.

Nolan, Janet A. *Ourselves Alone: Women's Emigration from Ireland 1885–1920*. Lexington: University of Kentucky Press, 1989.

Odd, Gilbert. *Encyclopedia of Boxing*. London: Hamlyn Publishing Group, 1983.

Odd, Gilbert. *Kings of the Rings: 100 Years of World Heavyweight Boxing*. Feltham, Middlesex: Newnes Books, 1985.

Odd, Gilbert. *The Fighting Blacksmith: A Biography of Bob Fitzsimmons*. London: Pelham Books, 1976.

Odd, Gilbert. *The Woman in the Corner*. London: Pelham Books, 1978.

Ó Duinnin, Eoghan. *Irish on the Playing Field: English-Irish Phrase book for Gaelic Football and Hurling*. Ath Cliath (Dublin): Studio Press, 1961.

Oman, John Campbell. *The Brahmans, Theists and Muslims of India*. London: T. Fisher Unwin, 1907.

O'Mara, Pat. *The Autobiography of a Liverpool Irish Slummy*. London: Martin Hopkinson, 1934.

Ong, Walter J. *Fighting For Life: Contest, Sexuality and Consciousness*. Ithaca: Cornell University Press, 1981.

O'Reilly, Bill. *Tiger*. Sydney: William Collins Pty., 1985.

Orwell, George. *Such, Such were the Joys*. New York: Harcourt, Brace, 1945.

Osborn, E.B. *The New Elizabethans: A First Selection of the Lives of Young Men Who have Fallen in the Great War*. London: John Lane, The Bodley Head, 1919.

O'Shea, James. *Priest, Politics and Society in Post-Famine Ireland: A Study of County Tipperary 1850–1891*. Dublin: Wolfhound Press, 1983.

Ó Tuama, Seán. *The Gaelic League Idea: The Thomas Davis Lectures*. Dublin: Mercier Press, 1972.

Page, Michael. *Bradman*. Melbourne: Macmillan Company of Australia, 1988.

Palmer, Joe. *Recollections of a Boxing Referee*. London: John Lane The Bodley Head, 1927.

Park, Roberta J. "A Decade of the Body: Researching and Writing About the History of Health, Fitness, Exercise and Sport, 1983–1993," *Journal of Sport History*, 21: 1 (1994).

Parker, Cecil. *Cricket Triumphs and Troubles*. Manchester: C. Nicholls, 1936.

Parratt, Catriona. "Athletic 'Womanhood': Exploring Sources for Female Sport in Victorian and Edwardian England," *Journal of Sport History* 16: 2 (1989).

Parry, Benita. *Delusions and Discoveries: Studies on India in the British Imagination, 1880–1930*. London: Allen Lane, 1972.

Parry, J.H., P.M. Sherlock, and A.P. Maingot. *A Short History of the West Indies*. New York: St. Martin's Press, 1987.

Peebles, I.A.R. *How to Bowl*. London: Chapman and Hall, 1934.

Perkins, E. Benson. *The Problem of Gambling*. London: The Epworth Press, 1919.

Perry, Roland. *The Don*. London: Sidgwik and Jackson, 1996.

Phillips, Jock. *A Man's Country? The Image of the Pakeha Male—A History*. Auckland: Penguin Books, 1987.

Phillips, W. Alison. *The Revolution in Ireland: 1906–1923*. London: Longmans, Green, 1923.

Pilger, John. *A Secret Country: The Hidden Australia*. New York: Alfred A. Knopf, 1991.

Pollard, Marjorie. *Cricket for Women and Girls*. London: Hutchinson, 1934.

Pollock, William. *The Cream of Cricket*. London: Methuen, 1934.

Poovey, Mary. *Uneven Developments: The Ideological Work of Gender in Mid-Victorian England*. Chicago: Chicago University Press, 1988.

Powell, William. *The Wisden Guide to Cricket Grounds*. London: Stanley Paul, 1992.

Pronger, Brian. *The Arena of Masculinity: Sports, Homosexuality, and the Meaning of Sex.* London: GMP Publishers, 1990.

Puirseal, Padraig. *The G.A.A in Its Time* (Dublin: privately published, 1982).

Pruvis, June, ed. *Women's History: Britain, 1850–1945.* London: University College London Press, 1995.

Pulling, Christopher. *Mr. Punch and the Police.* London: Butterworths, 1964.

Randall, Robert. *Memorandum on Book Readership in Jamaica.* London: Robert Randall, 1937.

Razzell, P.E. "Social Origins of Officers in the Indian and British Home Army," *The British Journal of Sociology* 14: 3 (1963), 248–60.

Rhodes, Rita M. *Women and the Family in Post-Famine Ireland: Status and Opportunity in a Patriarchal Society.* London: Garland Publishing Inc., 1992.

Roberts, E.L. *Test Cricket and Cricketers 1877–1934.* London: Hurst and Blackett, 1934.

Roediger, David R. *Towards the Abolition of Whiteness: Essays on Race, Politics, and Working Class History.* London: Verso, 1994.

Rosenwater, Irving. *Sir Donald Bradman: A Biography.* London: B.T. Batsford, 1978.

Ross, Barney and Martin Abramson. *No Man Stands Alone.* London: Stanley Paul, 1959.

Rudolph, Susan Hoeber, Lloyd I. Rudolph, and Mohan Singh Kanota, eds. *Reversing the Gaze: Amar Singh's Diary, A Colonial Subject's Narrative of Imperial India.* Cambridge, MA: Westview Press, 2002.

Said, Edward. *Orientalism.* New York: Vintage Books, 1979.

Said, Edward. *Culture and Imperialism.* New York: Vintage Books, 1993.

Saint-Thomas, H. *Paddy's Dream and John Bull's Nightmare: Notes During a "Passionate Pilgrimage" Through the Sister Country.* London: G. Vickers, ca. 1886.

Sammons, Jeffrey T. "Race and Sport: A Critical, Historical Examination," *Journal of Sport History* 21: 3 (1994).

Samuel, Raphael and Paul Thompson, ed. *The Myths We Live By.* London: Routledge, 1990.

Sandercock, Leonie and Ian Turner. *Up Where Cazaly? The Great Australian Game.* London: Granada, 1981.

Sandiford, Keith A.P. *Cricket and the Victorians.* Hants (England): Scholar Press, 1994.

Sawyer, Roger. *"We Are But Women" Women in Ireland's History.* London: Routledge, 1992.

Scobie, Edward. *Black Britannia: A History of Blacks in Britain.* Chicago: Johnson Publishing Company Inc., 1972.

Scott, Joan Wallach. *Gender and the Politics of History.* New York: Columbia University Press, 1988.

Sheppard, T. Wilfred. *A Guide to Training and Stable Management of Polo Ponies for Beginners in India.* Calcutta: Caledonian Printing, 1927.

Shipley, Stan. *Club Life and Socialism in Mid-Victorian London.* London: The Journeyman Press, 1983.

Shipley, Stan. *Bombardier Billy Wells: The Life and Times of a Boxing Hero.* Tyne and Wear: Bewick Press, 1993.

Singh, Benny. *Champions: Past and Present.* Durban: Luxmi Vilas Press, 1949.

Singh, Dhananajaya. *The House of Marwar.* New Delhi: Roli Books, 1994.

Sinha, Mrinalini. *Colonial Masculinity: The "Manly Englishman" and the "Effeminate Bengali" in the Late Nineteenth Century.* Manchester: Manchester University Press, 1995.

Sinha, Mrinalini. "Gender in the Critique of Colonialism and Nationalism: Locating the 'Indian Woman,'" in Ann-Louise Shapiro, ed. *Feminists Revision History.* New Brunswick: Rutgers University Press, 1994.

Sissons, Ric. *The Players: A Social History of the Professional Cricketer.* Sydney: Pluto Press, 1988.

Sissons, Ric and Brian Stoddart. *Cricket and Empire: The 1932–1933 Bodyline Tour of Australia.* London: George Allen and Unwin, 1984.

Smith, Bonnie G. *Changing Lives: Women in European History Since 1700.* Lexington, MA: D.C. Heath and Company, 1989.

Smith, Dai, "Focal Heroes: A Welsh Fighting Class," in Richard Holt, ed. *Sport and the Working Class in Modern Britain.* Manchester: Manchester University Press, 1990.

Smith, L.S. *West Indies Cricket History and Cricket Tours to England, 1900, 1906, 1923.* Port of Spain, Trinidad: Yulle's Printerie, 1922.

Smith, Vincent (Rewritten and edited by Percival Spear). *The Oxford History of India, fourth edition,* Delhi: Oxford University Press, 1981.

Sobers, Garfield and J.S. Baker. *Cricket in the Sun: A History of West Indies Cricket*. London: Arthur Barker, 1967.

Special Correspondent of The Times. *Letters from Ireland*. London: W.H. Allen, 1887.

Spivak, Gayatri, Chakravorty. "Psychoanalysis in Left Field and Fieldworking: Examples to Fit the Title," in Sonu Shamdasani and Michael Münchow, eds. *Speculations After Freud: Psychoanalysis, Philosophy and Culture*. London: Routledge, 1994.

Stallybrass, Peter and Allon White. *The Politics and Poetics of Transgression*. London: Methuen, 1986.

Stevens, F.S., ed. *Racism: The Australian Experience: Volume 1: Prejudice and Xenophobia*. Sydney: Australia and New Zealand Book Company, 1971.

Stevens, F.S., ed. *Racism: The Australian Experience: Volume 2: Black Versus White*. Sydney: Australia and New Zealand Book Company, 1972.

Stevens, F.S., ed. *Racism: The Australian Experience: Volume 3: Colonialism*. Sydney: Australia and New Zealand Book Company, 1973.

Stoddart, Brian. "Cricket, Social Formation and Cultural Continuity in Barbados: A Preliminary Ethnohistory," *Journal of Sport History* 14: 3 (1987).

Stoddart, Brian. *Saturday Afternoon Fever: Sport in the Australian Culture*. London: Angus and Robertson, 1986.

Stoler, Ann Laura. *Race and the Education of Desire: Foucault's History of Sexuality and the Colonial Order of Things*. Durham: Duke University Press, 1995.

Stoler, Ann Laura. "Rethinking Colonial Categories: European Communities and the Boundaries of Rule," *Comparative Studies in Society and History* 31 (1989).

Sugden, John and Alan Bairner. *Sport, Sectarianism and Society in a Divided Ireland*. Leicester: Leicester University Press, 1993.

Susuly, Richard. *Bookies and Bettors: Two Hundred Years of Gambling*. New York: Holt Reinhart and Winston, 1982.

Sutcliffe, Herbert. *For England and Yorkshire*. London: Edward Arnold, 1935.

Sutherland, Douglas. *The Yellow Earl: The Life of Hugh Lowther 5th Earl of Lonsdale, K.G., G.C.V.O., 1857–1944*. London: Cassell, 1965.

Tabili, Laura. *"We Ask for British Justice": Workers and Racial Difference in Late Imperial Britain*. Ithaca: Cornell University Press, 1994.

Taine, Hippolyte. *Taine's Notes on England*. Translated with an introduction by Edward Hyams. London: Thames and Hudson, 1957.

Tate, Maurice. *My Cricketing Reminiscences*. London: Stanley Paul, 1934.

The authors of "An Irish Cousin," *Through Connemara in a Governess Cart*. London: W.H. Allen, 1893.

Thompson, E.P. *The Making of the English Working Class*. New York: Vintage Books, 1966.

Thompson, L. O'Brien. "How Cricket is West Indian Cricket?: Racial and Colour Conflict," *Caribbean Review* 12 (1983).

Tierney, Mark. *Croke of Cashel: The Life of Archbishop Thomas William Croke, 1823–1902*. Dublin: Gill and Macmillan, 1976.

Tifft, Stephen. "The Parricidal Phantasm: Irish Nationalism and the 'Playboy' Riots," in Andrew Parker et al., eds. *Nationalisms and Sexualities*. New York: Routledge, 1992.

Tomlinson, John. *Cultural Imperialism: A Critical Introduction*. Baltimore: Johns Hopkins University Press, 1991.

Toole, Joseph. *Fighting Through Life*. London: Rich and Cowan, 1935.

Trainor, Luke. *British Imperialism and Australian Nationalism: Manipulation, Conflict and Compromise in the Late Nineteenth Century*. New York: Cambridge University Press, 1994.

United Provinces of Agra and Oudh. *Misc. Government Publications, Manual on Indian Etiquette for the use of European Officers Coming to India*. Allahabad: Government Press, 1910.

Vadivelu, A. *The Ruling Chiefs, Nobles and Zamindars of India*. Madras: G.C. Loganadham Bros., 1915.

Vamplew, Wray. "It's Not Cricket and Perhaps it Never was: Australian Crowd and Player Behaviour," *The Sport Historian: The Journal of the British Society of Sports History* 14 (1994).

Vamplew, Wray and Brian Stoddart, eds. *Sport in Australia: A Social History*. Cambridge: Cambridge University Press, 1994.

Vamplew, Wray et al., eds. *The Oxford Companion to Australian Sport*. Melbourne: Oxford University Press, 1994.

Van Wart, R.B. *The Life of Lieut.-General H.H. Sir Pratap Singh*. London: Oxford University Press, 1926.

Veitch, Colin. " 'Play Up! Play Up! and Win the War!' " Football, The Nation and the First World War," *Journal of Contemporary History* 20 (1985), 363–78.

Vertinsky. "Gender Relations, Women's History and Sport History: A Decade of Changing Enquiry, 1983–1993," *Journal of Sport History* 21: 1 (1994).

Visram, Rozina. *Asians in Britain: 400 Years of History*. London: Pluto Press, 2002.

Wakelan, H.B.T. *Half-Time: The Mike and Me*. London: Thomas Nelson and Sons, 1938.

Walcott, Clyde. *Island Cricketers*. London: Hodder and Stoughton, 1958.

Warner, P.F. *Cricket in Many Climes*. London: William Heinemann, 1900.

Warner, Sir P.F. *Cricket Between Two Wars*. London: Chatto and Windus, 1942.

Warner, Sir P.F. *Long Innings*. London: George G. Harrap, 1951.

Weber, Eugen. *Peasants into Frenchmen: The Modernization of Rural France 1870–1914*. London: Chatto and Windus, 1979.

Wells, Jeff. *Boxing Day: The Fight that Changed the World*. Sydney: Harper Collins, 1998.

Whelan, Kevin. "The Geography of Hurling," *History Ireland* 1 (1993), 28–31.

Whitington, Richard S. *Bodyline Umpire*. Adelaide: Rigby, 1974.

Whitington, R.S. *Time of the Tiger: The Bill O'Reilly Story*. London: Stanley Paul, 1970.

Whitney, Caspar W. *A Sporting Pilgrimage*. London: Osgood, McIlvaine, 1895.

Who's Who in World Cricket. London: Amalgamated Press, 1934.

Wiggins, David. "Great Speed But Little Stamina: The Historical Debate Over Black Athletic Superiority," *Journal of Sport History* 16: 2 (1989).

Wiggins, David. "Peter Jackson and the Elusive Heavyweight Championship: A Black Athlete's Struggle Against the Late Nineteenth Century Color Line," *Journal of Sport History* 12: 2 (1985).

Wilde, Simon. *Ranji: A Genius Rich and Strange*. The Kingwood Press, 1990.

Williams, Charles. *Bradman: An Australian Hero*. Little, Brown and Company, 1996.

Williams, Marcus, ed. *The Way to Lord's: Cricketing Letters to The Times*. London: Willow Books, 1983.

Williams, Marcus, ed. *Double Century: 200 Years of Cricket in The Times*. London: Willow Books, 1985.

Williams, Raymond. *Keywords: A Vocabulary of Culture and Society*. New York: Oxford University Press, 1983.

Wodehouse, John (Earl of Kimberly), ed. *Polo*. London: Seeley, Service, 1936.

Wohl, Robert. *The Generation of 1914*. Cambridge: Harvard University Press, 1979.

Wuthnow, Robert, James Davidson Hunter, Albert Bergesen, and Edith Kurzweil. *Cultural Analysis: The Work of Peter L. Berger, Mary Douglas, Michel Foucault, and Jürgen Habermas*. Boston: Routledge and Kegan Paul, 1984.

Younghusband, Francis. *The Light of Experience: A Review of Some Men and Events of My Time*. London: Constable, 1927.

Younghusband, Captain G.J. *Polo in India*. London: W.H. Allen, 1890.

INDEX

PATRICK F. McDEVITT is an assistant professor of history at the University at Buffalo, the State University of New York.